Hot & Cheesy

Also by Clifford A. Wright

Cooking

On Politics and History

Hot & Cheesy

Clifford A. Wright

WILEY

JOHN WILEY & SONS, INC.

For general information on our other products and services or for technical support, please contact our Customer Care Department within the United States at
(800) 762-2974, outside the United States at (317) 572-3993 or fax (317) 572-4002.

Wiley also publishes its books in a variety of electronic formats. Some content that appears in print may not be available in electronic books. For more information about Wiley products, visit our web site at www.wiley.com.

Visit the author at www.cliffordawright.com

Library of Congress Cataloging-in-Publication Data:

Wright, Clifford A.
Hot & cheesy / Clifford Wright.
  p. cm.
Includes index.
ISBN: 978-0-470-61535-5 (pbk); ISBN 978-1-118-11062-1 (ebk);
ISBN 978-1-118-11063-8 (ebk); ISBN 978-1-118-11064-5 (ebk)
1. Cooking (Cheese). 2. Cheese—Varieties. 3. Cookbooks. I. Title. II. Title: Hot and cheesy.
TX759.5.C48W75   2012
641.6'73—dc22   2011004543

Printed in the United States of America

10 9 8 7 6 5 4 3 2 1

For Michelle van Vliet

Contents

Acknowledgments

Our family ate a lot of cheese in the writing of this book. It was all delicious, but as a cookbook author one needs to pay attention to this kind of eating and incorporate plenty of exercise and keep portions small. Being a good eater is, for a cookbook author, no small matter and for that I would especially like to thank my children Ali Kattan-Wright, Dyala Kattan-Wright, and Seri Kattan-Wright and Michelle van Vliet and her daughters Alexandria Sitterly and Madeline Sitterly not only for all their appetites but also for their helpful and sometimes "cheesy" suggestions. I would also like to thank my agent Angela Miller for her support and belief in my abilities and to my editor Justin Schwartz, who edits and produces such great cookbooks and my copyeditor, Valerie Cimino.

Hot &
Cheesy

Introduction

Plunging your fork into a dish oozing with melted cheese is a joy everyone relishes. So it wasn't too much of a stretch for me to think of an entire book about cooking with cheese. Melted cheese is, after all, the star of so many favorite dishes, from the grilled cheese sandwiches of our childhood to the cheese pizza of our adolescence to the fondue of our adulthood. For some years now, we've noticed an explosion of interest in cheese. This interest manifests itself not only in a greater variety of imported cheeses from a greater variety of cheese-producing countries, but also in the actual cheese-making process itself, from home cooks to small mom-and-pop cheese operations. Artisanal cheese producers are popping up everywhere, and California rivals Wisconsin as the greatest cheese-producing state. There are cheese primers coming out every week, it seems, but I noticed a lack of a cheese cookbook. That is, how do we *cook* with all this available cheese?

Many home cooks know what to do with cheddar cheese or Swiss cheese, but what about manchego, Saint-André, Cowgirl Creamery Wagon Wheel, kashkaval, Fourme d'Ambert, vacherin, Colorado chèvre, queso fresco, and the hundreds of others that are now available? For the cheese-loving cook, this book offers 250 recipes in a variety of categories with explanatory notes delving into the wide world of dishes with melted cheese.

In a world of fusion this, junk that, foam, and sushi, sometimes what we crave is *real food*, like a cheeseburger or macaroni and cheese or a Lindy's New York cheesecake from the famous deli on Broadway in New York, immortalized in the musical *Guys and Dolls*.

Cheese is real food, good food, natural food, but tagged with a bad rap for too long. That's all changing now, as we see new artisanal American cheese makers from Vermont to California producing a bevy of alluring cheeses. Cheese is a terrific dairy product, and a world of delicious dishes can be made with cheese, all kinds of cheese. The grilled cheese sandwich you remember with fondness from your childhood no longer has to be made with the presliced processed cheese product called "American." Now you can make it with real cheddar cheese from Vermont, teleme from California, or goat cheese from Colorado.

In the past twenty years cheese appreciation has risen, along with cheese production. The artisanal cheese producers I mentioned earlier are springing up everywhere, not just in traditional cheese-producing states. More cheese is imported from France and Italy than ever before, and the introduction of cheeses from Spain is now in full swing. All this is enhanced by traditional cheeses from Great Britain and Ireland, the Balkans, Greece, and the Arab world. For some time now consumers have had an enormous choice with cheeses, both domestic and imported, mass-market and artisanal. Our sixty-year-old acceptance of "cheese-like products" such as Velveeta is now reversing direction and shifting toward real cheese. But there comes a time when putting samples of cheese on a board and serving it with red wine and crackers isn't enough, and we ask ourselves "Does it melt well?" and "Can I cook with this cheese?" and "What can I make with this cheese?"

Today, the wealth of possible cheeses one can eat is daunting. How simple it was to have less than ten choices forty years ago: cream cheese, American, Swiss, Jack, cheddar, and so on . . . and how boring. Today, there are five different cheddar cheeses from Vermont alone. Spanish cheeses, virtually unknown thirty years ago, are now being made by American companies, let alone all those that are newly imported from Spain itself. "Manchego" rolls off our tongues like we are cheese experts. France produces about four hundred cheeses, and probably a quarter of that number are now imported into the United States, up considerably from the time when only Brie and Camembert were available.

There's no denying that cheese is on the move . . . but we still don't have the guidance on how to cook with cheese.

Ever since the first fondue was made in the Swiss Alps, cheese has been recognized as a delicious and nutritious food, a dairy product par excellence. Although we don't know who first started cooking with cheese, we know that cheese was first used in prehistoric times. Cheese was probably not invented but rather discovered. Some long-ago people made the simple observation that milk left in a bag made from a calf's stomach coagulated after some time. They also noticed that when the climate changed from cold to hot, the milk curdled faster. This is probably why the richest cheese-producing countries are those with four distinct seasons. Today there are over a thousand different cheeses produced in hundreds of different types from the milk from cow, sheep, goat, buffalo, horse, yak, and camel. The milk might be raw, skimmed, or pasteurized.

Along with the explosion of cheeses now available on the market, there has also been a proliferation of books on cheeses, covering everything you could possibly want to know about a cheese and its production, storage, and serving. But outside of some fondue books, there are precious few cookbooks with recipes devoted to cooking with cheese. Cooking with cheese is actually more common than one would think at first blush, as we all cook with cheese. What, after all, is a grilled cheese sandwich, lasagne, macaroni and cheese, or pizza but cooking with cheese? But why stop there? The classics are great, and every cheese cookbook should provide an easy-to-find, simply written, recipe for these dishes. But there is so much more one can do with cheese. In fact, the greatest difficulty in writing this book was choosing only 250 recipes when one has thousands to consider.

I've included many classic dishes in this cookbook, but I've been mindful of including recipes in every category of food, from appetizers to soups to pasta to rice to main courses to salads to desserts. The world is our table, and luscious recipes come from all the great cheese-producing countries. America's contribution to cheese culture is becoming more important, and we have readily available, delicious, and unique cheeses with which to cook, so innovative recipes for these artisanal American cheeses are included too.

We Americans, new as we are to real cheese, need to learn a thing or two about the care and handling of this living thing called cheese. No longer can we be so casual as to leave a hunk of unwrapped sliced cheese product in our refrigerator. So do we need special equipment? Not at all, because the proper care and storage of cheese is not hard at all, and by observing a few tips for serving and storage, your cheese will last longer and taste better.

Serving and Storage Tips

- Store cheese in the refrigerator between 46° and 55°F.

- Store cheese separately from other foods. Refrigerator doors usually have a dedicated compartment for cheeses and/or butter.

- Remove cheese from the plastic wrap it is sold in, transfer to a wrapping of wax paper, and then place in a loose-fitting food bag so humidity is not lost and air circulates better.

- Blue cheese must be wrapped all over, as mold spores can spread readily to other cheeses.

- Cheeses are living organisms that need air to breathe, so it is important that they not be cut off from circulating air, yet they must be wrapped properly so the cheese does not dry out.

- If serving cheeses on their own (that is, not cooking them), remove them from the refrigerator 2 hours before serving. Cheese must always be served at room temperature for its full flavor to be appreciated.

- Don't slice cheese until needed; otherwise it will start to lose its subtlety and aroma.

Basics of Cooking with Cheese

It's one thing to eat cheese and crackers with a nice glass of red wine, but cooking with cheese has a few twists to it, so a little knowledge will enhance your culinary experience.

- When aged cheese melts, the texture will be grainy.

- When young cheese melts, the texture will be creamier.

- Cheese should be cooked briefly and gently, just until it has fully melted.

- Cheese can be incorporated into a stable base such as a cream sauce through gentle melting.

- Cheese mellows in flavor when it melts into other foods, so feel free to use stronger cheese if desired.

- When a recipe calls for grating, crumbling, or slicing cheese, you can take it directly from the refrigerator, as it is easier to handle when cold.

- When a recipe calls for mashing or spreading, allow the cheese to reach room temperature, as it is easier to handle when soft.

- Remember that cheese, when cooked beyond a certain point, will coagulate and turn into a stringy and hard glob; therefore, it only needs to be heated until it melts. If the cheese coagulates, you will not be able to return it to its smooth state.

- Cheese does not need high heat to melt, so if your cheese dish happens to be finished under the broiler, don't walk away, as it will be done in seconds.

- If not specified in a recipe, add cheese at the end of cooking.

- Grated and shredded cheese will melt more quickly and evenly than cubed cheese or cheese in chunks.

- The type of cheese used is always specified in the recipe, but it doesn't hurt to know what happens to cheese when it is cooked. Lower-fat cheeses such as halloumi, feta, cottage cheese, and ricotta react to heat differently than high-fat cheeses. They are ideal for frying or instances when you want warmed but not melted cheese in a dish.

- Nonfat cheeses never melt, but I don't use them, as they have no taste.

- Higher-fat cheeses such as full-fat mozzarella melt very well and are popular in a great variety of cooked dishes.

- If a cheese has been aged, it will be firmer and not melt in the same way that younger cheeses do. The cheese will be more "granular."

- The trickiest of the melted cheese dishes are fondues, which, if they reach coagulation, cannot be rescued. Therefore, the addition of wine and a starch such as cornstarch or flour aids in the fondue being smooth and perfectly melted.

- Buy cheese as you need it. There is a perfectly understandable temptation to buy all kinds of cheese when you're shopping, especially if you're shopping in a store with a top-quality cheese section. However, try to be sensible and buy the cheese you need for the dish and an amount that you can reasonably expect to finish in 2 weeks.

- Recipes usually specify both dry (volume) measurement and weight measurement, but when buying whole cheese you are only given weight measurements. Here is a general rule of thumb:

  ½ cup of shredded cheese, such as cheddar or Monterey Jack, weighs about 1½ ounces.

  1 cup of shredded or crumbled cheese weighs about 3 ounces.

  Remember that both the dry (volume) measurement and the weight measurement in the recipes are meant as a relative guide; they don't need to be exact.

A Note About the Recipes

I often call for a large flameproof casserole in the recipes. There are two types of casseroles, one that is both ovenproof and flameproof, the heavy enameled cast-iron ones made by Le Creuset being an example. The other casserole is strictly an ovenproof baking casserole, usually rectangular or oval. Earthenware casseroles may be both, but if you don't know if it's flameproof then use a heat diffuser.

You will have fun cooking from this book, and you'll be introduced to many new cheeses. I encourage you not to be limited by the cheeses in this book and to replace cheeses as you see fit, especially in the more nontraditional and malleable recipes. I'd also like to encourage you to shop for cheeses from the variety of Web sites suggested throughout the book—now that's really fun.

Soups, Sauces, and Dips

S ome of the soups in this chapter are substantial enough to be dinner, such as Chicken, Potato, and Cheese Soup (page 11) with its Mexican queso blanco. Others are the answer to leftovers, such as Turkey Soup with Cheese Pancake Strips (page 16), which is the perfect solution to your post-Thanksgiving dinner turkey carcass. The sauces and dips in this chapter are probably unfamiliar—and I intended it that way—because you don't need to know about melted Velveeta. Try the Mustard Gouda Sauce (page 19) over rutabagas and you'll be a convert. The next time you need a party dip, serve the Hot Crab Dip (page 22); it will definitely disappear, and you'll be giving out the recipe.

MEXICAN CHEESES

Every supermarket carries Mexican cheeses, all named "queso" something or other. How do you know what to get? Curiously, Mexico is not famous for its cheeses, and they tend to be used for two purposes: to melt or to crumble. That's why they are almost obligatory in so many Mexican and Mexican-inspired dishes. Here's all you really need to know: Queso fresco is a crumbly cheese, and under the rubric "queso blanco" are the melting cheeses, which include queso ranchero, queso Chihuahua, queso Oaxaca, queso amarillo, and some others. Need a substitute for queso blanco? You'll never go wrong using Muenster cheese, hard (not fresh) mozzarella cheese, Gouda cheese, Edam cheese, Monterey Jack cheese, and mild cheddar in any recipe calling for "queso."

Chicken, Potato, and Cheese Soup

THIS HEARTY SOUP is filled with a nice balance of vegetables and protein. The ideal cheese to use is the soft Mexican white cheese queso blanco. This soup doesn't hold up well as a leftover because the cheese, once cool, congeals on the bottom of the pot and does not re-melt well. For that reason, it's a great dish to serve to a group of about six people. Good boiling potatoes are Yukon Gold, white rose, or red potatoes.

Makes 4 to 6 servings

1. In a large pot, heat the oil over medium heat. Add the onion, garlic, half the cilantro, and the cumin and cook, stirring occasionally, until the onion is mushy, about 8 minutes.

2. Add the chicken and cook, stirring occasionally, until it turns color, about 5 minutes. Add the water, season with salt, and cook over medium heat without letting the water come to a boil for 15 minutes; reduce the heat to low if it is bubbling. It is important that the water not boil; otherwise the chicken will toughen.

3. Remove the chicken with a slotted spoon, shred it into very small pieces using two forks, then return it to the pot together with the potatoes and bring to a near boil over high heat. Then reduce the heat to low and simmer, stirring, until the potatoes are tender, about 15 minutes. Add the corn kernels, the remaining cilantro, and the milk, mix well, and check the seasoning. Return the broth to a simmering point over low heat, making sure it does not boil, then remove from the heat, add the cheese, and serve immediately.

1 tablespoon vegetable oil

1 medium onion, finely chopped

4 large garlic cloves, finely chopped

1 bunch fresh cilantro (coriander leaf), stems removed and leaves chopped

1 teaspoon ground cumin

2 boneless, skinless chicken breast halves (1 pound), cubed

6 cups water

Salt to taste

3 boiling potatoes (about 1 pound), peeled and diced

1 fresh ear of corn, husked and kernels removed

2 cups whole milk

6 ounces Mexican queso blanco or farmer's cheese, diced or shredded

Poblano Chile and Cheese Soup

1 pound poblano chiles

4 tablespoons unsalted butter

2 cups whole milk

½ cup Mexican crema or sour cream

2 ounces queso Chihuahua (or Muenster cheese)

2 ounces queso Oaxaca (or hard mozzarella cheese)

2 ounces queso amarillo (or Gouda or Edam cheese)

Salt and freshly ground black pepper to taste

POBLANO CHILES are dark green heart-shaped chiles that are mildly piquant, much less hot than a jalapeño chile. In some supermarkets, they are labeled pasilla chiles, which they are not. Pasilla chiles are very dark green, nearly black, long and thin chiles, which are, however, a fine substitute. Because supermarkets increasingly carry a variety of Mexican cheeses, I give you here the names of the Mexican cheeses to use, but the substitutes are excellent should you not find the Mexican ones.

Makes 4 servings

1. Preheat the oven to 425°F.

2. Place the chiles on a wire rack over a burner on high heat and roast, turning occasionally with tongs, until their skins blister black on all sides. Remove the chiles and place in a paper or heavy plastic bag to steam for 20 minutes, which will make peeling them easier. When cool enough to handle, rub off as much blackened skin as you can. Cut them open and remove the seeds by rubbing with a paper towel (to avoid washing away flavorful juices) or by rinsing under running water (to remove more easily). Cut the chiles into strips.

3. In a large pot, melt the butter over medium heat, then add the chile strips, milk, crema, and cheeses and cook, stirring constantly in a figure-8 pattern, until the mixture is homogeneous and the cheese is melted, about 8 minutes. Season with salt and pepper and serve.

Fregula and Cheese Soup

IN SARDINIA, mountain farmers make this soup with a sour goat's milk cheese called viscido. Feta cheese is an excellent substitute, especially if it's made out of goat's milk, which some are. The fregula (also fregola) called for is a kind of toasted Sardinian couscous or pasta ball made from durum wheat. It's usually sold in Italian markets and some gourmet stores or online at www.gourmetsardinia.com. If you make this recipe with regular soup pasta, it will be an entirely different dish, so I think it worth the effort to find fregula. *Makes 4 servings*

2 quarts cold water

3 boiling potatoes (about 1¾ pounds), peeled and cut into small cubes

1 to 2 ounces pork fatback or salt pork, rind removed and fat cut into ¼-inch-thick, 4-inch-long strips

⅓ cup dried white beans, soaked in water to cover overnight, drained

1 small garlic clove, crushed

1 teaspoon salt

4 ounces feta cheese (preferably made from goat's milk and in one piece), cut into 2 slices

¼ cup Sardinian fregula (see above for where to procure)

1. Put the water, potatoes, pork fatback, beans, garlic, and salt in a large pot and slowly bring to a boil over medium heat. Once it begins to bubble, reduce the heat to a gentle simmer and cook until the beans are half done, about 1 hour.

2. Rinse the salt off the feta cheese, crumble or cut it into large pieces, and add it to the soup. Let the soup cook until the cheese is very soft, about 1 hour. Add the fregula and cook, stirring often so it doesn't stick, until cooked, about 20 minutes. Serve immediately.

Cheddar Cheese and Beer Soup

4 tablespoons
unsalted butter

1 small onion,
finely chopped

1 small carrot, finely
chopped or grated

¼ cup all-purpose flour

½ teaspoon dry mustard

½ teaspoon paprika

8 ounces mild orange
cheddar cheese, shredded
or grated (about 2 cups)

7 cups chicken or
vegetable broth

1¼ cups half-and-half

One 12-ounce bottle ale

2 tablespoons chopped
fresh chives

ALTHOUGH YOU CAN USE white cheddar cheese (its natural color), orange-dyed cheddar cheese is particularly appetizing. You will want a cheddar cheese less than 2 years old, and use top-quality ale and not a lager beer. Once you put the cheese in, make sure the broth does not come to a boil.

Makes 8 servings

In a large pot, melt the butter over low heat. Add the onion and carrot, cover, and cook, stirring occasionally, until the onion is softened, about 5 minutes. Stir in the flour, dry mustard, and paprika until well blended. Add the cheese and broth and stir slowly until the cheese is melted, about 5 minutes. Add the half-and-half and ale and simmer over low heat, stirring occasionally, for 30 minutes. Serve, garnishing each bowl with some chives.

Leek, Mushroom, and Stilton Cheese Soup

THIS IS A MEMORABLE SOUP, and you may find yourself using the blue-veined Stilton cheese and the horseradish and sour cream garnish in many more dishes than this soup, as the taste is so appealing. It's best to use freshly grated horseradish, but if you can only find prepared horseradish, then that's what you will have to use. *Makes 4 servings*

1. Prepare the garnish by mixing together the horseradish, gherkin, and sour cream in a bowl. Set aside.

2. In a large pot, melt the butter over medium heat. Add the leeks and mushrooms and cook, stirring occasionally, until softened, about 10 minutes. Add the broth, milk, and potatoes and bring to a boil over high heat, then reduce the heat to low and simmer until the potatoes are tender, about 20 minutes.

3. Add the Stilton cheese by crumbling it into the soup, and stir for 1 to 2 minutes. Ladle into individual bowls and serve with a tablespoon of the garnish and a sprinkle of parsley on top.

For the garnish

¼ cup freshly grated horseradish

1 small gherkin pickle, finely chopped

¼ cup sour cream

For the soup

4 tablespoons unsalted butter

4 leeks (about 1 pound), white part only, split lengthwise, washed well, and finely chopped

8 ounces button (white) mushrooms, coarsely chopped

3 cups vegetable broth

1 cup whole milk

8 ounces boiling potatoes (such as Yukon Gold), peeled and finely diced

3 ounces Stilton cheese

1 teaspoon finely chopped fresh flat-leaf parsley

Turkey Soup with Cheese Pancake Strips

For the broth

1 roasted turkey carcass, remaining large chunks of meat removed and reserved for another purpose

1 leek, split lengthwise, washed well, and cut up

1 celery stalk, cut up

1 carrot, cut up

1 onion, quartered

8 fresh flat-leaf parsley sprigs

1 bay leaf

For the cheese pancakes

¾ cup all-purpose flour

1 teaspoon double-acting baking powder

½ teaspoon salt

¾ cup whole milk

1 large egg, separated

1½ tablespoons unsalted butter, melted and slightly cooled

3 ounces Fontina Val d'Aosta cheese or Gruyère cheese, shredded

2 tablespoons freshly grated Parmesan cheese

Freshly ground black pepper

GOOD COOKS GRAB the roasted turkey carcass at Thanksgiving and make a heavenly turkey broth for that weekend. After straining and de-fatting the broth, I like to reduce the broth a bit to enrich it and then serve it with cheese pancake strips. The pancakes are cooked while the broth simmers and are cut into strips. You lay the pancake strips in the soup bowl and pour the bubbling broth over them. This is a two-day affair. The first day you make the broth, usually the Friday after Thanksgiving, and the next day—that is, Saturday—you make the soup.

Makes 4 servings

1. Place the roasted turkey carcass in a large stockpot with the leek, celery, carrot, onion, parsley, and bay leaf. Cover with water (about 2 gallons) and bring to a boil over high heat. Reduce the heat to low and simmer uncovered for 8 hours.

2. Strain the broth and discard all the bones. Strain the broth twice more through triple-folded cheesecloth, then return to a clean pot. Bring to a boil over high heat and reduce the broth by half. Let cool, then refrigerate, and once the fat congeals on top, remove and discard the fat.

3. Preheat a cast-iron griddle or skillet over medium heat for at least 15 minutes.

4. In a bowl, mix the flour, baking powder, and salt. Pour the milk into a 1-cup measuring cup, add the egg yolk, and beat. Add the slightly cooled butter to the milk. In another bowl, whip the egg white with an electric or hand beater until peaks form. Pour the milk mixture into the bowl with the dry ingredients. Then add the egg white, Fontina cheese, and Parmesan cheese and fold, don't beat, all the ingredients together. Let sit for 15 minutes.

5. Pour one ladleful (or ½ cup) of batter onto the hot griddle or skillet and, with a circling motion, push the batter out until the pancake is about 6 inches in diameter. Cook until browned on the bottom, then flip and brown the other side. Do not turn more than once. Transfer to a plate and cook the remaining batter. Cut the pancakes into ½-inch-wide strips and lay in individual bowls. Bring the turkey broth to a furious boil, season with salt and pepper, if necessary, and spoon into the soup bowls over the pancake strips. Serve immediately.

Blue Cheese and Beef Soup

1 tablespoon vegetable oil

½ small onion, chopped

¼ teaspoon hot paprika

¼ teaspoon ground Sichuan peppercorns or black pepper

¼ teaspoon finely chopped garlic

¼ teaspoon finely chopped fresh ginger

4 ounces beef top sirloin, finely chopped

1 jalapeño chile, seeded and finely chopped

2 to 3 tablespoons blue cheese

5 cups water

1 large ripe tomato (about 10 ounces), peeled, seeded, and diced

1½ teaspoons salt, or more to taste

¼ cup cornstarch mixed with ¼ cup water

I FIRST CAME ACROSS THIS SOUP when writing my soup book, *The Best Soups in the World*. This Tibetan soup is made with a mold-ripened cheese, for which any strong-tasting blue cheese would be a fine substitute. You want that sourish taste. The hot chile mixed with the pungent blue cheese, seasoned with Sichuan peppercorns, creates an amazing flavor. You can find Sichuan peppercorns, which are not related to black peppercorns, under Szechuan peppercorns under Grocery & Gourmet Food at www.Amazon.com. *Makes 4 servings*

1. In a large pot, heat the oil over medium-high heat. Add the onion and cook, stirring occasionally, until golden, about 4 minutes. Stir in the paprika, Sichuan peppercorns, garlic, and ginger. Add the beef and cook, stirring constantly, until browned, 1 to 2 minutes. Add the chile, reduce the heat to low, and add the cheese. Cook, stirring, until the cheese melts, 2 to 3 minutes, then add the water, tomato, and salt. Reduce the heat to low, and simmer for 30 minutes.

2. Stir in the cornstarch mixture and bring to a boil over high heat. Cook until the mixture thickens a bit, about 5 minutes, then let rest for 10 minutes and serve.

Mustard Gouda Sauce

MY FAVORITE USE for this sauce is over the smoked pork chops I occasionally buy at the supermarket. It's also ideal for ham steak, roast pork, chicken, or vegetables such as Brussels sprouts, potatoes, turnips, or rutabagas. *Makes about 1½ cups*

In a small saucepan, melt the butter over medium-high heat, then add the flour to form a roux, stirring for about 1 minute. Remove from the heat, slowly pour in the evaporated milk, and stir until smooth. Return to the heat, add the cheese, dry mustard, caraway seeds, sour cream, Dijon mustard, and salt and pepper. Stir over medium heat until smooth and bubbling, about 5 minutes.

1 tablespoon unsalted butter

1 tablespoon all-purpose flour

1 cup evaporated milk

2½ ounces Gouda cheese, finely diced

1 tablespoon dry mustard

⅛ teaspoon ground caraway seeds

½ cup sour cream

1 tablespoon Dijon mustard

Salt and freshly ground black pepper to taste

Chef Thijs's Cheese Sauce

2 tablespoons
unsalted butter

¼ cup all-purpose flour

1¼ cups whole milk, hot

2½ ounces Edam
cheese, grated

½ teaspoon cognac
or brandy

⅛ teaspoon ground
fennel seeds

Salt and freshly ground
black pepper to taste

CHEF HENRI J. THIJS was an assistant to the famous French chef Auguste Escoffier when he returned to his native Holland in 1915 to become a partner in the famous Dikker & Thijs store in Amsterdam, now a lavish classic hotel. Chef Thijs created this cheese sauce for vegetables such as cauliflower, broccoli, or Brussels sprouts. Because the sauce is white, I find it ideal over green vegetables, such as a whole head of light green Romanesco cauliflower.

Makes 1½ cups

In a small saucepan, melt the butter over medium heat, then add the flour to form a roux, stirring for about 1 minute. Remove from the heat and slowly whisk in the milk. Return to the heat and bring to a boil over medium-high heat while whisking constantly. Reduce the heat to low and cook slowly until smooth, about 8 minutes. Add the cheese, cognac, fennel seeds, and salt and pepper, and mix well. Cook until the cheese melts completely and the sauce is smooth, about 5 minutes.

Norwegian Game Sauce

I FIRST ENCOUNTERED the odd little brick of caramel-colored Norwegian cheese called *gjetost* (pronounced YET-oast) in the 1960s, while passing through the Gudbrandsdalen Valley in central Norway as a hitchhiker. I later read that it was first made by a farmer's wife, Anne Hov, in the 1880s, who thought of pouring cream into the kettle of whey. The new cheese fetched a higher price than the ordinary cheese and is reputed to have saved Gudbrandsdalen Valley from financial ruin. There are two types of gjetost, Ski Queen in red packs, made from goat and cow's milk and whey, and Ekte, made only from goat's milk. This sauce for game meats is a wonderful way to use the cheese. The sauce is also excellent for turkey thighs.

Makes about 2 cups

2 tablespoons unsalted butter

2 tablespoons all-purpose flour

1 cup beef broth

½ cup crème fraîche or sour cream

5 ounces Ski Queen gjetost cheese, shredded

1 teaspoon salt

½ teaspoon freshly ground black pepper

In a medium saucepan, melt the butter over medium heat, then add the flour to form a roux, stirring constantly for 1 to 2 minutes. Slowly add the beef broth, crème fraîche, and cheese. Let it bubble gently while stirring until smooth and thickened slightly, about 10 minutes. Season with salt and pepper.

Hot Crab Dip

8 ounces cream cheese

8 tablespoons (1 stick) unsalted butter

1 pound lump crabmeat, picked over

1 small onion, finely chopped

2 teaspoons Tabasco sauce

2 teaspoons garlic powder

2 teaspoons cayenne pepper

2 teaspoons salt

2 teaspoons freshly ground white pepper

THIS LOUISIANA CREOLE hot crab dip is temperature-hot and chile-hot. You can use crackers, tart shells, or Fritos corn chip scoops for dipping, but celery or carrot sticks are equally nice, and then you can eat more of the dip and not feel so fat.

Makes 3 cups

In a double boiler over medium-high heat, melt the cream cheese and butter together, stirring. Once the mixture has become homogeneous, reduce the heat to medium-low, add the crabmeat, onion, Tabasco, garlic powder, cayenne, salt, and white pepper, and stir until the dip is heated through, about 5 minutes. Add additional seasoning to your taste and serve hot.

Fritters with Cheese

Cheesy fritters are not only popular at parties, but they also make wonderful snacks or appetizers before dinner. Sometimes fritters seem unappealing only because of their name. Case in point is the first recipe, Cauliflower-Cheese Fritters (page 24). But once you make them you'll marvel at the wonderful taste and the ease with which you can prepare them. If you want a little more of a challenge, then you can't pass up Zucchini Blossoms Stuffed with Mozzarella (page 25). Think it's too difficult? Even one of my twentysomething sons made it for a date once (he impressed her and didn't let on he didn't know what he was doing—just following the recipe). My personal favorite is the Cheese and Anchovy Fritters (page 30), which aren't for everyone, but for me they're impossibly delicious. Before making any recipe in this chapter I recommend you read the note on deep-frying on page 28.

Cauliflower-Cheese Fritters

1 head cauliflower
(about 1¾ pounds), cut
into florets and
stems discarded

6 cups olive oil, for frying

½ cup all-purpose flour

2 ounces Gruyère
cheese, shredded

2 large eggs

Salt to taste

1 lemon, cut into
6 wedges

THESE CROQUETTES are popular party fare. In this recipe, you drop spoonfuls of egg batter incorporating mashed cauliflower and Gruyère cheese into hot oil and fry them until golden brown. Let the oil cool down, strain it, and you can use it again for frying.

Makes 6 servings

1. Bring a large pot of water to a boil and cook the cauliflower until tender, about 25 minutes. Drain the cauliflower in a colander and crush with a potato masher.

2. Preheat the frying oil in a deep fryer or an 8-inch saucepan fitted with a basket insert to 375°F.

3. In a bowl, mix the cauliflower, flour, cheese, eggs, and salt together. Carefully slide heaping tablespoonfuls of the mixture into the hot oil (do not crowd them) and fry until golden brown, about 3½ minutes. Remove with a slotted spoon and drain on paper towels. Continue frying the remaining batches. Serve hot with the lemon wedges.

Zucchini Blossoms Stuffed with Mozzarella

YEARS AGO, the only zucchini blossoms to be found were in your garden. Today better supermarkets and greengrocers, and definitely farmers markets, carry them. The beautiful yellow flowers, which spread wide open in the daytime, are wonderful to behold and beg to be stuffed. Although this is a bit tricky and labor-intensive, your guests will be wowed if you're able not to eat them all yourself. *Makes 4 or 5 servings*

10 zucchini blossoms

10 fresh mozzarella cheese cubes (about 2 ounces in all)

5 salted anchovy fillets, rinsed and cut in half lengthwise

6 cups vegetable oil or sunflower seed oil, for frying

½ cup all-purpose flour

1 teaspoon extra-virgin olive oil

1 large egg white

Salt to taste

Water

1. Open the flowers and remove the pistil, then very carefully wash the inside by dunking each flower in a bowl of cold water. (Use tweezers if you have large fingers.) Dry the flowers by leaving them on some paper towels for 15 minutes.

2. Wrap each cube of mozzarella with half a piece of anchovy fillet, then stuff each blossom. The flowers can be refrigerated for up to 24 hours at this point.

3. Preheat the frying oil in a deep fryer or an 8-inch saucepan fitted with a basket insert to 360°F.

4. In a bowl, mix the flour, olive oil, egg white, salt, and enough water to make a slightly thick batter. Dip the blossoms in the batter, letting the excess drip off, then deep-fry several at a time (don't crowd them) in the hot oil until golden, turning once, about 30 seconds. Remove with a slotted spoon and drain on paper towels for a minute before serving hot.

Kefalotyri Cheese Croquettes

3 cups grated kefalotyri cheese (about 8 ounces)

1 teaspoon baking powder

½ teaspoon salt

5 large egg whites, beaten until stiff peaks form

2 tablespoons all-purpose flour (optional)

6 to 8 cups olive oil, for frying

THE ONLY DOWNSIDE to this wonderful meze I first had in Greece is that the cheese, kefalotyri, is hard to find. It is a hard, light yellow grating cheese made from either sheep's milk or goat's milk and can be found in Greek markets. I usually buy it from www.igourmet.com or www.christosmarket.com. You can replace it with a young pecorino cheese that is not as old or hard as grating pecorino or with kashkaval cheese.

Makes 16 croquettes to serve 8

1. In a bowl, mix the cheese, baking powder, and salt. Slowly add the cheese mixture to the egg whites, beating constantly. The mixture should be very thick. If it isn't, add some or all of the flour.

2. Preheat the frying oil in a deep fryer or an 8-inch saucepan fitted with a basket insert to 360°F.

3. Shape the mixture into croquettes about 2 inches long using a teaspoon. It's okay if they are rounder. Fry them several at a time (don't crowd them) in the hot oil until golden, about 3 minutes. Remove with a slotted spoon, drain on paper towels, and serve hot.

Buckwheat and Taleggio Fritters

TALEGGIO IS A STRONG, CREAMY cow's milk cheese made in the mountains of Lombardy in northern Italy. These fritters will be dark brown in appearance once cooked. When you cook the fritters, make sure to refrigerate the batter first, then drop it into the oil in heaping teaspoonfuls. Do not make them any bigger than called for; otherwise they will taste pasty. Grappa is a grape-based clear brandy from northern Italy.

Makes 5 servings

1 cup buckwheat flour

½ cup all-purpose flour

2 teaspoons salt

1 cup plus 2 tablespoons water, or a little more

6 to 8 cups olive oil, for frying

3 ounces Taleggio cheese, diced

1 tablespoon grappa

1. In a large bowl, sift together the flours. Add the salt, then enough water to make a stiff batter. Cover with a cloth and let rest for 1 hour.

2. Preheat the frying oil in a deep fryer or an 8-inch saucepan fitted with a basket insert to 300°F.

3. Stir the cheese and grappa into the batter. Fry heaping teaspoonfuls several at a time (don't crowd them) in the hot oil until golden brown, about 8 minutes. Remove with a slotted spoon, drain on paper towels, and serve immediately.

ON DEEP-FRYING

Although everyone loves deep-fried anything, it's amazing how few people—including well-known cookbook authors—deep-fry at home. A lot of that reluctance derives from fear of lots of boiling oil and from an image of fried food as being unhealthy and providing excessive calories. Here are a few tips and suggestions for you to deep-fry food perfectly and to reduce your worry about fat in your diet. The most important thing to remember about deep-frying is that your cooking oil must be and must remain hot while cooking, usually a temperature between 350° and 370° F. This is why a home-use deep-fryer or a deep-fry thermometer is essential. The first is a great convenience because you can leave the oil in the frying receptacle and once it cools, store for repeated use. Always make sure the oil reaches the specified temperature. Never fry too many pieces of food at once; otherwise the oil temperature will drop too much and result in greasy food. It's that greasy food that one must avoid, because that's where the fat calories come from and it also makes for unpleasant-tasting food. Lastly, remember that eating deep-fried foods everyday *is* unhealthy; that's why deep-frying is for special treats and occasions. Deep-frying in itself is not unhealthy; it's just another cooking method for you to master.

Fried Provolone Fritters

THESE FRITTERS start out looking like coins, then once they are fried, they turn golden brown and puff up slightly. They make a wonderful little snack or an appetizer tidbit to munch on before a dinner party. *Makes 24 fritters to serve 10 to 12*

2 cups unbleached all-purpose flour

1 large egg, beaten

2 tablespoons unsalted butter, melted

1 teaspoon salt

½ cup water

4 ounces provolone or caciocavallo cheese, cut into 1-inch pieces

12 salted anchovy fillets, rinsed and cut in half

6 to 8 cups olive oil, for frying

1. In a medium bowl, put the flour and make a well. Add the egg, melted butter, salt, and water to the well, mix well to form into a ball, cover with plastic wrap, and let rest for 30 minutes.

2. Roll the dough out thinly on a lightly floured work surface and cut out 3-inch diameter disks. Reroll the scraps to cut out more disks. Place a piece of cheese on half the disks, then lay a piece of anchovy on top. Cover with the remaining disks and seal the borders by crimping them together with a fork.

3. Preheat the frying oil in a deep fryer or an 8-inch saucepan fitted with a basket insert to 360°F.

4. Fry several disks at a time (don't crowd them) in the hot oil until golden, about 3 minutes, turning once. Remove with a slotted spoon, drain on paper towels, and serve hot or warm.

Cheese and Anchovy Fritters

1 package (about 2¼ teaspoons) active dry yeast

2 cups tepid whole milk

2½ cups all-purpose flour

1 teaspoon salt

16 salted anchovy fillets, rinsed and chopped

6 ounces caciocavallo or mild provolone cheese, cut into small dice

Freshly ground black pepper to taste

6 to 8 cups olive oil, for frying

THESE FRITTERS ARE MADE WITH a yeasted batter, with cheese and anchovies mixed into the batter itself. Ideally, you will use caciocavallo, a hard southern Italian cow's milk cheese usually made in the shape of a gourd. Caciocavallo cheese is usually found in Italian markets, but can be replaced by a mild provolone. These fritters are addictive and usually served as a snack, but they also make a great passed antipasto at a cocktail party. *Makes 40 fritters to serve 10*

1. In a medium bowl, dissolve the yeast in the milk and leave for 5 minutes. Add the flour and salt and incorporate to form a very thick batter that can still flow very slowly. Cover with a kitchen towel and let rise for 1 hour.

2. Stir the anchovies, cheese, and pepper into the dough and let rise for another 2 hours.

3. Preheat the frying oil in a deep fryer or an 8-inch saucepan fitted with a basket insert to 350°F.

4. Drop large spoonfuls of the dough into the hot oil (don't crowd them) and fry, turning, until golden, about 4 minutes. Remove with a slotted spoon, drain on paper towels, and serve hot or warm.

Fried Goat Cheese Pudding Squares

THESE SQUARES are a kind of cross between a pudding and a custard. The French call it a clafouti, and it's usually a fruit-based dessert. Here you make the pudding with cherry tomatoes and goat cheese, chill it, then cut it into squares that are dipped in egg white and bread crumbs and deep-fried. It's quite a nice hors d'oeuvre. "Fresh" goat cheese refers to the soft, crumbly goat cheese sold in logs.   *Makes 6 servings*

Butter, for greasing pan

8 ounces fresh goat cheese, diced

1 pound cherry tomatoes, cut in half

5 large eggs

¾ cup whole milk

½ cup crème fraîche

½ cup chopped fresh chives

Salt and freshly ground black pepper to taste

Pinch of ground nutmeg

5 tablespoons cornstarch

6 cups vegetable oil, for frying

2 large egg whites

1 cup dried bread crumbs

1. Preheat the oven to 350°F.

2. Grease a 9-inch deep-dish pie pan with butter. Put the cheese and tomatoes in the pan. In a bowl, beat the eggs, milk, crème fraîche, three-quarters of the chives, the salt, pepper, and nutmeg. Add the cornstarch to the mixture, stir it in, then pour over the tomatoes and cheese. Bake until golden and set, 1 to 1¼ hours. Remove from the oven and cool to room temperature before placing in the refrigerator for 2 hours.

3. Preheat the frying oil to 325°F in a deep fryer or an 8-inch saucepan fitted with a basket insert.

4. Cut the pudding into 1- to 2-inch squares. Beat the egg whites until frothy, dip the squares into the beaten egg whites, then dredge in the bread crumbs. Deep-fry until golden, about 2 minutes. Season with salt and the remaining chives and serve hot.

Savory Pastries with Cheese

This may be my favorite chapter in the book, because I just love little pastries that satisfy one's hunger and desire before any of the main food comes out of the kitchen. When I first learned how to make the Gougères on page 35, I couldn't stop making them and filling them with all kinds of stuffings. You will feel the same way, too. I could probably say the same thing about the Pan-Fried Cheese Pies recipe from Greece (page 40) that I nearly ate all by myself. They make wonderful party appetizers. Another great party appetizer, because of both its delicious taste and its startling color, is Cheese and Potato Cigars (page 44), stuffed pastries rolled up like a cigar with a very appetizing golden yellow interior.

BEIGNET DOUGH

In French, this kind of beignet dough is called *pâte à choux* or *pâte à beignets soufflés* or, more colorfully, *pets-de-nonne*, ("nun's farts"), and it is made with flour and butter stirred into boiling water, with eggs then incorporated one at a time. It is an ordinary cream puff pastry—the same kind used for making cream puffs and éclairs. There are two kinds of beignet dough, one for baking (this one) and the other used for deep-frying (see my book *Little Foods of the Mediterranean*, Harvard Common Press).   *Makes 30 medium or 60 small beignets*

　　1 cup whole milk
　　8 tablespoons (1 stick) unsalted butter
　　¾ teaspoon salt
　　1 cup unbleached all-purpose flour
　　6 large eggs
　　Ground nutmeg (optional)

1. Put the milk, butter, and salt in a large heavy saucepan and set over medium-high heat. Once the butter has melted, add the flour all at once. Stir with a wooden spoon until it creates a dough that pulls away from the sides of the saucepan easily, and the butter begins to ooze a little, 1½ to 2 minutes. Transfer to a bowl.

2. Preheat the oven to 400°F.

3. Beat the eggs vigorously into the flour mixture one at a time with a fork. Make sure each egg is absorbed and the dough is smooth before you add the next one. Sprinkle with nutmeg, if desired.

4. Butter a large baking sheet and, using a tablespoon, drop large tablespoonfuls of the dough in rows on the sheet 1½ inches apart. Each droplet of dough should be about 1 inch in diameter for small ones and 2 inches for medium ones. Bake until golden brown, 22 to 25 minutes. Do not be tempted to peek in the oven, but if you simply must, crack the oven door slowly open; otherwise the puffs may collapse. They will look and seem done at 20 minutes, but they are not; continue to bake until they are firm when pressed down on top with your finger, another 2 to 5 minutes.

Gougères

GOUGÈRES, A KIND OF CHEESE PUFF, are traditional hors d'oeuvres from Burgundy, made with pâte à choux or ordinary cream puff pastry. The cheese puffs are also filled (see next recipe) and in France may be eaten between the main course and the dessert as a course of their own.

Makes 50 to 60 gougères

1 Beignet Dough recipe
(page 34; see step 1 below)

4 ounces Gruyère
cheese, diced

1. Prepare the beignets through step 1 of the Beignet Dough recipe, blending the Gruyère in with the nutmeg.

2. Preheat the oven to 400°F.

3. Butter a large baking sheet and drop large tablespoonfuls of the dough in rows on the sheet 1½ inches apart. Bake until golden brown, 22 to 25 minutes. Do not be tempted to peek in the oven but if you do, crack the oven door slowly open; otherwise the puffs may collapse. They will look and seem done at 15 minutes, but they are not; continue to bake until they are firm when pressed down on top with your finger. You can serve them hot as is, or let them cool, then stuff them or freeze them for later use.

Gougères with Creamy Cheese Sauce

2 cups milk

One ¼-inch-thick slice onion

6 black peppercorns

1 bay leaf

2 tablespoons unsalted butter

2 tablespoons all-purpose flour

Salt and freshly ground black pepper to taste

Pinch of ground nutmeg

2 tablespoons crème fraîche

⅔ cup shredded Gruyère cheese (about 2 ounces)

60 Gougères (page 35)

THIS RECIPE is the classic Gougères (page 35) filled with a cheese sauce. *Makes 50 to 60 Gougères*

1. In a medium heavy saucepan, heat the milk over medium heat until bubbles form around the edge, then add the onion, black peppercorns, and bay leaf and remove from the heat. Let steep for 10 minutes, covered.

2. Make a thin béchamel sauce (white sauce) by melting the butter in a saucepan and incorporating the flour to form a roux. Slowly whisk in the reserved hot milk by pouring it through a strainer, discarding the onion, bay leaf, and peppercorns. Bring to a boil and season with salt and pepper and a pinch of ground nutmeg.

3. Reduce the heat to low and simmer, stirring, until dense, 10 minutes. Add the crème fraîche and shredded Gruyère cheese and stir until it melts and is smooth. Check the seasoning. Slice the puff pastries open, stuff with a spoonful of the sauce, and serve hot.

Gruyère Half-Moons

SERVE THE HALF-MOONS as little party tidbits. You may eat them hot or cool, and they are the perfect do-ahead hors d'oeuvre for the time-pressed host. When you form the dough, make it into a ball with a minimum of kneading.

Makes 6 to 8 servings

1¼ cups all-purpose flour

8 tablespoons (1 stick) unsalted butter, at room temperature

6 ounces Gruyère cheese, shredded

1 large egg

Pinch of salt

1. Pour the flour on a work surface or in a bowl and make a well in the center. Work the butter, cheese, egg, and salt into the flour to form a ball of dough. Wrap the dough in wax paper and let rest in the refrigerator for 30 minutes.

2. Preheat the oven to 400°F.

3. Remove the dough and roll it out on a flour-strewn counter with a rolling pin until ⅛ inch thick. Cut as many 2-inch disks as you can, and cut each disk in half to form a half-moon. Continue to gather and roll out the remaining dough until it is all used. Butter a large baking sheet, then sprinkle flour on top and shake so the whole tray has a light dusting of flour. Place the half-moons on the sheet and bake until golden on top, about 10 minutes. Serve hot or at room temperature.

Cheddar Cheese Twists

3½ cups finely grated sharp
white Vermont Cheddar
cheese (about 12 ounces)

1½ teaspoons dried thyme

1½ teaspoons dried sage

1 teaspoon coarsely
ground black pepper

1 pound frozen puff pastry,
defrosted according to
package instructions

AT THANKSGIVING our family spends a lot of time hanging around in the kitchen, and these cheese twists give everyone something to nibble on while we wait for dinner. They are best when right out of the oven, but you can serve them room temperature, too. We double this recipe if there are more than nine people.

Makes about 36 twists

1. In a bowl, mix the cheese, thyme, sage, and pepper.

2. Lightly flour a work surface and roll out the puff pastry until 18 × 10 inches. Sprinkle one-third of the cheese mixture over half of the pastry. Fold the plain half over the cheesy half and press with a rolling pin so it adheres. Roll out again to 18 × 10 inches, sprinkle the next third of the cheese, and fold the dough over. Repeat the process a third time with the remaining cheese, rolling the dough out to a final shape of 18 × 10 inches. Place in the refrigerator for 30 minutes.

3. Preheat the oven to 425°F.

4. Line two 10 × 14-inch baking sheets with parchment paper. Cut the pastry in half crosswise to form two 10 × 9-inch rectangles. Trim off the uneven pieces of pastry. Cut each rectangle crosswise into ½-inch-wide strips. Twist each strip a few times and place on the baking sheet about ¾ inch apart, damping the ends with water and pressing them to adhere to the parchment.

5. Bake until golden brown, reversing the position of the sheets halfway through baking, about 10 minutes total. Remove from the oven and let cool on the baking sheet. Serve warm or at room temperature.

Rustic Pastries

THE STAR CHEESE OF THESE PASTRIES is scamorza, a soft provolone-like cheese originally made in the Abruzzo and Molise provinces of Italy with water buffalo's milk. Today it is made with cow's milk. The short dough pastries are stuffed with ricotta, too. Scamorza can be hard to find, but good Italian markets will have it, and you can order it at www.realmozzarella. com, www.mozzco.com, or www.igourmet.com. It's also made in a smoked variety, which is excellent on pizza. You can use a mild provolone in its place. *Makes 32 pastries to serve 16*

4 ounces ricotta cheese, preferably homemade (page 65)

2 large eggs, separated

2 ounces salami, cut into small dice

Salt and freshly ground black pepper to taste

4 ounces scamorza cheese, cut into small dice

2 Short Dough recipes (page 77)

1. In a medium bowl, whisk the ricotta, egg yolks, 1 egg white, and the salami together and season with salt and pepper. Stir in the scamorza.

2. Preheat the oven to 400°F.

3. Roll the short dough out until very thin and cut out as many 2½-inch diameter rounds as you can, collecting the dough and rerolling the scraps as necessary. Place a heaping teaspoonful of stuffing on top of one round and cover with another, pinching the sides closed with a fork. Arrange the pastry disks on a greased baking sheet, brush with the remaining beaten egg white, and bake until golden, about 25 minutes. Remove from the oven and let rest for 10 minutes before serving.

Pan-Fried Cheese Pies

For the dough

1¼ teaspoons (½ envelope) active dry yeast

1 cup milk

2½ cups all-purpose flour

¼ teaspoon salt

½ cup fresh orange juice, strained of pulp

1 large egg, lightly beaten

For the filling

8 ounces ricotta cheese

2½ ounces feta cheese

1 large egg

2 teaspoons dried mint

Extra-virgin olive oil, for frying and handling the dough

THERE ARE QUITE A FEW different pies called *kalitsounia* in Greece and Crete. They can be vastly different from each other. In the town of Rethymnon, with its grand castle walls of the old Venetian fortress, the largest Venetian fortress ever built, there are tavernas nestled here and there near the walls, and that's where I had a delicious *kalitsounia*, almost pancake-like. Although I don't remember having these pies made with orange juice, Diane Kochilas, from whose recipe this is adapted, does use it in *The Glorious Foods of Greece*.

Makes 15 pies

1. In a bowl, dissolve the yeast in the milk and let rest for 5 minutes. Stir in ½ cup of the flour and the salt and mix well. Add the orange juice, egg, and ½ more cup of the flour and stir to mix. Add the remaining flour in ¼-cup increments, stirring with a wooden spoon, until a soft mass of dough forms. Turn out onto a floured work surface and knead for 8 minutes. The dough should be very sticky. Place in an oiled bowl, cover with a kitchen towel, and let double in size, about 2 hours. The dough will rise and be spongy.

2. In a bowl, combine the cheeses, egg, and mint.

3. In a large cast-iron skillet, heat 1 tablespoon oil over medium heat. Oil your hands with some olive oil. Press a golf ball–size piece of dough into the palm of one hand, pushing down with the fingertips of the other hand to form a small, thick disk. Place a heaping tablespoon of the cheese mixture into the center of the disk and close up to form a ball, making sure there are no holes for cheese to escape. Flatten the stuffed ball of dough with an oiled palm until 4 inches in diameter and 1 inch thick. Cook the stuffed disk until the bottom is golden brown, 3 to 4 minutes. Turn and cook the other side until golden brown. Transfer to paper towels. Continue with the remaining dough and cheese and replenish the olive oil as you cook. Serve warm.

Empanadilla de Queso de Cabrales

6 to 8 cups olive oil, for frying

5 ounces Cabrales or any blue cheese

3 tablespoons heavy cream

1 large egg

Salt to taste

15 empanadilla skins, defrosted according to package instructions

CABRALES CHEESE is a famous cheese from the Asturias region of northern Spain. It is blue cheese made from a mixture of cow's, goat's, and sheep's milk and has a rough rind. Its texture is creamy but the flavor is complex, with a powerful bouquet resulting from its maturation wrapped in leaves and left to age in caves. Order it from www.tienda.com or www.igourmet.com. It is sometimes found at better supermarkets. Empanadilla skins are found in many ethnic markets ranging from Mexican to Italian; you can also try the Web sites mentioned above. *Makes 15 empanadillas to serve 7 or 8*

1. Preheat the frying oil to 360°F in a deep fryer or an 8-inch saucepan fitted with a basket insert.

2. In a bowl, mix together the cheese, cream, and egg until well blended. Taste and season with salt if necessary.

3. Place a small amount of cheese stuffing in the center of each disk of dough. Fold over and crimp the edges with the tines of a fork. Set aside while you finish making the rest. They can be frozen or refrigerated at this point, separated by plastic wrap so they don't stick to each other.

4. Fry in batches (do not crowd the fryer) until golden brown on all sides, about 2 minutes. Transfer to paper towels to drain, and serve hot.

Cigar Böreks

IF YOU TRAVEL IN TURKEY, you will eat these ubiquitous fried roll-ups of phyllo, served as meze and found in every little restaurant, until they come out of your ears. That's a good thing, as they are impossibly delicious. The name comes from the fact that the phyllo pastry is stuffed with cheese and rolled up like a cigar. Three kinds of cheese are used in this börek, ideal for parties because you make a lot and store them in a cool place covered with a damp cloth, then fry them at the last minute. The Greek and Turkish kashkaval cheese I usually buy from www.igourmet.com or www.christosmarket.com.

Makes 16 to 18 roll-ups

8 ounces soft white cheese, such as Syrian white cheese, Mexican queso blanco or queso Oaxaca, farmer's cheese, or firm mozzarella, finely chopped

4 ounces feta cheese, crumbled

¼ cup shredded kashkaval or Monterey Jack cheese

1 large egg, beaten

1 tablespoon finely chopped fresh flat-leaf parsley

12 ounces frozen phyllo pastry, defrosted according to package instructions

2 cups sunflower seed oil or vegetable oil

1. In a bowl, mix the cheeses, egg, and parsley.

2. Cut the phyllo pastry in half so the dimensions are 14 × 9 inches. Take two sheets of dough and lay them on top of one another. Place a small amount of cheese filling, about 1 tablespoon, in the center of the short end, spreading it out into the length of a cigarette, and roll several times. Fold about 2 inches of each side over toward the center to partially cover the stuffing, then continue rolling until you have a cigar shape. Dip your finger in a bowl of water and seal the edges by rubbing them together with the water. Repeat with the remaining filling and phyllo. As you set the rolled böreks aside, cover them with a damp kitchen towel.

3. In a 9- or 10-inch skillet, heat the oil over medium heat to 365°F. Fry the roll-ups in batches (don't crowd them) until golden brown, about 15 seconds, turn with tongs, and cook for another 15 seconds. Transfer to paper towels to drain, and serve hot.

Cheese and Potato Cigars

1 large baking potato
(about 12 ounces)

8 ounces Gruyère
cheese, shredded

2 large eggs

1 teaspoon salt

1 teaspoon freshly
ground black pepper

2 teaspoons ground nutmeg

2 teaspoons ground turmeric

Fourteen 6-inch-
square Chinese egg roll
wrappers (7 ounces)

1 large egg white,
lightly beaten

6 cups olive oil or
vegetable oil, for frying

THIS PREPARATION is a Tunisian version of the cigar börek from Turkey (page 43). It is a cheese- and potato-stuffed pastry rolled up like a cigar. The turmeric turns the inside a very appetizing golden yellow, and it's hard not to just keep popping these tidbits into your mouth. You can cut the roll-ups in half or in quarters for bite-size pieces. *Makes 14 roll-ups*

1. Place the whole potato in a saucepan and cover with cold water by several inches. Bring to a gentle boil over medium heat and cook for about 20 minutes, then continue to cook at a strong simmer until a skewer glides easily to the center of the potato, about another 25 minutes. Drain, peel when cool enough to handle, and mash.

2. In a bowl, mix the potato, cheese, eggs, salt, pepper, nutmeg, and turmeric.

3. Arrange an egg roll wrapper in front of you and place a portion of stuffing, about 2 tablespoons, along the end nearest to you. Roll it up one roll, fold the sides in, and continue rolling it up like a cigar. Seal the edges by rubbing them with egg white with your finger. Set aside as you repeat with the remaining wrappers and filling. They can be frozen at this point if you like.

4. Preheat the frying oil in a deep fryer or an 8-inch saucepan fitted with a basket insert to 360°F.

5. Fry a few of the roll-ups at a time (do not crowd them) until golden, 2 to 3 minutes. Transfer to paper towels to drain. Cut in half on the bias, and serve immediately.

Boiled Croatian Cheese Strudel

THIS PREPARATION, called *Zagorski štrukli* in Croatian, is a boiled puff pastry pie made with farmer's or cottage cheese and is a specialty of the Zagorje, Prigorje, and Međimurje regions around the city of Zagreb in northern Croatia. It will seem completely counterintuitive to boil puff pastry, but that's what you do here, and it will work. Just remember, you don't boil them for long.

Makes 8 servings

1 pound puff pastry, defrosted according to package instructions

8 ounces farmer's cheese or cottage cheese, at room temperature

8 ounces imported feta cheese, at room temperature

3 large eggs

½ teaspoon salt, plus more to taste

Butter, for greasing

1 cup sour cream

1. Preheat the oven to 365°F.

2. On a floured surface, roll out each puff pastry sheet (usually 2 to a box) until it is a large rectangle about 18 × 11 inches.

3. In a bowl, stir together the cheeses, 2 of the eggs, and the ½ teaspoon salt. Spread this mixture in a line, below center, lengthwise along the puff pastry. Fold the puff pastry over the stuffing and shape into a cylinder, sealing the long edge by rubbing with water with your finger. Cut into 2-inch lengths and pinch the ends shut with the tines of a fork.

4. Bring a large saucepan of water to a gentle boil and boil the puff pastry pieces until softened, about 1 minute. Some cheese will escape. Transfer with a slotted spoon to paper towels to drain a bit, then place in a buttered 13 × 9 × 2-inch baking dish.

5. In a bowl, whip together the sour cream and remaining egg and a pinch of salt. Pour over the pastries and bake until golden brown, about 30 minutes. Remove from the oven and serve once they are warm.

Roquefort Allumettes

1 cup mashed Roquefort cheese (3 to 4 ounces)

¼ cup coarsely crushed walnuts

2 tablespoons heavy cream

1 tablespoon finely chopped fresh flat-leaf parsley

Freshly ground black pepper to taste

8 ounces frozen puff pastry, defrosted according to package instructions

1 large egg, beaten

THE BLUE-VEINED ROQUEFORT cheese comes from the town of Roquefort-sur-Soulzon in the Haut Languedoc region of France. The constant and reliable airflow, humidity, and temperature of the caverns and grottos of the region have the ideal conditions for the growth of a certain bacteria that turns ordinary white sheep's milk cheese into blue cheese. One such system of grottos is at Roquefort, and it gave birth to that famous cheese. These allumettes are the common hors d'oeuvre of the Rouergue region of Languedoc in southwestern France. They are short and squat puff pastries that are ideal for parties.

Makes 12 pastries to serve 6

1. Preheat the oven to 400°F.

2. In a bowl, mix the Roquefort cheese, walnuts, cream, parsley, and pepper until smooth. Fill a small pastry bag fitted with a ¼-inch tip with the stuffing.

3. Prepare the puff pastry by rolling it out into two rectangles about ⅛ inch thick, not wider than 9 inches, and about 12 inches long. Have the shorter side nearest to you.

4. Using the pastry bag, pipe six ½-inch-wide rows of stuffing on the lower half of each sheet of the puff pastry, leaving a space at each end and in between each row of stuffing. If you are not using a pastry bag, spoon the stuffing in neat rows. Fold the top portion over the bottom portion of the puff pastry with its columns of stuffing and seal the edges. Cut into 6 long batons (allumettes) in between the rows of stuffing and crimp the edges closed with the tines of a fork. Make sure that the pastries are well sealed so no stuffing oozes out. Arrange the pastries on an ungreased baking sheet. Brush the tops with the beaten egg. Bake until golden, about 20 minutes. Serve warm.

Feta Cheese Puff Pastry #1

8 ounces frozen puff pastry, defrosted according to package instructions

2 to 3 ounces imported feta cheese, washed of salt and crumbled

1 small egg mixed with 1 tablespoon water

1 tablespoon sesame seeds

THIS SIMPLE LITTLE MEZE is a delight when served as a passed hors d'oeuvre with a typical Greek drink such as ouzo. My favorite feta cheeses are Greek or Bulgarian, and those are what you should look for.

Makes 48 pastries to serve 8

1. Preheat the oven to 425°F.

2. Roll out the puff pastry on a lightly floured work surface until a little thinner. Cut into 48 rectangles about 2½ × 1¼ inches long and place on a baking sheet. Divide the feta between the rectangles and brush with the egg wash. Sprinkle the tops with the sesame seeds. Bake until golden, about 15 minutes. Serve immediately.

Feta Cheese Puff Pastry #2

THIS DELICIOUS APPETIZER seasons the feta cheese with the Middle Eastern spice mix known as za'tar. You can find it in Middle Eastern markets, although it's not difficult to make your own (see box).

Makes 12 servings

8 ounces frozen puff pastry, defrosted according to package instructions

2 tablespoons za'tar (see box)

3 ounces feta cheese (preferably Greek or Bulgarian), crumbled

Extra-virgin olive oil, for drizzling

1. Preheat the oven to 385°F.

2. On a lightly floured surface, roll out the pastry until a bit thinner, then cut into twelve 2½-inch squares.

3. Arrange the squares on a baking sheet, sprinkle with a little za'tar, then push some feta cheese down into the center of the pastry. Drizzle with very little olive oil and place in the oven. Bake until golden brown, about 20 minutes. Serve hot.

HOW TO MAKE ZA'TAR

This Lebanese spice mix can be bought online or in Middle Eastern markets, but it is very easy to make yourself. In a bowl, mix ½ cup dried thyme, 2 tablespoons sesame seeds, 2 teaspoons ground sumac, and a little salt. Store in a jar in a dark place. If you have made or bought a lot, freeze some of the mix.

Savory Crêpes and Pancakes with Cheese

Crêpes and pancakes are among the most appealing foods. Combine them with cheese and they're heavenly. Delicate or fluffy, they can encapsulate a range of foods, which are then transformed into something greater than the parts. Certainly the first recipe, Porcini Mushroom Crêpes with Creamy Cheese Sauce (page 52), qualifies as one of these transcendental-type dishes that will remain memorable long after you eat it. Personally, I find the Saffron Crêpe Cake with Swiss Chard and Ricotta Cheese (page 54) to be the most extraordinary recipe in this chapter. Make it and impress your guests and yourself. It's not hard; it just requires paying attention.

Porcini Mushroom Crêpes with Creamy Cheese Sauce

2 ounces freshly grated Parmesan (preferably Parmigiano-Reggiano cheese) or shredded Fontina Val d'Aosta cheese or both

1 cup Béchamel Sauce (see box)

2 tablespoons unsalted butter, plus more for baking dish

1 tablespoon extra-virgin olive oil

4 ounces fresh porcini mushrooms, thinly sliced

Salt and freshly ground black pepper to taste

3 Crêpes (page 60)

IF YOU EVER TRAVEL at the height of the porcini mushroom season in Italy, every restaurant will have a porcini mushroom dish they will insist you try. That's how I came upon this preparation one autumn at the Ristorante Gianni e Amadeo, in the city of Sassari on Sardinia. It was porcini mushroom season and there were porcini mushrooms galore. The restaurant's version was a very light and soft crêpe wrapped around sautéed porcini and covered with a creamy cream of Parmigiano-Reggiano sauce that melted in your mouth. If you can't find (or afford!) porcini mushrooms, I suggest using shiitake mushrooms. *Makes 2 or 3 servings*

1. Add half the cheese to the warm béchamel sauce until it melts.

2. Preheat the oven to 350°F.

3. In a skillet, melt the butter with the olive oil over medium heat, then cook the porcini mushrooms, stirring, until softened, about 6 minutes. Season with salt and pepper. Add half of the béchamel sauce, or more if you like it saucier, and cook for 1 minute. Divide the porcini mixture between the crêpes, placing it in the center, and fold over 4 times to form a square crêpe. Place the crêpes in a buttered baking dish. Sprinkle the remaining cheese on top and bake until the cheese is melted and very hot, about 12 minutes.

BÉCHAMEL SAUCE

Makes 1½ cups

 2 tablespoons unsalted butter
 3 tablespoons all-purpose flour
 1½ cups hot milk
 Salt and freshly ground white pepper to taste
 Pinch of ground nutmeg

In a medium saucepan, melt the butter, then stir in the flour to form a roux, cooking for 1 minute over medium heat while stirring. Remove the saucepan from the heat and whisk in the milk a little at a time until it is all blended. Sprinkle with salt, white pepper, and nutmeg. Return to the heat and cook, stirring almost constantly, until thick, 10 minutes.

Saffron Crêpe Cake with Swiss Chard and Ricotta Cheese

For the crêpes

2 cups whole milk

1½ cups all-purpose flour

10 tablespoons water

3 large eggs

2 tablespoons extra-
virgin olive oil

1 teaspoon saffron threads

1 teaspoon salt

½ teaspoon freshly
ground black pepper

2 tablespoons finely
chopped scallions

1 tablespoon
unsalted butter

(continued)

IN THE BASQUE COUNTRY of northwestern Spain, cooks make this quite extraordinary crêpe cake. Each layer is filled with Swiss chard, prosciutto, and ricotta cheese. Typically served as a lunch dish, it also makes a wonderful appetizer. No matter how you serve it, your guests will be very impressed.

Makes 6 to 8 appetizer servings or 4 lunch servings

1. Prepare the crêpes. In a blender, combine the milk, flour, water, eggs, olive oil, saffron, salt, and pepper and blend until smooth. Transfer the mixture to a bowl and stir in the scallions. Let the batter rest for 30 minutes.

2. In a 9-inch crêpe pan or nonstick skillet, heat a film of butter over medium heat. Pour about ⅓ cup of crêpe batter into the pan and twirl the pan as you do so that the bottom is covered. Cook on one side only until golden brown, about 1 minute for the first one, and 15 to 20 seconds for the remaining ones. Remove from the pan and continue with the remaining batter, buttering the pan only if necessary to keep the crêpes from sticking as you cook them. As you finish cooking each crêpe, lightly butter them to prevent their sticking to one another as you stack them, or separate each with plastic wrap. (The crêpes can be stacked and wrapped in plastic wrap and kept in the refrigerator for 3 days or in the freezer, wrapped further in a freezer bag, for 6 months if not using immediately.) You will need 9 crêpes for this recipe, and you can save the remainder.

3. Make the stuffing. In a large skillet, heat 2 tablespoons of the butter over low heat. Add the onions and cook, stirring, until softened, about 10 minutes. Add the Swiss chard and cook, stirring, for 3 minutes. Remove from the heat and let cool for 5 minutes. Stir in the eggs, then ½ cup of the ricotta cheese. Season with salt and pepper.

4. Preheat the oven to 350°F and place an oven rack in the center position

5. Grease a 9-inch cake pan with the remaining 1 tablespoon butter. Place 1 crêpe cooked side down in the pan. Cover with one-third of the prosciutto slices and top with a crêpe, cooked side down. Spread with one-third of the remaining ricotta cheese. Top with a crêpe, cooked side down, then spread with another one-third of the Swiss chard. Sprinkle with 2 tablespoons of Parmesan. Repeat this layering in this order two more times, pressing each layer down with your hands or the back of a spatula.

6. Drizzle the cake with olive oil. Cover loosely with aluminum foil, making sure the foil doesn't touch the top of the cake but is sealed tightly around the edges. Place in the middle of the oven and bake for 1 hour. Remove the aluminum foil and bake for another 10 minutes. Remove from the oven and let rest for 10 minutes. Invert the cake onto a warm serving plate. Serve and slice at the table.

For the stuffing and assembly of the cake

3 tablespoons unsalted butter

2 cups chopped onions

3 cups cooked, drained, and chopped Swiss chard (about 3¼ pounds raw)

2 large eggs, lightly beaten

1¼ cups ricotta cheese (page 65)

Salt and freshly ground black pepper to taste

3 ounces thinly sliced prosciutto

6 tablespoons freshly grated Parmesan cheese

2 tablespoons extra-virgin olive oil

Ham Crêpes Casserole

4 tablespoons unsalted butter, clarified (see Note

Salt and freshly ground black pepper to taste

½ recipe batter for Crêpes (page 60), made with beurre noisette instead of regular butter

8 ounces cooked ham, thinly sliced

1 teaspoon beurre noisette (see headnote)

1 cup heavy cream

½ cup shredded Gruyère cheese (about 1½ ounces)

1 tablespoon unsalted butter, cut into small dice

IN THIS RECIPE, said to come from the little town of Ambert in the heart of the mountains of Livradois of the Auvergne region of France, local cooks make the crêpes with buerre noisette, clarified butter heated until golden brown in color. They're stuffed with strips of cooked ham, rolled up, and arranged in the casserole. Although you can use any cooked sliced ham, if you have a good deli nearby that sells Bayonne ham, Black Forest ham, or Virginia Smithfield ham, I think it is worth the effort. In this recipe you will use 1 tablespoon of the buerre noisette in making the half recipe of crêpes.

Makes 4 servings

1. Preheat the oven to 325°F.

2. In a small saucepan or butter warmer, make the beurre noisette by melting or heating the clarified butter over medium heat until it turns golden brown after a couple of minutes. Watch it all the time so it doesn't become too brown. Season with salt and pepper and set aside.

3. Make 8 or 9 crêpes using the batter made with beurre noisette. Stuff each crêpe with the ham. Roll the crêpes up, butter a 12 × 9 × 2-inch casserole, using a teaspoon of the beurre noisette and arrange the crêpes in it. Pour the cream over them, sprinkle

the cheese on top, and dot with the remaining butter. Bake until the top is browned, 15 to 20 minutes.

NOTE: There are two methods you can use to clarify butter. First, melt salted or unsalted butter in a small pan, then pour the butter through several layers of cheesecloth to capture the milk solids. The resulting melted butter is now clarified. Second, put the butter in a microwavable container, cover, and melt in the microwave before pouring through the cheesecloth.

Chicken and Mushroom
Crêpes au Gratin

3 boneless, skinless
chicken breast halves
(about 1 pound)

2 teaspoons extra-
virgin olive oil

Salt to taste

6 tablespoons unsalted
butter, plus more for
buttering the casserole

2 large eggs, well beaten

6 ounces button (white)
mushrooms, sliced

Freshly ground black
pepper to taste

3 tablespoons all-
purpose flour

2 cups whole milk

1 cup shredded Swiss
(Emmenthaler) cheese
(about 2½ ounces)

1 cup shredded Gruyère
cheese (about 2½ ounces)

Pinch of ground nutmeg

6 Crêpes (page 60)

3 tablespoons dried
bread crumbs

WHEN MY CHILDREN WERE LITTLE, I occasionally made this crêpe casserole for dinner. Sometimes I stuffed them with broccoli and cheese (page 278). The kids loved the idea that they were eating "pancakes for supper." A side of butter-steamed broccoli with a touch of ground dried red chiles is an ideal accompaniment. *Makes 6 servings*

1. Preheat a cast-iron skillet or carbon steel pan over high heat until very hot.

2. Meanwhile, flatten the chicken breasts between 2 sheets of wax paper or plastic wrap with a mallet or the side of a cleaver until thin. Lightly oil the chicken and season with salt. Add the chicken to the hot skillet and cook until golden on both sides, 3 to 4 minutes. Remove and set aside.

3. Melt 1 tablespoon of the butter in the skillet, add the eggs, and cook without stirring but making sure they don't burn, until set, 20 to 30 seconds. Remove and set aside. Melt 1 more table-spoon of the butter in the skillet, add the mushrooms, and cook, stirring constantly, until softened, about 4 minutes. Season with salt and pepper. Remove and set aside.

4. In a saucepan, melt 3 tablespoons of the butter over medium heat, then add the flour to form a roux. Cook, stirring, for 2 minutes, then remove the saucepan from the heat and slowly pour in the milk, stirring constantly. Return to the burner and cook until dense, about 5 minutes. Set aside ¼ cup of the mixed cheeses, add the remaining cheeses to the sauce, and cook until melted. Season with salt, pepper, and nutmeg and keep warm.

5. Thinly slice the chicken breasts and add to the sauce. Slice the cooked egg into strips and add to the sauce. Add the mushrooms to the sauce.

6. Preheat the oven to 350°F.

7. Lay a crêpe in front of you. Divide the chicken filling mixture into 6 parts. Spread a portion of the filling just below the center of the crêpe, roll up and place in a lightly buttered baking dish. Continue with the remaining crêpes, laying them next to each other in the baking dish. Sprinkle the top of the crêpes with the reserved cheeses and the bread crumbs. Cut the remaining 1 tablespoon of butter into 6 thin slivers and place a pat on top of each crêpe. Bake until the tops are golden, about 20 minutes. Serve hot.

CRÊPES

A crêpe is a very thin pancake made by spreading batter over a hot flat cooking surface, either a griddle or a low-sided pan called a crêpe pan. Crêpes are always stuffed and can be either savory or sweet. When they are savory, the batter does not contain sugar, and when they are dessert crêpes, they do contain sugar. The word *crêpe* comes from the Latin *crispus*, which means a fried thin pancake, the same as today. Because crêpes freeze so well, this recipe will make twelve to fourteen 9-inch crêpes. Unlike pancake or waffle batter that gets folded together, crêpe batter gets blended quite vigorously. The actual making of a crêpe is a bit tricky, so you will want to pay attention to the direction in the method below. The recipes in the book requiring crêpes will often call for half a recipe (or specify a number), but I advise you to make this whole recipe, as the crêpes freeze so well and having already prepared crêpes is handy. The range given in the yield depends on how thick you make the crêpes and whether you rip any or not.

Makes twelve to sixteen 9-inch crêpes

2 large eggs, lightly beaten
2 cups whole milk
1¾ cups all-purpose flour
2 tablespoons unsalted butter, melted (check the recipe you're making to see
    if it calls for a specific kind of butter, otherwise use unsalted butter)
2 tablespoons sugar (only if making dessert crêpes)
½ teaspoon salt
Vegetable oil or butter, for greasing pan

1. In a blender, blend the eggs for a few seconds, then add the milk, flour, butter, sugar (if making dessert crêpes), and salt and blend until frothy. Pour into a bowl, cover, and let rest for 30 minutes.

2. In a large crêpe pan or nonstick skillet, heat a film of vegetable oil or butter over medium heat until very hot, then pour in about three-quarters of a ladleful of batter (about ¼ cup), tilting and twirling the skillet at the same time so the batter runs. Quickly spread the batter in the skillet even thinner with the front edge of a spatula, carefully (so you don't break it) spreading the batter to the outer part of the skillet in a circular motion so the crêpe remains round. Cook until the top is dry with a few air holes and the bottom is lightly brown. Look by gently and carefully lifting an edge of the crêpe. Loosen the crêpe all around the edge with the spatula, then flip and cook the second side for a minute or so. Set aside on a plate while you cook the remaining crêpes, re-greasing the skillet if necessary. Let each crêpe cool down quite a bit before you stack them; otherwise they might stick together.

3. Stack the crêpes on a sheet of aluminum foil, cover with another sheet of aluminum foil, and seal the edges well. Freeze until needed, and defrost at room temperature before trying to separate them. As you can calculate two stuffed crêpes per serving, you may want to divide the crêpes into serving sizes.

Buckwheat Crêpes with Bacon and Cheese

½ cup buckwheat flour

1 cup all-purpose flour

½ teaspoon salt

4 large eggs

1 cup apple cider

1 cup whole milk

½ cup water

6 tablespoons unsalted butter, melted, plus more for brushing skillet

Vegetable oil, for skillet

1 cup crumbled, crispy cooked bacon (8 slices)

2½ cups grated Gruyère cheese (about 8 ounces)

IN BRITTANY, THESE CRÊPES are justly famous . . . and you won't be able to stop eating them. The authentic crêpe is large, about a foot in diameter, but it's unlikely you'll have a nonstick skillet that large, so you will have to make them smaller. You can cut the crêpe recipe in half (this recipe makes nine), but since they freeze well, I recommend making the whole recipe even though you will only use four here. Lay the cooked and cooled crêpes on greased pieces of aluminum foil and wrap with plastic wrap before freezing. *Makes 4 servings*

1. Place the buckwheat flour, all-purpose flour, and salt in a blender. Pulse several times to blend, then add the eggs, cider, milk, water, and melted butter. Blend until smooth. Let the mixture stand in the blender for 1 hour, covered. Blend briefly before using.

2. Very lightly oil a 12-inch nonstick skillet or crêpe pan until smoking over medium-high heat, then brush the surface with some butter, and pour in about 6 tablespoons of the batter (⅓ cup), twirling the skillet as you do so it coats the whole bottom and a part of the sides. Spread further with the edge of a spatula. Cook

until golden brown, about 1 minute. Prepare all the crêpes and freeze for future use as described above, but reserve the last 4 for this recipe.

3. Sprinkle the top of each of the last 4 crêpes you make with one-quarter of the crumbled bacon and one-quarter of the cheese while it's still in the skillet. Cook for about 15 seconds, fold in half, remove from the skillet, let rest for 1 minute, and serve, or keep warm in a low oven covered with a buttered piece of aluminum foil.

Goat Cheese and Curdled Milk Crêpes

2 cups unbleached all-purpose flour

½ cup tepid water

12 ounces fresh homemade goat's milk ricotta (page 65, using all goat milk) or store-bought soft goat cheese, crumbled

2 cups curdled milk (see step 1 of the homemade ricotta recipe, page 65)

Salt to taste

Pork lard for greasing griddle

THE SHEPHERDS OF CORSICA prepare a traditional food they can cook on stone slates in their pastures while tending their sheep. They are called *mullades*, large rustic crêpes made with fresh cheese. These crêpes are eaten plain for lunch or with various garnishes such as more cheese, or fruit, or jam.

Makes 4 servings

1. Pour the flour into a large heavy saucepan and stir in the water and cheese. Mix well. Add the curdled milk and salt and mix until you have a slightly liquidy batter. Add some water if it is too thick; it should be thinner than pancake batter. Heat the batter gently over very low heat or in a preheated 200°F oven.

2. Grease a cast-iron griddle with lard and set over medium heat until a droplet of water sizzles rapidly on the griddle. Ladle about ¼ cup of the batter onto the hot griddle, spreading it thin with the bottom of the ladle. When the bottom browns, like a pancake, flip to the other side with a spatula, and continue cooking crêpes in this manner until they are all cooked.

NOTE: Taste the first crêpe to check the salt. Add some to the batter if necessary. The crêpes can be wrapped in plastic wrap and then frozen in a zipper-top plastic bag for up to 6 months.

HOW TO MAKE YOUR OWN RICOTTA CHEESE

Making your own ricotta cheese is an easy, fun, and surprisingly rewarding weekend project. The equipment you'll need is cheesecloth, a colander, a large pot, a quick-read thermometer, and a skimmer. You can also follow the recipe at www.cliffordawright.com/caw/tips.php/id/19/. Ricotta is known as an albumin or serum cheese, a cheese made as a by-product of provolone cheese from the re-cooked whey, hence the name *ricotta*, which translates from the Italian as "re-cooked." To make the Corsican *brocciu*, used in the recipe on page 64, replace the whole milk with whole goat's milk and the cream with goat's or cow's buttermilk.

Makes 2 pounds

4 quarts whole milk
3 cups heavy cream (preferably not ultra-pasteurized)
5 tablespoons fresh lemon juice

1. Pour the milk, cream, and lemon juice into a large nonreactive saucepan or stockpot. Turn the heat to low and bring to 194°F. Use a candy/deep-fry thermometer (also called a quick-read thermometer), making sure it does not touch the bottom or sides of the saucepan or pot. This will take about 2 hours. (You can do this faster, but you'll need to attend to the heat with more concern.)

2. Line a strainer or small colander with cheesecloth. When curds form on the surface of the liquid, remove them with a skimmer or slotted spoon and transfer to the strainer. Increase the heat to medium and after 8 minutes skim some more. Increase the heat to medium-high and skim until no more curds form, about 10 minutes of skimming.

3. Leave the curds to drain for 1 hour, then transfer them to a container and refrigerate. Fresh homemade ricotta will stay fresh for about 4 days in the refrigerator.

Cheese Roll with Mushroom Sauce

For the mushroom sauce

3 tablespoons pork lard or butter

½ small onion, chopped

6 ounces button (white) mushrooms thinly sliced

1 small bunch fresh flat-leaf parsley, leaves only, finely chopped

2 tablespoons all-purpose flour

1 cup beef broth

¼ teaspoon salt

⅛ teaspoon freshly ground black pepper

¾ cup sour cream

(continued)

THIS CHEESE ROLL is made by first making a kind of rectangular puffy pancake. The pancake is stuffed with a thick cheese sauce and then rolled up like a jelly roll. It's cut into slices, floured, dipped in beaten egg, and then fried in butter and served with a rich mushroom sauce. *Makes 6 servings*

1. Preheat the oven to 350°F.

2. Prepare the mushroom sauce. In a large skillet, melt the lard over medium heat. Add the onion and cook, stirring, until softened, about 3 minutes. Add the mushrooms and parsley, reduce the heat to low, and simmer, stirring, until the mushrooms are tender, 7 to 8 minutes. Sprinkle the flour over the mushrooms, stir, then pour in the beef broth. Stir until smooth, then simmer for 10 minutes. Season with the salt and pepper. Add the sour cream and stir until smooth. Set aside.

3. Prepare the cheese roll batter. In a saucepan, melt 3 tablespoons of the butter. Stir in 3 tablespoons of the flour to form a roux and cook, stirring all the time, for 2 minutes. Remove the saucepan from the burner and slowly pour in 10 tablespoons of the milk while whisking. Stir until smooth and dense, about 3 minutes. Season with salt and stir in the 3 egg yolks, incorporating one at a time, and half the shredded cheese. Let cool, then fold in the beaten 3 egg whites, incorporating it by folding.

4. Butter the bottom and sides of a 12 × 9-inch baking casserole. Lightly flour the casserole, shaking the flour to coat the bottom and sides. Shake out any excess flour. Pour the batter into the casserole and spread it evenly. Bake until golden, about 30 minutes.

5. Meanwhile, make the cheese filling. In a saucepan, melt the remaining 3 tablespoons butter over medium heat. Add the remaining 3 tablespoons flour to form a roux, stirring constantly. Remove from the burner and pour in the remaining milk, whisking until smooth with a whisk. Mix in the 2 egg yolks, the remaining shredded cheese, and a little salt. Let this filling cool slightly, then spread it while still warm over the entire surface of the baked pastry and roll up like a jelly roll. Slice on a slanted diagonal about ½ inch thick.

6. In a large skillet, melt the butter over medium-high heat. Bring the mushroom sauce to a gentle bubble. Meanwhile, dredge the slices in flour, then dip in beaten egg and fry once the butter has stopped foaming until golden on both sides, 3 to 4 minutes. Remove with a spatula and arrange on a serving platter. Spoon the mushroom sauce over the slices of cheese roll and serve.

For the cheese roll batter and cheese filling

6 tablespoons unsalted butter, plus extra for greasing casserole

6 tablespoons all-purpose flour, plus extra for flouring casserole

1¼ cups whole milk

½ teaspoon salt

3 large eggs, separated, whites beaten to stiff peaks, egg yolks put in bowl

4 ounces Edam cheese, shredded

2 large egg yolks

For the finish

4 tablespoons unsalted butter

all-purpose flour for dredging

1 large egg, beaten

Swiss Pancakes

1½ cups grated Swiss (Emmenthaler) cheese (about 3½ ounces)

3 large egg yolks, beaten

¾ cup sour cream

2 tablespoons all-purpose flour

½ teaspoon salt

½ teaspoon dry mustard

¼ teaspoon dried thyme

2 tablespoons unsalted butter

THESE GOLDEN BROWN cheese pancakes make a nice accompaniment to some pan-fried chicken breasts or pork chops. You can double the recipe if you would like this recipe to be more abundant, but I don't find that necessary, as they are rich and delicious.

Makes 4 pancakes to serve 2 to 4

1. Place the cheese in a bowl, add the egg yolks one at a time, then add the sour cream. In a separate bowl, mix the flour, salt, dry mustard, and thyme, then add to the cheese mixture and mix well.

2. In a cast-iron skillet, grease the skillet with some of the butter and pour about ⅓ cup of batter in to form a pancake. Cook until golden brown on both sides, about 3 minutes. Remove and keep warm while you cook the rest.

Pies, Tarts, and Quiches with Cheese

I n this chapter you'll find a veritable world of exciting pies, tarts, and quiches, all made with cheese, that you will go back to countless times. I just couldn't believe the Gibanica (page 72), a luscious and rich cheese strudel from the former Yugoslavia. Every time I make it, I cut off a little square to taste, arguing with myself that "I better make sure it's okay." Then I cut off another square to be really sure. You'll learn a variety of cheese pies using short dough, puff pastry, and phyllo dough.

Leek Phyllo Pie

12 ounces (3 sticks) unsalted butter

3 pounds leeks, white and very light green parts only, quartered, chopped into ⅛-inch pieces, and washed well

7 large eggs

12 ounces feta cheese, crumbled

2 ounces kefalotyri or kashkaval cheese, grated

½ cup finely chopped fresh flat-leaf parsley

½ cup finely chopped fresh dill

3 tablespoons all-purpose flour

¼ teaspoon ground cinnamon

¼ teaspoon ground allspice

Salt and freshly ground black pepper to taste

12 sheets phyllo pastry (about 12 ounces), defrosted according to package instructions

THE BEST LEEK PIES in Greece come from the northern regions of Thrace and Greek Macedonia, where they make phyllo pastry with butter rather than olive oil. Some cooks also cook the leeks until they almost disintegrate, and others use yogurt instead of cheese. Phyllo pastry is sold frozen, and once defrosted and the package opened, can dry out very quickly, so always keep the phyllo covered with a damp kitchen towel while you assemble the pie. This dish can be served as a meze or as a main course, in which case the portion sizes should be appropriately sized. Kefalotyri and kashkaval cheeses can be ordered from www.igourmet.com or www.christosmarket.com. If those cheeses are unavailable, you might substitute with kasseri, cheddar, Monterey Jack, or Gouda. This recipe calls for an alarming amount of butter; however, most of it drains away and you're not consuming it. *Makes 8 servings*

1. In a large skillet, melt the butter over medium heat, then remove ½ cup and reserve, keeping it warm and melted. Add the leeks to the remaining butter and cook, stirring occasionally, until softened and their liquid has evaporated, about 20 minutes. Transfer to a strainer set over a bowl and let cool.

2. Preheat the oven to 350°F.

3. In a bowl, beat the eggs until frothy. Add the feta cheese, kefalotyri cheese, parsley, dill, flour, cinnamon, allspice, salt, pepper, and the cooled leeks to the eggs and mix well.

4. Butter a 13 × 9 × 2-inch baking pan. Lay 5 sheets of phyllo on the bottom of the pan, brushing each sheet with butter. Spread half of the leek mixture over the phyllo. Cover with 2 more sheets of phyllo over the leek mixture, brushing each layer with butter. Spread the remaining leek mixture over the phyllo pasty. Cover the leek mixture with the remaining 5 sheets of phyllo, handling the phyllo sheets carefully and brushing each sheet with the melted butter. Seal the edges by pressing the leaves of phyllo together with moistened forefinger and thumb. Brush any remaining butter over the top. Score the phyllo with a sharp knife to mark where you will cut into serving portions.

5. Bake until golden on top, about 40 minutes. Serve hot or warm cut into portions.

Gibanica

6 large eggs

½ cup all-purpose flour

1 teaspoon salt

2 pounds large-curd cottage cheese, creamed with a whisk

1 cup kaymak (for a substitute, see Note below)

8 ounces (2 sticks) unsalted butter, melted

1 pound phyllo dough, defrosted according to package instructions

PRONOUNCED GHEE-bah-neet-sah, gibanica is one of the most popular pies to be found in Slovenia, Serbia, Bosnia, and other regions of the old Yugoslavia. Variants of this rich cheese strudel are found in Hungary, Bulgaria, Macedonia, Greece, Turkey, and Syria. This recipe uses phyllo dough and cottage cheese to replace the crumbly white cheese used in Serbia. Depending on who's making it and for what reason, gibanica can be savory or sweet. As a savory, one mixes a copious amount of white cheese and kaymak, a kind of thick cream, with eggs and layers them between multiple buttered layers of phyllo sheets. For the kaymak, I substitute a mixture of thick yogurt, ricotta cheese, and sour cream. There is a variation called *guzvara* where the phyllo dough is dipped in the filling and crumpled in the pan, hence the name *guzvara*, which means "crumpled." The sweet version might contain poppy seeds and walnuts. This is the savory version. *Makes 6 to 8 servings*

1. Preheat the oven to 325°F.

2. In a large bowl, beat the eggs until light and fluffy. Add the flour and salt and mix thoroughly. Add the cottage cheese and kaymak and combine.

3. Lightly brush a 12 × 9 × 2½-inch baking casserole with melted butter. Place 2 sheets of phyllo pastry in the casserole and lightly brush each sheet with melted butter. Spread about ⅔ cup of the cheese filling on top. Repeat with 2 sheets of phyllo and

⅔ cup cheese, buttering each sheet and continuing until all the phyllo and cheese is used up, ending with 2 sheets of phyllo. Tuck in ends, if necessary. Brush with remaining butter. Bake until golden brown, 1 to 1¼ hours. Let stand for 20 minutes. Cut into squares and serve warm.

NOTE: Kaymak is a kind of thick cream and can be replaced with 1 cup of sour cream or a mixture of 6 tablespoons ricotta cheese (page 65), 6 tablespoons sour cream, and 4 tablespoons *labna* (very thick strained yogurt, also called *lubny*).

Fontina Val d'Aosta Cheese Pie

2 cups unbleached
all-purpose flour

7 tablespoons unsalted
butter, melted

½ teaspoon salt

7 tablespoons dry
white wine

2 large eggs, beaten

2 tablespoons freshly
grated Parmesan cheese
(preferably Parmigiano-
Reggiano cheese)

Salt to taste

Pinch of ground nutmeg

4 ounces Fontina
Val d'Aosta cheese,
thinly sliced

GIVEN THE NAME of this cheese pie typically served as a simple antipasto in the Piedmont in northern Italy, you really must use the most famous cheese of that region, the fontina from the valley called Val d'Aosta. There are other inferior fontina cheeses, made outside Italy, but the best is the genuine Fontina Val d'Aosta, which can be found at better supermarkets and on the Internet at www.igourmet.com and other food Web sites. *Makes 8 servings*

1. Place the flour in a large bowl and make a well in the center. Add the melted butter and salt to the well. Working gently with your fingers, incorporate 6 tablespoons of the wine to form a dough and shape it into a smooth ball. Wrap in wax paper and leave in the refrigerator for 1 hour.

2. Preheat the oven to 350°F.

3. Cut the dough in half and roll each ball out on a lightly floured work surface into a thin sheet large enough to cover the bottom and sides of an 8-inch pie pan. Butter the pie pan and cover with 1 sheet of dough.

4. In a small bowl, beat 1 egg, the Parmesan cheese, salt, and nutmeg together and dilute with the remaining 1 tablespoon wine. Pour three-quarters of the egg mixture into the crust and layer the fontina cheese on top of the egg mixture. Coat the cheese with the remaining beaten egg. Cover the pie with the top crust and crimp the edges together, cutting off any excess dough with kitchen scissors. Bake until light golden on top, 35 to 40 minutes. Let rest for a few minutes before serving warm, cut into small serving portions.

Chäschüechli

DON'T WORRY, I can't pronounce this either; and even when I lived in Switzerland and learned German, I still could not pronounce the name of this cheese tart. In Switzerdeutsch, it's also known by the equally unpronounceable *chuchichäschtli*. You can call it a Swiss cheese tart. It has a mild taste and makes a great appetizer. *Makes 8 appetizer servings*

Butter, for greasing pans

10 ounces puff pastry, defrosted according to package instructions

2 cups grated Swiss (Emmenthaler) cheese (about 5 ounces)

1 cup heavy cream

2 large eggs

Freshly ground black pepper to taste

Pinch of ground nutmeg

1. Preheat the oven to 400°F. Generously butter eight 4-inch tart pans.

2. Roll out the puff pastry with a rolling pin on a floured surface until ⅛ inch thick. Cut out 8 disks to fit into the tart pans. Gather and reroll the pastry when necessary.

3. In a bowl, mix the cheese, cream, eggs, pepper, and nutmeg and spoon into the tarts. Bake until puffy until light golden, 15 to 20 minutes. Serve hot. The tarts can be cooled and reheated later.

Einsiedeln Cheese Tart

1 Short Dough recipe
(page 77), rolled out
(save excess dough
for another use)

3 tablespoons
unsalted butter

3 medium onions,
chopped

12 ounces Gruyère
cheese, finely shredded

12 ounces Vacherin du
Jura cheese, cut up

5 large eggs

1½ cups whole milk

⅛ teaspoon salt

THIS DENSE, CHEESY QUICHE comes from the town of Einsiedeln, in the canton of Schwyz, one of the three original cantons of Switzerland. It is a rich and filling but surprisingly light-tasting tart that highlights the cheeses used. If you are unable to find vacherin, a washed-rind soft cow's milk cheese, you could use Brie. For online shopping for these cheeses, try www.fromages.com.

Makes 8 servings

1. Preheat the oven to 350°F Roll out the short dough for a 9-inch deep-dish pie pan. Save excess short dough.

2. In a skillet, melt the butter over medium-high heat. Add the onions and cook, stirring, until translucent, about 8 minutes.

3. In a bowl, mix the onions, cheeses, eggs, milk, and salt. Line the pie pan with the rolled-out short dough, crimping and forming the edges. Pour the onion mixture into the pie pan and bake until brown on top and a skewer stuck in the middle comes out clean, about 1 hour 10 minutes. The top of the pie will wiggle, but it's cooked. Remove and let rest for 10 minutes. Serve hot.

Short Dough

PIE CRUSTS ARE MADE WITH short dough. Short dough is the name for the yeast-less pastry made of flour and fat used for both sweet and savory pies, as well as a variety of pastries ranging from empanadas to some calzone-like pies. Short dough is also known by its French name, pâte brisée.

Makes enough for 1 double-crust 10-inch pie or

ten 4-inch empanadas/calzones

1¼ cups unbleached all-purpose flour, sifted

6 tablespoons cold unsalted butter, cut into bits

2 tablespoons cold vegetable shortening or pork lard

¼ teaspoon salt

2 to 3 tablespoons ice water, or more as needed

1. Blend the flour, butter, shortening, and salt together in a large, cold mixing bowl using a pastry blender until the mixture looks like coarse meal. Add 2 tablespoons of ice water. Mix again until the water is absorbed. Add the remaining 1 tablespoon ice water (or more) if necessary to form the dough.

2. Shape the dough into a ball, handling it as little as possible (so do this quickly), then dust it with flour and wrap in wax paper. Refrigerate for at least 1 hour before using, then let rest at room temperature for a few minutes before rolling out according to the recipe.

Gomser Cholera

4 Yukon Gold potatoes
(about 1¾ pounds)

8 ounces (2 sticks)
unsalted butter

3½ ounces thick-cut bacon,
cut into 1-inch pieces

8 ounces onions,
finely chopped

1 pound leeks, white and
light green parts only,
split lengthwise, washed
well, and thinly sliced

1 pound tart apples, peeled,
quartered, and sliced

Salt and freshly ground
black pepper to taste

Pinch of ground nutmeg

1 pound puff pastry,
defrosted according to
package instructions

10 ounces Gomser cheese
(raclette cheese)

1 large egg, beaten

GOMS IS A VALLEY in the rugged mountainous canton of Valais in Switzerland, where this pie originated. The unusual name of this pie derives from the cholera epidemic that hit Switzerland hard in 1836. Rather than leave the house and risk infection, people tended to prepare meals with the food they had on hand. In nineteenth-century Switzerland, this was typically apples, pears, potatoes, onions, leeks, raclette cheese, local bacon, and the pastry ingredients. The cheese called for is one particular kind of raclette cheese known as Gomser; other raclette cheeses are Belalp, Valais Raclette, and Bagnes. They are sold under the generic name "raclette cheese." As befits a home-prepared dish of many families, there are many recipes. This recipe is adapted from the one posted on the Goms tourist bureau Web site. However, the pie is hardly known in Switzerland today; in fact, most Swiss will look at you confusedly if you were to mention it.   *Makes 8 to 10 servings*

1. Place the potatoes in a pot full of water, bring to a boil over medium heat, then cook until a skewer glides easily into the center, about 40 minutes in all. Remove the potatoes, peel, cut into quarters, slice, and set aside.

2. In a large flameproof casserole, melt the butter with the bacon over low heat and cook until the bacon is slightly crispy, about 10 minutes. Add the onions and leeks and cook, stirring, until softened and slightly caramelized, about 20 minutes. Add the apples and cook, stirring, for 5 minutes. Season with salt, pepper, and nutmeg.

3. Preheat the oven to 400°F.

4. Roll out two-thirds of the puff pastry dough to fit into a 9-inch diameter deep-dish pie pan. Spread half the onion mixture over the dough and top with half of the potatoes and then half the cheese. Cover the cheese with the remaining filling in the same order. Roll out the remaining puff pastry and cover the filling with it. Score in several places and brush with the beaten egg. Bake until golden brown, about 35 minutes. Serve hot.

Pine Nut and Bacon Quiche

1 tablespoon
unsalted butter

8 ounces smoked slab
bacon, cut into lardons

1 tablespoon dried savory

2 tablespoons water

4 ounces Gruyère cheese,
coarsely shredded

½ cup half-and-half

2 tablespoons crème fraîche

5 large eggs, 2 left whole
and 3 separated

Salt and freshly ground
black pepper to taste

⅛ teaspoon ground nutmeg

1 garlic clove, lightly crushed

8 ounces frozen puff
pastry, defrosted according
to package instructions
and rolled out thinner
to cover the bottom and
sides of the tart pan

½ cup pine nuts

1 tablespoon finely
chopped fresh flat-
leaf parsley

ALTHOUGH THE QUICHE has its origins in Lorraine in eastern France, this dish, called *quiche aux pignons*, traces its roots to the *garrigue* (moors) of the Camargue of Provence. It's a simple quiche, but the taste is not: it is luscious. To make this properly, you will need to focus on the bacon lardons. Make sure you only use a smoked bacon slab cut into sticks about ¼ inch thick and 1½ inches long. Don't use your typical supermarket bacon, because it is sliced and too fatty. If you must use fatty bacon, blanch the bacon first in boiling water for about 10 minutes.

Makes one 10-inch quiche to serve 10

1. In a medium skillet, melt the butter with the bacon lardons over medium-high heat, then cook, stirring, until the bacon is releasing some fat, 4 to 5 minutes. Add the savory and cook, stirring, until the bacon sticks, adding 2 tablespoons of water to scrape up the bits, about 3 minutes. Transfer the bacon to a bowl to cool. Add the Gruyère to the bowl and toss.

2. Preheat the oven to 400°F.

3. In another bowl, mix together the half-and-half, crème fraîche, 2 whole eggs, and the 3 egg yolks. Season with salt, pepper, and nutmeg and let rest for a moment. Rub the sides and bottom of a 10-inch tart pan with the crushed garlic clove. Cover with the rolled-out puff pastry, fitting it in snugly. Puncture the puff pastry with a fork and crimp the border attractively. Arrange the bacon-cheese mixture and pine nuts evenly over the puff pastry.

4. In a small bowl, beat 2 of the egg whites until frothy, then brush the edges of the puff pastry with it. Beat the cream-and-egg mixture vigorously for 1 minute with an electric mixer. Add the remaining egg white to the mixture and stir in gently. Pour into the tart pan. Sprinkle the parsley on top of the quiche and bake until golden brown on top, 25 to 30 minutes. Remove from the oven, let rest for 20 minutes, then cut into wedges and serve.

Muenster Cheese Leek Quiche

For the short dough

¾ cup all-purpose flour

¼ cup cold pork lard
or unsalted butter

⅛ teaspoon salt

2 tablespoons ice water

For the quiche

3 tablespoons
unsalted butter

1 tablespoon vegetable oil

4 large leeks, white and
light green parts only,
split lengthwise and
washed well, sliced

1½ cups half-and-half

½ cup heavy cream

4 large eggs

1 tablespoon caraway seeds

1 teaspoon freshly
ground black pepper

½ teaspoon salt

¼ teaspoon ground nutmeg

1 cup grated Muenster
cheese (about 3 ounces)

10 fresh chive stems, cut
into ½-inch lengths

SOMETIME AROUND the seventh century, Münster cheese originated in an Alsatian monastery. It is a soft, washed-rind cheese made from raw cow's milk. It has no resemblance to American Muenster cheese, which is a bland cheese with no distinctive taste because it is not aged for more than a few weeks. The Alsatian Münster cheese is more flavorful and stronger. However, there's a good use for the American-style Muenster, and it's this flavorful leek quiche in which the Muenster is perfect.

Makes 8 servings

1. Prepare the short dough. In a bowl, mix the flour, lard, salt, and water together with a pastry blender or 2 knives until it looks like coarse meal. Gather the dough together, handling it as little as possible, and form into a ball. Wrap in wax paper and refrigerate for 1 hour.

2. Preheat the oven to 350°F.

3. For the quiche, in a large skillet, melt the butter with the oil over medium heat. Add the leeks and cook, stirring, until softened, about 5 minutes.

4. In a bowl, stir together the half-and-half, cream, eggs, half the caraway, the pepper, salt, and nutmeg. Whisk to blend well.

5. Remove the short dough from the refrigerator. On lightly floured parchment paper, roll the short dough out with a floured rolling pin until ⅛ inch thick and about 12 inches in diameter, spreading flour so the dough doesn't stick or break. Place a 10-inch tart pan upside down on the short dough and lift up with the parchment paper and turn right side up. Carefully peel away the parchment paper and gently press the dough into the pan. Trim away the excess overhanging dough with scissors or a paring knife and use it to patch any holes.

6. Fill the tart with the cooked leeks. Pour the egg-and-cream mixture over the leeks. Sprinkle the surface with the cheese and the remaining caraway. Sprinkle the chives on top, place the tart pan on a round baking sheet or pizza pan, and bake until golden, about 35 minutes. Serve warm.

Quiche with Kielbasa and Cheese

1 Short Dough
recipe (page 77)

3 large eggs

1 cup whole milk

½ cup sour cream

4 ounces cooked kielbasa
sausage, chopped

1 cup shredded Gouda
cheese (about 3 ounces)

1 cup shredded queso
asadero or sharp cheddar
cheese (about 3 ounces)

¼ cup chopped fresh dill

5 scallions, top 2 inches
trimmed, remainder sliced

Salt to taste

THIS QUICHE HAS A WONDERFUL flavor from just a little amount of sausage and is very satisfying as a lunch dish.

Makes 4 to 6 servings

1. Preheat the oven to 425°F. Roll out the short dough to form a disk that can fit into a 9-inch pie pan. Crimp the edges and cut away excess dough, using it if needed to patch holes. Save the excess short dough for another purpose.

2. In a bowl, mix the eggs, milk, sour cream, sausage, cheeses, dill, scallions, and salt. Pour the cheese mixture into the pie pan, leveling it off, and bake until golden brown, firm, and a skewer stuck in the middle comes out clean, about 35 minutes. Cool a little bit and serve.

Roquefort Tart

ONE OF THE MOST FAMOUS of French cheeses, Roquefort is made by mixing the curds of ewe's milk to make a cheese with the distinctive blue veins of *Penicillium roqueforti*. This rich and heavenly tart will delight everyone at the table.

Makes 6 servings

8 to 10 ounces frozen puff pastry, defrosted according to package instructions

2 large eggs

1 cup crème fraîche

4 ounces Roquefort cheese, crumbled

Freshly ground black pepper to taste

1. Preheat the oven to 425°F.

2. Roll the puff pastry out slightly on a floured work surface so that it can cover the bottom of an 8- to 9-inch tart pan or shallow pie pan. Fit the puff pastry into the pan and prick the bottom carefully with a toothpick. Trim the edges if desired.

3. In a bowl, beat together the eggs, crème fraîche, Roquefort, and pepper. Pour the mixture into the pan and, if you have not trimmed the pastry, flip the edges over on top of the filling. Bake until the top is speckled brown, about 25 minutes. Serve hot or warm.

Swiss Chard Tart

For the tart shell

½ cup whole wheat flour

½ cup all-purpose flour

½ teaspoon salt

⅓ cup very cold pork lard or unsalted butter

2 to 3 tablespoons ice water

For the filling

1¼ pounds Swiss chard, leaves only

1 tablespoon extra-virgin vegetable oil

1 medium onion, sliced

3 tablespoons pine nuts

1 garlic clove, finely chopped

2 teaspoons fresh lemon juice

¾ cup shredded Gruyère cheese (about 2 ounces)

¼ cup freshly grated Parmesan cheese (about 1 ounce)

3 tablespoons heavy cream

1 large egg

1 tablespoon finely chopped fresh flat-leaf parsley

¼ teaspoon salt

Pinch of ground nutmeg

Fresh ground black pepper to taste

SWISS CHARD is one of the favorite vegetables of Provence, which is not surprising, as it grows well along coasts. There are two well-known recipes for Swiss chard pies in Provence, one a covered pie that is called a *tourte* in French and the other an open pie called a *tarte* in French. The first, called *tourte de blettes*, has a biscuit-like crust and is filled with Swiss chard, raisins, apples, red currant jelly, brown sugar, and rum, served as either a dessert or an appetizer. This recipe is the *tarte de blettes* made with Swiss chard, cheese, and pine nuts. Typically, one would serve it as a first course. You will need the leaves from about two bunches of Swiss chard for this recipes, and the stems can be saved for making the Swiss chard stem recipe (page 331).

Makes 6 servings

1. For the tart shell, in a large bowl, mix the flours and salt with the lard using a pastry blender or your fingertips until the mixture is in pea-size clumps. Sprinkle the mixture with the ice water and mix very gently. Form the dough into a ball. Flatten the ball slightly with your hands. Lay a sheet of parchment paper on a round pizza pan or baking sheet. Place the ball on the sheet and cover with plastic wrap. Roll the dough out thin with a rolling pin until about 11 inches in diameter. Chill in the refrigerator for 1 hour.

2. Meanwhile, for the filling, lay the Swiss chard leaves on top of each other and slice into 1-inch pieces crosswise.

3. In a flameproof casserole, heat the oil over medium-high heat. Add the onion, pine nuts, and garlic and cook, stirring, until softened, about 7 minutes. Add the Swiss chard leaves and lemon

juice, cover, and cook, stirring once, until the leaves have wilted, about 3 minutes. Reduce the heat to medium and cook, uncovered, and stirring occasionally, until the liquid has evaporated completely, about 6 minutes. It is important that the liquid is evaporated. Let the Swiss chard cool to room temperature.

4. Preheat the oven to 375°F.

5. In a large bowl, combine the Gruyère cheese, Parmesan cheese, heavy cream, egg, parsley, salt, nutmeg, and pepper and mix well. Add to the cooled chard and onion mixture.

6. Remove the dough from the refrigerator and remove the plastic wrap. Spoon the filling mixture into the center of the tart dough, then spread to within 2 inches of the edges. Carefully fold the dough edges up and over the edge of the filling by lifting the parchment paper, crimping the dough as needed.

7. Place the pizza pan with the tart in the oven and bake until the filling mixture is cooked through and bubbling and the tart dough is golden brown, 45 minutes. Remove and let rest for a few minutes, and serve warm.

Vols-au-Vent with Creamed Pearl Onions

For the Mornay sauce

2 tablespoons unsalted butter

2 tablespoons all-purpose flour

1 cup hot milk

½ cup freshly grated Parmesan cheese

Salt and freshly ground black pepper to taste

¼ cup ricotta cheese (page 65)

3 tablespoons crumbled feta cheese

1 tablespoon finely chopped fresh dill

For the vols-au-vent and onions

4 frozen puff pastry shells, defrosted according to package instructions

1 tablespoon unsalted butter

12 white pearl onions (about 5 ounces)

1 large shallot, chopped

THIS IS AN EASY BUT ELEGANT dish to accompany a preparation such as Stuffed Veal Chops Valdostana (page 347). Pearl onions can be peeled by plunging them into boiling water for about 2 minutes, then removing them and cutting off the tip of the stem end and squeezing them so the onion pops out. Vols-au-vent puff pastry shells are sold in the frozen food section of supermarkets. Pepperidge Farm makes a nice frozen puff pastry shell. The recipe begins with a Mornay sauce, which is nothing but a béchamel sauce (white sauce) with cheese.

Makes 4 servings

1. Preheat the oven to 400°F.

2. Prepare the Mornay sauce. In a skillet, melt the butter over medium heat, then stir in the flour to form a roux. Cook, stirring, for 2 minutes, then remove from the heat and stir in the milk. Return to the heat and cook until thick and dense, about 10 minutes. Add the Parmesan cheese, stir, season with salt and pepper, and cook until the cheese melts. Add the ricotta, feta, and dill and stir until blended.

3. For the vols-au-vent and onions, place the vols-au-vent on a baking sheet and bake until golden brown and risen, 20 to 25 minutes. Remove from the oven, and once they are cool enough to handle, remove the cut-out top and set aside. With a small fork, scrape out any loose pastry.

4. In a skillet, melt the butter over high heat. Add the pearl onions and shallot and cook, stirring, until softened, about 5 minutes. Add to the cheese sauce and stir well. Spoon the onions and sauce into the vols-au-vent. Place the tops on and heat in the oven until hot, about 4 minutes. Serve hot.

Tomato Tart with Figs, Fontina, and Goat Cheese

8 ounces puff pastry, defrosted according to package instructions

3 tablespoons extra-virgin olive oil

1 large garlic clove, crushed

2 pounds ripe and juicy tomatoes, peeled and cut into large chunks

Salt and freshly ground black pepper to taste

2 sprigs fresh mint

4 ounces Fontina Val d'Aosta cheese, cut into 8 thin wedges

4 ounces fresh goat cheese, broken apart

4 fresh figs, quartered

THIS TART IS A FAVORITE in mid-summer when Black Mission figs appear at farmers markets. I think Black Mission are the most flavorful of figs and this tart is perfect for them and luscious, too. You'll need to blind-bake the puff pastry first, which means baking the dough without the filling so that it does not become soggy later. *Makes 4 servings*

1. Preheat the oven to 400°F.

2. Roll the puff pastry out on a lightly floured surface with a floured rolling pin to cover the bottom and sides of a 10-inch tart pan, pressing the pastry against the bottom and sides and folding over excess dough to make a thick rim. Prick the bottom of the pastry with a fork. Cut out a 10-inch round of parchment paper and place on top of the pastry. Fill with 1 pound ceramic pastry baking balls or 1 pound dried beans and bake until the edges are golden, about 20 minutes. Let cool on a rack. Remove the ceramic balls or dried beans.

3. Increase the oven temperature to 425°F.

4. In a skillet, heat the olive oil over high heat with the garlic clove, and when it starts smoking, add the tomatoes and cook,

stirring occasionally, until it is thick with large soft chunks, about 8 minutes. Season with salt and pepper, add the mint sprigs, and let cool a bit while the pastry shell cools.

5. Remove and discard the mint sprigs. Spoon the chunky tomato sauce over the bottom of the pastry. Lay the fontina cheese, goat cheese, and figs on top attractively. Bake until the cheese is bubbling, about 20 minutes. Serve hot or warm.

Pizzas, Calzones, and Breads with Cheese

You'll revisit this chapter many times because of all the incredible pizzas and calzones that are here. Try some of the more unfamiliar ones, such as the Corsican Pizza Flamiche (page 101) with its mix of goat and cow's milk cheese, onions, and bacon, and enter a new world. Another new experience will be the Rotoloni with Leeks and Sausage (page 112), a popular southern Italian stuffed cheese bread. This is a great recipe and always surprises everyone.

Basic Pizza Dough

One ¼-ounce package
(2¼ teaspoons)
active dry yeast

1 cup warm water
(105° to 115°F)

¾ to 1¼ teaspoons
salt, to your taste

3½ cups bread flour or
all-purpose flour, sifted

3 tablespoons extra-virgin
olive oil (do not add if
making bread or calzones)

THIS DOUGH IS USED for all pizza and calzone recipes in the book. To make the dough in a mixer or food processor, see the box on page 96. This amount of dough will make five very thin 14-inch diameter pizzas, the kind of pizza you are most likely to find in Italy. If you don't have a baking stone, follow the same directions below without it.

Makes 2 thin 16-inch pizzas, 5 very thin 14-inch pizzas,
4 slightly thick 12-inch pizzas, ten 4-inch empanada
or calzone disks, or 1 large round loaf bread

1. Warm a large metal bowl under hot running water, then dry. In the warmed bowl, dissolve the yeast in the warm water. Let it rest for 5 minutes, then add the salt and shake gently.

2. Add the flour and olive oil (only if you are making pizza) and mix until you can knead it with your hands. The dough should stick a little bit for the first few minutes but will then form itself into a ball with more kneading and folding. Once it is formed into a ball, turn it onto a lightly floured work surface and knead for 8 to 12 minutes.

3. Once the ball of dough is smooth, place it in a lightly floured or oiled bowl, cover with a clean kitchen towel, and let rise in a warm place (80°F), such as inside a turned-off oven, for 2 hours.

4. Punch down the dough after 1 hour, cover, and let rise for another hour. For more flavor, let the rising process go on longer: Cover the dough with plastic wrap and place in the refrigerator overnight (this is called a cold rise), but let the dough return to room temperature before working it again. Now it is ready for making into a pizza. If you are making bread, go on to step 5, otherwise, use this dough for any recipe calling for Basic Pizza Dough.

Further Instructions for Baking Bread

5. Set one rack at the topmost rung in the oven and set the other two racks at the two lowest rungs. Place a baking stone on the second lowest rack, leaving the rack below it free and, if you have a second stone, place it on the topmost rack. Preheat the oven to 475°F.

6. Transfer the dough to a pizza pan. Form into the shape you wish, let rest 1 hour, then score with a razor blade or very sharp knife. Place a pan of water on the bottommost oven rack, then place the bread dough on the pizza pan on the second lowest rack on top of the baking stone. Reduce the oven temperature to 425°F and bake until golden brown on top, 45 to 50 minutes, spraying it with water at first. Let cool on a wire rack before slicing.

VARIATION: Use 6 tablespoons milk and ¾ cup water instead of 1 cup water for a richer flavor.

BASIC PIZZA DOUGH IN AN ELECTRIC MIXER OR FOOD PROCESSOR

Read the instructions for your mixer or food processor. This recipe was tested with a Kitchen-Aid mixer and a Cuisinart food processor.

Makes 2 thin 16-inch pizzas, 5 very thin 14-inch pizzas,
4 slightly thick 12-inch pizzas, ten 4-inch empanada or calzone disks,
or 1 large round loaf bread

One ¼-ounce package (2¼ teaspoons) active dry yeast
1 cup warm water (105° to 115°F)
¾ to 1¼ teaspoons salt, to your taste
3½ cups bread flour or unbleached all-purpose flour, sifted
3 tablespoons extra-virgin olive oil (only add if making pizza)

1. Warm the bowl of a stand mixer under hot running water, then dry. Dissolve the yeast in the warm water. Let it rest for 5 minutes, then add the salt and shake gently. (For the food processor: Mix the yeast and warm water in a small bowl, let rest for 5 minutes, then add the salt.)

2. Add 2½ cups of the flour and the olive oil (only if you are making pizza dough), affix to the mixer, and attach the dough hook. Run according to the directions of the manufacturer for about 2 minutes, adding the remaining flour in ½-cup increments. Let the mixer run until the dough is pulled off the walls of the bowl and is being pushed by the dough hook. (For the food processor: Place the flour in the processor and pulse a few times. Run the processor and pour the water and yeast through the feed tube. Once it forms a ball on the blades, remove to a lightly floured surface and knead into a ball for 2 minutes with the palms of your hands.)

3. Once the ball of dough is smooth, whether using the mixer or processor, place it in a lightly floured or oiled bowl, cover with a clean kitchen towel, and let rise in a warm place (80°F), such as inside a turned-off oven, for 2 hours. Proceed as the recipe instructs.

Pizza Rustica

THIS NEAPOLITAN PIZZA PIE filled with cheeses and eggs is an enclosed pizza made from short dough or pizza dough, so it is more like a torta or savory pie than a pizza. I prefer it with pizza dough, and that's the recipe I give you here. There are many versions of pizza rustica throughout Italy, and the word *rustic*, when used in this context, means the tastes are simple and elemental. *Makes 16 appetizer servings*

1. Divide the dough into 2 balls and let rise as instructed in the Basic Pizza Dough recipe.

2. Preheat the oven to 375°F with a baking stone, if you have one, for 30 minutes.

3. Pass the ricotta cheese through a strainer or food mill into a bowl if fresh or homemade, then beat in 4 large eggs, the Parmesan, provolone, mozzarella, salami, and parsley and season with salt and pepper. If using supermarket-bought ricotta, add only 2 large eggs.

4. On a lightly floured work surface, roll out the 2 balls of dough about ⅛ inch thick and place one on a 16-inch pizza pan. Spread the stuffing evenly over the surface, leaving about an inch border along the edge. Cover with the other piece of dough and crimp the edges together to seal in the stuffing. Brush the top with the egg white.

5. Place the pizza pan in the oven and bake until golden, about 30 minutes. Slice into 16 segments, either wedges or squares.

1 Basic Pizza Dough recipe (page 94; see step 1)

8 ounces ricotta cheese, preferably homemade (see box, page 65)

2 or 4 large eggs (see step 3)

½ cup freshly grated Parmesan cheese (preferably Parmigiano-Reggiano cheese)

5 ounces mild provolone, provola, or caciocavallo cheese, cut into small dice

5 ounces fresh mozzarella cheese, cut into small dice

5 ounces salami, cut into small dice

2 tablespoons finely chopped fresh flat-leaf parsley

Salt and freshly ground black pepper to taste

1 large egg white, beaten until foamy

Pizza al Formaggio #1

1 Basic Pizza Dough recipe (page 94; see step 1)

Cornmeal, for sprinkling

Extra-virgin olive oil, as needed

12 ounces fresh mozzarella cheese, shredded

4 ounces ricotta cheese (page 65)

Salt and freshly ground black pepper to taste

20 large fresh basil leaves, thinly sliced

THIS PIZZA IS MADE only with cheese. Supermarket ricotta cheese is usually not dense enough, fresh enough, or flavorful enough to use on this pizza. One can find excellent and fresh ricotta cheeses in many Italian markets. You could also buy some for shipping at www.pastacheese.com or make your own (see page 65). Also, make sure to drain the mozzarella. If you must use supermarket-bought ricotta, let it drain in a strainer for 2 hours. *Makes two 16-inch pizzas*

1. Divide the dough into 2 balls and let rise as instructed in the Basic Pizza Dough recipe.

2. Preheat the oven to 450°F with a large baking stone, if you have one, for 30 minutes.

3. Roll or stretch each ball of dough out until 16 inches in diameter using a rolling pin on a lightly floured work surface or by rotating the pizza while it's draped over your fist until about ⅓ inch thick. Place on a 16-inch solid pizza pan sprinkled with cornmeal to prevent sticking or, preferably, use a 16-inch perforated pizza pan, making sure the border of the dough is a little higher than the center. Make indentations all over the pizza with your fingertips and lightly oil the top, including the borders, with the olive oil.

4. Place the pizzas in the oven until light brown, about 8 minutes. (If you don't have 2 pizza pans and/or you don't have a convection oven, bake one at a time.) Remove from the oven and lay the mozzarella and ricotta all over the pizzas, leaving a 1-inch border all around. Season with salt and pepper, drizzle with a little more oil, and return to the oven until the borders are charred in places and the top is dappled brown in some places on the cheese, 12 to 15 minutes.

5. Remove from the oven and sprinkle the basil over the pizza. Cut each pizza into 16 slices and serve hot.

Pizza al Formaggio #2

1 Basic Pizza Dough recipe (page 94), prepared through step 3, substituting ¾ cup cool water and ¼ cup warm milk for the warm water

2 large eggs

¾ cup freshly grated Parmesan cheese (preferably Parmigiano-Reggiano cheese)

½ cup freshly grated pecorino cheese

½ cup shredded mild provolone or caciocavallo cheese

2 tablespoons extra-virgin olive oil, plus more as needed

Flour, as needed

THIS ALL-CHEESE PIZZA is not as thin as the previous recipe, Pizza al Formaggio #1. It is thicker and baked in a baking pan, not a pizza pan. *Makes 16 hors d'oeuvres servings*

1. In a bowl, beat the eggs with all the cheeses. After the dough has risen the first time, punch it down and knead in the olive oil, then form the dough so it has a well in the center and pour in the cheese and eggs. Knead the dough again, making sure the eggs don't run out at first until you have a smooth ball of dough with all the eggs and cheese incorporated. At this point, it will be very wet and sticky. Turn the dough out onto a well-floured work surface and sprinkle more flour on top. Knead the dough until a soft ball forms and all the ingredients are incorporated. Cover and let rise for another hour.

2. Preheat the oven to 400°F.

3. Grease a 12 × 9-inch baking pan with olive oil. Roll the dough out on a floured surface until it is the same size as the pan. Transfer it to the pan and bake until light golden on top, about 20 minutes. Cut into portions and serve hot.

Pizza Flamiche

A FLAMICHE is a kind of leek tart made in northern France, Burgundy, and Picardy, but when I had it in Corsica, it was an incredibly delicious sweet onion and smoked bacon pizza with lots of local cheese that probably can't be found in this country, with a little red chile, bay leaf, and olive oil. The toppings go right to the edge of the pizza. If you can't find some of the cheeses I call for, then use a combination of ricotta, Gruyère, and goat cheese. The cheeses called for may be found in better supermarkets and at www.igourmet.com.

Makes 16 hors d'oeuvres servings

1 cup extra-virgin olive oil

3 ¾ pounds sweet onions, such as Vidalia, thinly sliced

1 Basic Pizza Dough recipe (page 94)

3 ounces fresh goat cheese, crumbled

3 ounces Tronchon cheese (semisoft Spanish mixed milk cheese), thinly sliced

4 ounces fresh mozzarella cheese, thinly sliced or shredded

4 ounces ricotta cheese (page 65)

4 ounces smoked slab bacon, cut into 1-inch matchsticks

2 dried red chiles, seeded and crumbled

9 small bay leaves

Salt and freshly ground black pepper to taste

1. In a large skillet, heat the olive oil over medium heat. Add the onions and cook, stirring occasionally, until golden, about 35 minutes.

2. Preheat the oven to 400°F.

3. On a lightly floured work surface, roll the dough out so it fits into a 17 × 12-inch (approximately) baking sheet and is ¼ inch thick, and make indentations over its entirety with your fingertips. Arrange the cheeses over the top of the pizza. Spread the onions evenly over the top, then sprinkle the bacon strips around at intervals. Sprinkle with the chile, place the bay leaves around, and season with salt and black pepper.

4. Bake until golden and the bacon is a little crispy, 30 to 35 minutes. Cut into serving portions and serve hot.

Pizza Sarde

1 Basic Pizza Dough recipe (page 94; see step 1)

8 ounces eggplant, peeled and cut in ⅛-inch-thick slices

Extra-virgin olive oil, as needed

Cornmeal, for sprinkling

4 ounces black olives, drained, pitted, and cut in half

8 ounces fresh mozzarella cheese, thinly sliced

3 ounces prosciutto di Parma, very thinly sliced

I HAD THIS WONDERFUL Sardinian pizza at the Ristorante Il Girasole da Pepper, in Sant Teresa di Gallura on the very northern tip of Sardinia, many years ago; I still remember it. It was topped with very thin slices of the earthy local prosciutto di cinghiale, a cured haunch of wild boar. This is not a product imported into this country, and I don't know anyone who makes it other than some restaurant chefs, so you will have to use prosciutto. A search on the Internet might turn up something; in any case, boar or not, it's not a boring pizza.

Makes two 16-inch pizzas

1. Prepare the pizza dough. Divide the dough into 2 balls and let rise as instructed in the Basic Pizza Dough recipe.

2. Preheat a ridged cast-iron skillet or griddle over high heat for 20 minutes. Brush the eggplant with olive oil and cook until browned with grid marks on both sides, 6 to 8 minutes. Remove from the pan and set aside.

3. Preheat the oven to 450°F with a large baking stone, if you have one, for 30 minutes.

4. Roll or stretch both balls of dough out until 16 inches in diameter, using a rolling pin on a lightly floured work surface or by rotating the pizza while it's draped over your fist until about ⅛ inch thick. Place on a 16-inch solid pizza pan sprinkled with cornmeal to prevent sticking or, preferably, use a 16-inch perforated pizza pan, making sure the border of the dough is a little higher than the center. Make indentations all over the pizza with your fingertips and grease the top, including the borders, with olive oil. Layer the eggplant, olives, and mozzarella over both pizzas.

5. Bake until the cheese is dappled with brown spots and the crust is golden, 13 to 15 minutes. (If you don't have 2 pizza pans and/or you don't have a convection oven, bake one at a time.) Remove from the oven, layer the prosciutto slices on top, cut into slices, and serve.

Pizza con Pancetta

1 Basic Pizza Dough recipe
(page 94; see step 1)

Extra-virgin olive
oil, as needed

Cornmeal, for sprinkling

1½ cups chopped pancetta
(about 5 ounces)

1 cup chopped scamorza
cheese (about 3½ ounces)

1 cup chopped pecorino
pepato cheese (about
3½ ounces)

Dried oregano to taste

Salt and freshly ground
black pepper to taste

PANCETTA IS A CURED PORK BELLY product used in Italian cooking. In other words, it's cured bacon, not smoked like the American pork belly. It's not eaten in the morning but, rather, gives a basic flavor to a variety of foods. Here it goes on top of a pizza with two kinds of cheeses. The pancetta should be chopped until it's about ⅜-inch cubes. Pecorino pepato cheese is a young pecorino cheese with peppercorns thrown into the curd; it is commonly found in many markets today, beyond the usual Italian markets where it is always found. Scamorza, a cheese in the same family as mozzarella and provolone, is hard to find, but good Italian markets will have it and you can order it at www.realmozzarella.com, www.mozzco.com, or www.igourmet.com. It's also made in a smoked variety, which is excellent on pizza. *Makes two 16-inch pizzas*

1. Divide the dough into 2 balls and let rise as instructed in the Basic Pizza Dough recipe.

2. Preheat the oven to 450°F with a large baking stone, if you have one, for 30 minutes.

3. Roll or stretch the dough out until 16 inches in diameter using a rolling pin on a lightly floured work surface or by rotating the pizza while it's draped over your fist until about ⅛ inch thick. Place on a 16-inch solid pizza pan sprinkled with cornmeal to prevent sticking or, preferably, use a 16-inch perforated pizza pan, making sure the border of the dough is a little higher than the center. Make indentations all over the pizza with your fingertips and grease the top, including the borders, with olive oil. Sprinkle the pancetta, cheeses, and oregano evenly over the surfaces of both pizzas, leaving a 1-inch border. Season with salt and pepper.

4. Bake until the cheese is dappled with brown spots and the crust is golden, 10 to 13 minutes. (If you don't have 2 pizza pans and/or you don't have a convection oven, bake one at a time.) Cut into slices and serve immediately.

Catalan Pizza with Duck, Prunes, and Roquefort

1 Basic Pizza Dough recipe (page 94)

6 ounces prunes, cut in half

½ cup brandy or Armagnac

1 pound boneless duck breasts

1 tablespoon extra-virgin olive oil

2 large, fleshy roasted red bell peppers, peeled, seeded, and cut into thin strips

1 large onion, thinly sliced

Salt and freshly ground black pepper to taste

5 ounces Roquefort cheese or other blue cheese

A COCA IS A KIND OF Catalan calzone (if folded over) or pizza (if not). The word *coca*, used in the Occitan and Catalan languages, comes from the Latin word for "to cook." It's a pizza, really, and this pizza is a *coca d'ànec amb pruna seca i Roquefort* in Catalan. Roquefort cheese from France is very popular in Catalonia—they put it on everything—but you can also use the slightly stronger blue cheese, Cabrales, from Asturia, or Mitica brand Valdeon cheese, a pasteurized cow's and goat's milk cheese with blue veins.

Makes 4 main-course servings or 8 appetizer servings

1. Divide the dough into 2 pieces. Soak the prunes in the brandy for at least 1 hour and drain before using.

2. Preheat a cast-iron or carbon-steel skillet over high heat, then cook the duck breasts, skin side down, until golden brown, about 4 minutes. You can use a lid to reduce splatter of duck fat. Remove after having cooked on one side only. Let cool, then slice the duck breasts thinly and set aside.

3. Preheat the oven to 450°F.

4. Lightly oil 2 large baking sheets (about 17 × 12 inches). Roll the 2 balls of pizza dough into large oblong shapes 18 × 8 inches. Divide the duck, prunes, bell peppers, and onion in half and spread over the two *coques* (the plural) and season with salt and pepper. Bake until the crust is golden and the onions soft, about 25 minutes. Add the Roquefort cheese on top and bake until it begins to melt, about 2 minutes. Serve warm or at room temperature.

Calzones

1 Basic Pizza Dough recipe
(page 94; see step 1)

⅓ cup raisins

1 cup tepid water

10 ounces spinach,
stems removed

3 tablespoons extra-
virgin olive oil

1 garlic clove, crushed

⅓ cup pine nuts

1 pound ricotta
cheese (page 65)

Semolina (durum
wheat) flour, for
sprinkling (optional)

CALZONES are large stuffed, baked, or fried crescent-shaped dough crusts encasing various ingredients along with cheese. This calzone from the southern Italian region of Apulia could contain Swiss chard, beet greens, spinach, or escarole. I use spinach in this recipe, but you could use any of the other greens or two or three of them. *Makes 8 calzones*

1. Divide the pizza dough into 8 balls before letting it rise.

2. Preheat the oven to 400°F.

3. Put the raisins in the water to soak until you need them. Place the spinach with only the water adhering to its leaves from the last rinsing in a large saucepan and steam over medium-high heat until it wilts, 4 to 5 minutes. Drain well in a colander, pressing the excess liquid out with the back of a wooden spoon, and chop coarsely.

4. In a large casserole, preferably earthenware (which enhances the flavor), heat the olive oil over medium heat, then add the garlic and cook, stirring occasionally, until it just begins to turn light brown. (If using earthenware, you may need to use a heat diffuser. Earthenware heats up slower but retains its heat longer than other casseroles. When using earthenware, food may cook slower when first heating up and then cook very quickly and retain its heat longer.) Remove and discard the garlic. Add the pine nuts and cook, stirring, until they are almost golden, about 2 minutes, being careful not to burn them. Add the spinach and cook, stirring, for about 3 minutes. Drain the raisins, add them to the casserole, and cook for another 2 minutes. Remove from the heat.

5. Push the balls of dough down with the palm of your hand and roll or stretch them into 8 disks with the thickness of a pizza, about ⅛ inch thick and 8 to 10 inches in diameter. Add some of the spinach mixture and a heaping tablespoonful of ricotta cheese to one half of each disk. Fold the other half of the dough over to form a half-moon and pinch closed with the tines of a fork.

6. Place the calzone on an oiled or semolina-strewn baking sheet or a flour-strewn pre-heated baking stone and bake until golden on top, 15 to 20 minutes. Remove and cool on a wire rack.

VARIATION: Steam a head of escarole until wilted and the core or heart is softer. Drain well and chop together with several anchovy fillets and some pitted imported black olives. Stuff the calzones with this mixture.

Calzones Napoletana

1 Basic Pizza Dough recipe
(page 94; see step 1)

2 large eggs

8 ounces ricotta
cheese (page 65)

Salt to taste

½ cup freshly grated
Parmesan cheese

6 ounces fresh mozzarella
cheese, cut into tiny dice

2 ounces salami,
sliced ¹⁄₁₆ inch thick
and slivered

THE WORD *CALZONE* comes from the Italian word meaning "pant leg," after the style of pants worn in centuries past. This half-moon of dough is filled with delicious cheeses and a variety of meats. Originally from Naples, this recipe is considered by many to be the classic one and it is indeed probably the most popular.

Makes 8 calzones

1. Let the dough rise once until it has doubled in size. Divide the dough into 8 balls, arrange on a tray, cover with a clean kitchen towel, and let rise a second time, about 1¼ hours.

2. Preheat the oven to 400°F with a large baking stone, if you have one, for 30 minutes..

3. Lightly beat 1 egg in a medium bowl. Stir in the ricotta, beating well with a fork or whisk. Season with salt and stir in the Parmesan, mozzarella, and salami.

4. Roll each ball of dough out on a lightly floured work surface into disks as thin as a pizza and about 7 inches in diameter. Divide the ricotta mixture between the disks. Fold one edge of the disk over onto the other to form a half-moon and pinch the ends together with a fork. When crimping the calzones, make sure you press firmly down and that there are no spaces, or else cheese will ooze out when baking. Puncture the tops with the tip of a knife so that the calzones can breathe while baking. Beat the remaining egg and brush each calzone with it. Place on the baking stone strewn with flour or a pizza pan in the oven and bake until golden brown on top, about 20 minutes. Let cool on a wire rack for a few minutes before serving.

Sausage and Provolone Calzones

IN SICILIAN, these calzones are called *ravazzati*, a word described in an old Sicilian dictionary as a kind of focaccia stuffed with a variety of ingredients. Although traditionally formed with two 5-inch disks of dough that are sealed around the stuffing, in this recipe I form them like a calzone and deep-fry them until an appetizing orange color. Some Sicilian cooks dip them in eggs, then dredge them in bread crumbs, before frying.

Makes 8 calzones

1 Basic Pizza Dough recipe (page 94; see step 1), made with the addition of 2 large beaten eggs and 2 tablespoons melted pork lard (or unsalted butter) to replace the olive oil

¾ cup fresh or canned tomato purée mixed with 1 tablespoon tomato paste

8 ounces ricotta cheese (page 65)

¾ cup cooked fresh or frozen peas (not canned)

8 ounces cooked mild Italian sausages, thinly sliced

1 ounce salami, thinly sliced

2 large hard-boiled eggs, shelled and each cut into 8 slices

4 ounces provolone cheese, thinly sliced

Salt to taste

6 cups vegetable oil or sunflower seed oil, for frying

1. After you mix the dough, form the dough (it will be sticky) into 8 balls about the size of a large lemon and lay on a floured baking sheet, covered with a kitchen towel, to rise for 2 hours in a warm place, such as a turned-off oven.

2. Roll each ball of dough out into an 8-inch diameter disk on a well-floured work surface. As the dough will be sticky, it's important to make sure the surface and both sides of the disk are floured. Smear 1 tablespoon of tomato sauce over the disk, leaving at least a 1-inch border. In the center, place a dollop of ricotta, pushing it down slightly, then push about 1 tablespoon of peas into the ricotta. Lay a slice each of sausage and salami, 2 egg slices, and a slice of provolone on top. Season with salt, then fold one side over to the other to form a half-moon and crimp the edges together with a fork.

3. Preheat the frying oil in a deep fryer or an 8-inch saucepan fitted with a basket insert to 360°F.

4. Fry the calzones in batches (do not crowd them), turning once, until orange, 6 to 7 minutes. Drain on paper towels, and cut in half or leave whole for a larger-than-appetizer portion. Serve immediately.

Rotoloni with Leeks and Sausage

For the dough

One ¼-ounce package
(2¼ teaspoons)
active dry yeast

1 cup warm water
(105°F to 115°F)

1 teaspoon salt

3½ cups bread flour or
all-purpose unbleached
flour, sifted

For the stuffing

1 pound mild Italian
sausage, removed from
the casing and crumbled

3 tablespoons extra-
virgin olive oil

6 leeks, white and light
green parts only, trimmed,
split lengthwise, washed
well, and sliced ¼ inch thick

1 large shallot, sliced

4 large garlic cloves,
finely chopped

Salt and freshly ground
black pepper to taste

8 ounces scamorza or
mozzarella cheese,
shredded

8 ounces provolone
cheese, shredded

RELATED TO CALZONES, rotoloni are stuffed breads, a very popular family preparation in southern Italy. My grandfather and two of his nine siblings emigrated to America from the village of Pago Veiano in the Campania region of Italy in about 1911, and this stuffed bread must have reminded them of home. These kinds of "big calzones" are still made by us, and they are forever popular in our family. This recipe is made with sautéed leeks, sausage, scamorza cheese, and provolone cheese. It's rather easy to do and you can mix up the ingredients if you want—for example, by adding sun-dried tomatoes or red chile. I use my electric mixer to make the dough, but you could also use a food processor, and if you have neither I give some instructions for doing it by hand. *Makes 4 to 6 servings*

1. Warm the bowl of a stand mixer under hot running water, then dry. In the warmed bowl, dissolve the yeast in the warm water. Let it rest for 5 minutes, then add the salt and shake gently.

2. Add 2½ cups of the flour, affix the bowl to the mixer, and attach the dough hook. Run according to the directions of the manufacturer, adding the remaining flour in ½-cup increments, until the dough is pulled off the walls of the bowl and is being pushed by the dough hook, about 2 minutes. Continue running for another 2 minutes.

3. Once the ball of dough is smooth, remove the dough from the bowl. Place it in a lightly floured or oiled bowl, cover with a clean kitchen towel, and let rise in a warm (80°F) place, such as inside a turned-off oven, for 2 hours. (If using a food processor, follow the same method but run in pulses for about 1 minute. If making by hand, turn the dough ball out onto a floured surface and knead for 8 minutes.) If you like, for a lighter taste, you can punch the dough down and let it rise for another 2 hours.

4. Prepare the stuffing. In a skillet over low heat, add the sausage and cook, breaking it up further with a wooden spoon, until browned, about 20 minutes. Transfer to a bowl. In the same skillet, heat the olive oil over medium-low heat. Add the leeks and shallot and cook, stirring, until softened, about 5 minutes. Add the garlic and cook, stirring, until everything is slightly caramelized, about 30 minutes. Season with salt and pepper. Mix the sausage and leek mixture together.

5. Roll the bread dough out until 18 × 14 inches. Place the sausage-leek mixture and the cheeses over the surface, leaving a 2-inch border on the edges. Roll up the bread, pinching the seams and end closed by crimping with the tines of a fork. Place the stuffed bread on a baking sheet or pizza pan and let rest while the oven heats.

6. Preheat the oven to 475°F, with a baking stone if you have one.

7. Place the bread in the oven. Immediately reduce the temperature to 425°F. Bake until golden brown, about 40 minutes. Remove, let rest for 10 minutes, then slice and serve.

Rotoloni with Sausage and Broccoli Rabe

For the dough

One ¼-ounce package
(2¼ teaspoons)
active dry yeast

1 cup warm water
(105° to 115°F)

1 teaspoon salt

3½ cups bread flour
or unbleached all-
purpose flour, sifted

For the stuffing

1 pound hot Italian
sausage, removed from
the casing and crumbled

1 pound broccoli rabe,
tops and stems separated

1 tablespoon extra-
virgin olive oil

2 large garlic cloves,
finely chopped

1 teaspoon red chile flakes

Salt and freshly ground
black pepper to taste

8 ounces fresh mozzarella
cheese, chopped or sliced

3 ounces provolone cheese,
chopped or sliced

THE STUFFING is a family preparation popular in Naples called *salsicce e friarelli* and is eaten plain, on pizza, or rolled into bread, as in this rotoloni. *Makes 4 to 6 servings*

1. Warm the bowl of a stand mixer bowl under hot running water, then dry. In the warmed bowl, dissolve the yeast in the warm water. Let it rest for 5 minutes, then add the salt and shake gently.

2. Add 2½ cups of the flour, affix to the mixer, and attach the dough hook. Run according to the directions of the manufacturer, adding the remaining flour in ½-cup increments, until the dough is pulled off the walls of the bowl and is being pushed by the dough hook, about 2 minutes. Continue running for another 2 minutes.

3. Once the ball of dough is smooth, remove the dough from the bowl. Place it in a lightly floured or oiled bowl, cover with a clean kitchen towel, and let rise in a warm (80°F) place, such as inside a turned-off oven, for 2 hours. (If using a food processor, follow the same method but run in pulses for about 1 minute. If making by hand, turn the dough ball out onto a floured surface and knead for 8 minutes.) If you like, for a lighter taste, you can punch the dough down and let it rise for another 2 hours.

4. Prepare the stuffing. Bring a large pot of water to a boil over high heat, then cook the broccoli rabe stems for 4 minutes. Add the broccoli rabe tops and cook until softened, about 6 minutes. Drain well and chop coarsely. In a skillet, cook the sausage over medium heat, breaking it up further with a wooden spoon, until browned, about 20 minutes. Add the drained broccoli rabe, olive oil, garlic, and chile and cook, stirring occasionally, for another 5 minutes. Season with salt and pepper.

5. Roll the dough out until 18 × 14 inches. Place the sausage mixture and cheeses over the surface, leaving about a 2-inch border on the edges. Roll the bread dough away from you once, fold a bit of the sides inwards, and continue rolling, then pinch the seams and end closed by crimping with the tines of a fork. Place the stuffed bread on a baking sheet or pizza pan to rest while the oven heats.

6. Preheat the oven to 475°F, with a baking stone if you have one.

7. Place the bread in the oven. Immediately reduce the temperature to 425°F. Bake until golden brown, about 40 minutes. Remove, let rest for 10 minutes, then slice and serve.

Gruyère Cheese Bread

For the starter

1¼ cups unbleached
bread flour

1 teaspoon salt

½ teaspoon active dry yeast

½ cup cool water

For the dough

1¼ cups lukewarm water,
plus more as needed

1 teaspoon salt

3½ cups unbleached
bread flour

½ teaspoon active dry yeast

For the filling

2½ cups grated Gruyère
cheese (about 6½ ounces)

WHEN THIS BREAD COMES OUT of the oven, the cheese is spilling out of the top and the bread looks a bit like a crown. The bread is famous at the French Pastry School in Chicago, whose recipe I've adapted. The head bakers/chefs Jacquy Pfeiffer and Sébastien Canonne say that this is probably their most popular bread. You will be instructed to make the starter the day before you make the bread. *Makes 4 small loaves*

1. Prepare the starter. Mix the flour, salt, yeast, and cool water in a bowl. Cover and let rest overnight at room temperature.

2. Prepare the dough. The starter will look bubbly. In the bowl of an electric mixer, combine the starter with the lukewarm water, salt, flour, and yeast and mix with the dough hook for about 5 minutes at medium speed. (If making it by hand, form the dough into a ball and knead for 10 minutes. You may need another 2 tablespoons of water if the air is dry.) Transfer the dough to a lightly greased bowl, cover, and let rest in a warm, draft-free place (such as a turned-off oven) until nearly doubled in bulk, about 2 hours. Remove the dough, punch it down, and let rise for another hour, covered as before.

3. On a floured work surface, punch down the dough with your fist and pat and stretch it into a 12 × 9 × ¾-inch rectangle. Spray water on the dough with a spritz bottle and sprinkle the surface with the cheese. Roll into a log starting with the long side, gathering cheese with your fingers as you roll so that it doesn't spill out. Pinch the seam to seal. Place the bread log seam side down on a lightly greased baking sheet. Cover with a clean kitchen towel and let it rise until puffy but not doubled in bulk, 1 to 1½ hours.

4. Preheat the oven to 425°F.

5. Cut the dough log into four pieces. Place them on a parchment paper–lined baking sheet, cut side up. Gently spread them open to expose the cheese a little. Spray with warm water and bake until the cheese is melted and the loaves are golden brown, about 25 minutes. Remove from the oven and let cool on a rack.

Sandwiches with Cheese

One cannot write a chapter about sandwiches with cheese and not have a Grilled Cheese Sandwich (page 120). But here you'll find a twist that takes advantage of all the real cheeses being produced in this country today. All kinds of sandwiches are here that you may not have encountered before, such as Grilled Pork, Black Bean, and Cheese Sandwich with Chipotle Mayonnaise (page 130), as well as famous classics like Welsh Rabbit (page 122) and Croque-Monsieur (page 123). Once you've made a few sandwiches from this chapter, I'm sure you'll be inspired to create your own.

Grilled Cheese Sandwich

2 to 3 tablespoons
unsalted butter, at
room temperature

Eight 6¼ × 4½ × ¾-inch
slices artisan-style white
or mild sourdough bread

3⅓ ounces Fontina
Val d'Aosta cheese,
grated (about 1 cup)

3⅓ ounces Gorgonzola
dolce, cut into small
pieces (about 1 cup)

3⅓ ounces raclette cheese,
grated (about 1 cup)

THIS WAS MY FAVORITE sandwich as a kid. But think about it: It's bread and cheese, so why did we stick with Wonder bread and American cheese slices when the sandwich begs for only the best? Although originally derived from cheddar cheese, American cheese slices aren't even cheese, for goodness sake! It is a processed cheese product that does not meet the legal definition of cheese. Processed cheese is made with unfermented dairy ingredients, emulsifiers, whey, and food colorings. This grilled cheese sandwich is in another category: artisanal bread with three kinds of natural cheeses for what will be the best grilled cheese sandwich you've ever had. *Artisanal bread* is the term being used today for those breads in your supermarket that are baked fresh and do not come, generally, in plastic bags.

Here are some tips: Use the best loaf bread you can get, slicing it yourself if necessary; grate the cheese rather than using slices; make sure your butter is at room temperature for easy spreading; use lots of cheese (after all, it's called a grilled cheese sandwich, not a diet sandwich); press down with a spatula while it cooks; cook the sandwich covered; and try some of the variations listed below. In my mind, a grilled cheese sandwich should be only melted cheese and bread. When one starts adding other ingredients, such as ham or tomatoes, you've got a different sandwich. That being said, those different sandwiches will be great, too. *Makes 4 servings*

1. Butter one side of each of the 8 slices of bread. Place 4 slices butter side down on a tray and divide the cheeses among the slices. Cover the cheeses with the 4 remaining slices, butter side up.

2. Heat 2 large skillets over medium-high heat for 2 minutes. Put 2 sandwiches in each skillet (or cook in two batches in one skillet), cover, and cook until the bottoms are golden brown, about 2 minutes. Uncover, turn over with a spatula, and cook, pressing with the spatula, until golden brown and the cheese is melted completely. Serve immediately.

VARIATION 1: Use Gruyère, Saint-Nectaire, and Swiss (Emmenthaler) cheese.

VARIATION 2: Use Edam, cheddar, and Muenster.

VARIATION 3: Use cheddar, Monterey Jack, and Muenster.

VARIATION 4: Use only orange-colored shredded cheddar for a traditional sandwich.

VARIATION 5: Put a layer of cooked ham on top of the cheese. (You can also spread some honey mustard on the ham.)

VARIATION 6: Put a layer of cooked ham, a drizzle of truffle oil, and some thin tomato slices on top of the cheese. Dip the whole sandwich in beaten egg before cooking. (Remember that truffle oil is a chemical additive and is not made from truffles.)

VARIATION 7: Use only one cheese of your choice.

Welsh Rabbit

8 ounces cheddar cheese, cut into small dice

1 tablespoon unsalted butter

1 tablespoon all-purpose flour

1½ teaspoons dry mustard

¼ teaspoon cayenne pepper, or to taste

½ cup beer (ale)

1 teaspoon Worcestershire sauce

1 large egg

Salt to taste

4 bread slices, lightly toasted

ALTHOUGH EVERYONE calls it Welsh rarebit and no one seems to make it anymore, this dish is properly called Welsh rabbit, and it is nothing but melted cheese covering toast. It is also known as Scotch rabbit. Although the dish is quite old—the term *Welsh rabbit* was first recorded in 1725—the origin of the name is unknown. It's a very nice lunch dish and worth knowing how to make. The quality of the bread and the cheddar cheese are key to the preparation; this is no time for plastic-wrapped presliced sandwich bread and Velveeta.

Makes 4 servings

1. Preheat the broiler.

2. In the top of a double boiler, add the cheese, butter, flour, mustard, and cayenne and cook, stirring constantly in a figure 8, until the cheese begins to melt. Whisk in the beer and Worcestershire sauce and continue cooking, stirring in a figure-8 motion, until the melted cheese is uniform. Beat the egg in a bowl and mix in a couple of tablespoons of the melted cheese mixture. Then return the egg mixture to the cheese sauce in the double boiler. Season with salt. Continue to cook, stirring occasionally, until fragrant and smooth, 3 to 5 minutes.

3. Spread the cheese mixture evenly over the toast and put under broiler until bubbly and the edges of the toast are crisp, about 2 minutes. Serve immediately.

Croque-Monsieur

CROQUE-MONSIEUR is the French version of a grilled ham-and-cheese sandwich. This recipe is the traditional croque-monsieur recipe, the closest to the original sandwich served in Parisian cafés in the early 1900s. Today, it's a popular snack all over France, and the variations are countless. Remember, the better your bread, the better the sandwich. *Makes 4 servings*

8 slices sandwich bread, crust removed

4 tablespoons clarified butter (see Note, page 171), at room temperature

2 tablespoons Dijon mustard

4 ounces baked ham, thinly sliced

3 cups grated Gruyère cheese (about 8 ounces)

1. Set an oven rack 8 inches below the broiler heating element. Preheat the broiler.

2. Brush 4 slices of the bread on one side with half the clarified butter. Place the slices butter side down on a broiler or baking sheet. Spread half the mustard on the top side of the bread slices on the sheet, to the edge of each slice. Place 1 ounce of sliced ham on each slice. Divide 2 cups of the Gruyère cheese among the 4 slices. Spread the remaining mustard on the remaining 4 slices of bread and press down on top of the cheese, mustard side down. Brush the tops and sides of the sandwiches with the remaining butter.

3. Broil until golden brown on top, 3 to 4 minutes, then turn over, cover the sandwiches with the remaining cheese, and continue cooking until they are crispy and golden brown, about 3 additional minutes.

Croque-Madame

8 slices sandwich bread

5 tablespoons clarified butter (see Note, page 171), at room temperature

2 tablespoons Dijon mustard

4 ounces baked ham, thinly sliced

3 cups grated Gruyère cheese (about 8 ounces)

4 large eggs

¼ cup Béchamel Sauce (page 53)

THE CROQUE-MADAME IS SIMPLY a traditional croque-monsieur served with a fried egg and a bit of béchamel sauce spooned over the finished sandwich. *Makes 4 servings*

1. Set an oven rack 8 inches below the broiler heating element. Preheat the broiler.

2. Brush 4 slices of the bread on one side with 2 tablespoons of the clarified butter. Place the slices butter side down on a broiler or baking sheet. Spread half the mustard on the top side of the bread slices on the sheet, to the edge of each slice. Place 1 ounce of sliced ham on each slice. Divide 2 cups of the Gruyère cheese among the 4 slices. Spread the remaining mustard on the remaining 4 slices of bread and press down on top of the cheese, mustard side down. Brush the tops and sides of the sandwiches with 2 tablespoons of the butter.

3. Broil until the top is golden brown, 3 to 4 minutes, then turn them over, cover each sandwich with the remaining cheese, and continue cooking until they are crispy and golden brown, about 3 minutes longer.

4. Meanwhile, melt the remaining 1 tablespoon butter in a large nonstick skillet over medium-high heat, then cook the eggs until the whites set. Carefully slide 1 egg onto the top of each sandwich. Top with a spoonful of béchamel sauce and serve.

Bruschetta with Ricotta and Spinach

BRUSCHETTA (pronounced broo-SKET-ta) is an Italian toast spread with olive oil or other ingredients and usually served as an antipasto. In this preparation, it's turned into a large open-faced dinner sandwich. You will want to use dense Italian or French country bread with its earthy taste. For a less substantial meal, the bread slices can be cut smaller and the preparation served as a snack or appetizer. If you use a baguette in slices, you can serve this as a passed party hors d'oeuvre.

Makes 4 servings

10 ounces fresh spinach, heavy stems removed

3 tablespoons unsalted butter

4 tablespoons extra-virgin olive oil

1 garlic clove, crushed

Salt and freshly ground black pepper to taste

Four 6 × 5 × ¾-inch (approximately) slices French or Italian country bread

1 pound ricotta cheese (page 65)

1. Preheat the oven to 350°F.

2. Put the spinach in a large saucepan with only the water adhering to its leaves from its last rinsing. Cover the pot and wilt the spinach, turning occasionally, over medium-high heat, 4 to 5 minutes. Drain well in a strainer, using the back of a wooden spoon to squeeze out all the water. Chop coarsely.

3. In a medium skillet, heat the butter over medium heat with 2 tablespoons of the olive oil and the crushed garlic until the butter melts. Add the spinach and cook, stirring, for 5 minutes. Season with salt and pepper. Remove and keep warm.

4. Meanwhile, coat the slices of bread with the ricotta cheese. Drizzle 1¼ teaspoons olive oil over each slice and season with salt and pepper. Set on a baking sheet and place in the oven until the oil starts bubbling, about 10 minutes. Remove from the oven and cover each slice with the spinach. Return to the oven and bake for 2 minutes. Serve immediately.

Francesinha

2 tablespoons
unsalted butter

1 tablespoon extra-virgin
olive oil, plus more for
oiling the skillet

1 medium onion, chopped

2 bay leaves, crushed

4 large garlic cloves,
finely chopped

1 tablespoon tomato
paste mixed with
2 tablespoons water

1 cup beer (lager) or
white wine and port
in equal portions

1 cup beef broth

1 tablespoon red
chile flakes

Salt and freshly ground
black pepper to taste

8 slices good-quality
sandwich bread or
country bread

4 thin slices (about
5 ounces) beef bottom
round (sandwich steaks),
pounded thinner

2 ounces fresh or smoked
linguiça sausage or
fresh or smoked kielbasa,
removed from the
casing and thinly
sliced

(continued)

PRONOUNCED fran-san-SEEN-yesh, it means "little French" in Portuguese and is a sandwich originally from Oporto. Typically, it is made with two slices of bread and cooked ham slices; linguiça sausage; fresh sausage like chipolata, a thin breakfast-like pork sausage made with onions, paprika, and thyme; pan-fried thin beef steaks; and melted cheese, and it is served with a dense and piquant tomato and beer sauce. According to Wikipedia, Francesinha is said to have been invented in the 1960s by Daniel da Silva, a returned emigrant from France and Belgium who wished to adapt the croque-monsieur (page 123) to Portuguese tastes. ***Makes 4 servings***

1. In a saucepan, melt the butter with the 1 tablespoon olive oil over medium-high heat. Add the onion and bay leaves and cook, stirring, until softened, about 5 minutes. Add the garlic and cook, stirring, for 1 minute. Stir in the dissolved tomato paste and then the beer, beef broth, red chile flakes, salt, and pepper. Reduce the heat to medium-low and simmer the sauce until denser, about 15 minutes.

2. Meanwhile, heat a cast-iron skillet or griddle with a little olive oil over medium heat. Cook the bread slices in batches until crispy golden on both sides, about 3 minutes. Remove and set aside. Season the beef slices lightly with salt and pepper and lightly oil them, then sear on both sides until golden brown, 1 to 2 minutes. Set aside. Add the juices from the skillet to the sauce. Add the linguiça and chorizo to the skillet and cook until browned, about 5 minutes.

3. Set a rack in the middle of the oven and preheat the broiler.

4. Add the flour mixed with a bit of water to the sauce. Mix well, cook for 1 to 2 minutes, then strain the sauce through a wire-mesh strainer into a saucepan and keep warm. Place 4 slices of the bread on a broiler or baking sheet and top with the beef slices. Place the sausages on top of the beef. Place the ham slices on top of the steak. Cover with the 4 remaining bread slices. Place the cheese on top of the bread. Broil until the cheese is melted and bubbling, 5 to 7 minutes. Spread some sauce on individual plates, place a sandwich in the middle of each, and serve.

2 ounces Spanish chorizo sausage or mild Italian sausage, removed from the casing and thinly sliced

2 teaspoons all-purpose flour mixed with a little water

4 slices (about 3 ounces) cooked ham, such as Black Forest

8 ounces Edam cheese, sliced

Fried Cheese Pita

1 tablespoon
unsalted butter

1 pound Syrian white
cheese or queso ranchero
or queso fresco, cut
into ¼-inch-thick
2-inch squares

1 cup strained
yogurt (*labna*)

Eight 6-inch diameter
pita pocket breads,
warmed and cut
into sixths

THIS PREPARATION is fantastically simple, yet because it is so well received, I am always asked for the recipe. It consists of four foods. First, you need to find Syrian white cheese, which is available in Middle Eastern markets. A Mexican queso ranchero or queso blanco is an excellent substitute, as are several dense white farmer's cheeses, and there are always the cheeses sold as "frying cheeses" that some supermarkets carry. You will also need *labna* (or *lubny*), which is strained yogurt you can make yourself (see Note below) or buy at a Middle Eastern market, and you will need small fresh pita bread loaves (Arabic flatbread), which you will warm up and cut into sixths. One should be able to eat these starters in one or two bites.

Makes 10 appetizer servings

1. In a large nonstick skillet, melt the butter over medium-high heat, then lay down the cheese squares and cook until crispy brown, about 3 minutes. Turn with a spatula and cook the other side until crispy brown, about 2 minutes.

2. Meanwhile, open the pocket bread wedges, making sure the top and bottom remain attached. Spread a little strained yogurt inside each wedge, lay the fried cheese square on top, and close. Serve immediately as a passed appetizer.

NOTE: To make your own *labna*, place 1 quart of the best-quality plain whole yogurt you can buy in some cheesecloth set in a strainer and set the strainer over a bowl in the refrigerator. Let it drain for 12 hours. Refrigerate the resulting strained yogurt.

Brioche Pork and Cheese Sandwich

FOR THIS SANDWICH, you do not use the small breakfast-type brioche baked in fluted molds but brioche made into a hamburger bun–type shape. Many supermarkets, especially those with their own bakeries, have this brioche bun, and certainly one could find it at Trader Joe's. I very much like the cheeses I call for here; however, you can use what's most available.

Makes 4 servings

4 slices thick-cut bacon, cut in half

4 thin slices onion

8 ounces boneless pork loin, cut into strips

Salt and freshly ground black pepper to taste

4 brioche buns or honey wheat buns

8 lettuce leaves

3 tablespoons mayonnaise

4 thin slices medium tomato

3½ ounces Asiago cheese, sliced

1 small avocado, pitted, peeled, and thinly sliced

3½ ounces Fontina Val d'Aosta cheese, sliced

1. Preheat the oven to 350°F.

2. Preheat a cast-iron or carbon-steel skillet over medium heat, then cook the bacon until nearly crispy, about 5 minutes. Remove the bacon and set aside. Leave 2 tablespoons bacon fat in the skillet and discard the rest. Increase the heat to high, then add the onion slices and cook, turning once, until softened and blackened a bit on both sides, about 3 minutes. Remove and set aside.

3. Season the pork with salt and pepper. Add to the skillet and cook, tossing, until golden and crispy, about 3 minutes.

4. Slice the buns open. On the bottom half of each, lay a lettuce leaf, spread with a little mayonnaise, then lay a tomato slice, Asiago cheese, avocado, bacon, fontina cheese, pork, mayonnaise, and lettuce, in that order. Wrap the brioche sandwiches in aluminum foil. Place on a baking sheet and bake the sandwiches until the cheese melts, 20 to 25 minutes.

Grilled Pork, Black Bean, and Cheese Sandwich with Chipotle Mayonnaise

For the chipotle mayonnaise

1 large egg

2 canned chipotle chiles in adobo

1 large garlic clove

1¼ cups extra-virgin olive oil

1 teaspoon white wine vinegar

½ teaspoon salt

For the sandwich

6 slices bacon

One 1-pound pork chop (leave fat on)

Salt and freshly ground black pepper to taste

4 fresh New Mexico (Anaheim or Hatch) chiles

One 7-ounce can black beans, drained and rinsed

½ cup chopped red onion

8 pickled pearl onions (from a jar), chopped

1 small avocado, pitted, peeled, and chopped

1 small tomato, chopped

1 small habanero chile, seeded and finely slivered

(continued)

THIS IS MY EXTRAPOLATION on a Cuban sandwich (an invention of Cuban-American street vendors in Miami and Tampa and not from Cuba). It's a grilled pork chop that is sliced thin and arranged on bolillo bread, a wide soft roll used for Cuban sandwiches, with bacon, chopped red onion, grilled mildly hot New Mexico chiles, a superhot habanero chile, picked pearl onions, black beans, tomato, avocado, cilantro, Monterey Jack, queso fresco, cheddar, and homemade chipotle mayonnaise. It's wrapped in aluminum foil and placed back on the grill to become hot so the cheeses melt. Much of the preparation can be done ahead of time and then the sandwiches finished on the grill as the coals die down. I serve chopped lettuce on the side, and you can't go wrong with beer and some tequila and limes.

Makes 6 servings

1. Prepare the chipotle mayonnaise. Place the egg, chipotle chiles, and garlic in a food processor, then run for 30 seconds. While the processor is running, pour the olive oil through the feed tube in a very slow, narrow stream. Add the vinegar and salt, pulse the processor a few times, then transfer the mayonnaise to a container and refrigerate for 2 hours before using.

2. Prepare a hot charcoal fire to one side of the grill box or preheat a gas grill on high for 20 minutes.

3. In a wide skillet over low heat, cook the bacon, turning once, until crispy, about 15 minutes. Remove and cut into 1-inch pieces. Reserve 3 tablespoons of the bacon fat.

4. Season the pork chop with salt and pepper and place on the grill directly above the heat. Cook until golden brown on both sides, springy to the touch, and medium cooked, turning once, 10 to 12 minutes in all. Remove the pork chop, let rest for 5 minutes, then cut into thin slices and discard the bone. Meanwhile, place the New Mexico chiles on the grill directly above the heat and cook until blistered black all over, turning with tongs. Remove the chiles and place in a plastic bag to steam for 20 minutes to make peeling them easier.

5. In a bowl, mix the bacon, black beans, red onion, pickled onions, avocado, tomato, habanero chile, and cilantro. Remove the seeds and skin of the grilled chiles and cut into strips.

6. Slice open the bolillo bread and arrange the pork slices on one half. Brush the pork slices with about 2 tablespoons chipotle mayonnaise. Spoon the vegetable mix over the pork and sprinkle the cheeses on top. Close the sandwich, pressing down a bit, then wrap in aluminum foil and place on the grill, away from the fire, until very hot, about 15 minutes, although you can leave it longer if you don't want to eat right away. Serve hot.

¼ cup chopped fresh cilantro

6 bolillo bread rolls, hoagie rolls, or kaiser rolls

¾ cup chipotle mayonnaise

2½ ounces Monterey Jack cheese, shredded

2½ ounces Mexican queso blanco, shredded

2½ ounces orange cheddar cheese, shredded

Grilled Flap Steak and Vegetable Sandwich

14 ounces beef flap steak

1 teaspoon ground allspice

1 teaspoon ground cumin

1 teaspoon ground coriander seeds

1 teaspoon garlic powder

Salt and freshly ground black pepper to taste

1 small onion, cut in half and thinly sliced

Extra-virgin olive oil, for drizzling

2 red bell peppers

1 eggplant (about 1¼ pounds), cut in half, then cut into ¼-inch-thick slices

8 scallions, trimmed

6 pocketless flatbreads

1 cup loosely packed coarsely chopped fresh cilantro

4 ounces kashkaval cheese (preferably) or Monterey Jack cheese, cut into sticks

Yogurt-Garlic Sauce (optional; see Note #1)

Muhammara (optional; see Note #2)

FLAP STEAK IS A CHEAP CUT of beef from the short loin section that is an extension of the T-bone and porterhouse steaks. When you remove the flank and take the layers of fat off, the resulting meat is flap meat. It is a good meat to marinate or grill. Some supermarkets mislabel it, though, calling it skirt steak, which it is not, or sirloin tips, which it is not, or hanger steak, which it is not. It looks like a very wide skirt steak and is popular with Mexican cooks who use it for carne asada. In the summer, the grilled sandwiches are perfect on their own or with one or both of the sauces. A great accompaniment is a tomato-watercress or tomato-wild arugula salad dressed only with olive oil and salt.

Makes 6 servings

1. Season the flap steak with the allspice, cumin, coriander, garlic powder, salt, and pepper. Sprinkle on the onion slices and drizzle with olive oil. Set aside.

2. Prepare a hot charcoal fire or preheat a gas grill on high for 20 minutes.

3. Grill the red bell peppers until blistered black all over, about 10 minutes. Remove and place in a paper bag to steam. Meanwhile, grill the eggplant slices and scallions until brown and slightly crispy, about 10 minutes. Transfer the eggplant and scallions to a cutting board. Remove the bell peppers from the bag and brush off the skin and seeds with a paper towel. Place on the cutting board and chop all the vegetables in strips or coarsely. Toss the chopped vegetable with your hands. Drizzle with a little olive oil.

4. Grill the flap steak until golden brown, crisp, and medium-rare, about 8 minutes in all. Transfer to the cutting board, slice into thin strips, then cut the strips into thirds.

5. Place the beef on the flatbreads, cover with the cilantro and cheese, then cover with the mixed chopped vegetables. Fold the flatbreads to enclose the ingredients and wrap each in aluminum foil. Grill until the sandwiches are very hot and the cheese melted, about 5 minutes. Serve with the sauces if desired.

NOTE #1: In a mortar, pound 1 large garlic clove with ¼ teaspoon salt until mushy. Stir this into ¾ cup plain whole yogurt with 1 tablespoon extra-virgin olive oil.

NOTE #2: Visit www.cliffordawright.com, and under "Recipes" look for "Arab Levant" and you will find a recipe for muhammara, a spread or dip made with red peppers, walnuts, and garlic.

Veal Parmesan Hero

For the marinara sauce

One 15-ounce can whole plum tomatoes

1½ tablespoons extra-virgin olive oil

3 tablespoons finely chopped onion

1 small garlic clove, finely chopped

1 small bay leaf

¼ teaspoon dried oregano

⅛ teaspoon dried thyme

½ tablespoon finely chopped fresh flat-leaf parsley

¼ teaspoon salt

⅛ teaspoon freshly ground black pepper, or more to taste

¼ teaspoon sugar (optional)

(continued)

THIS HERO IS AN OLD FAVORITE from when I was a teenager on Long Island. I'm sure that the veal Parmesan hero is an Italian-American invention. Typically, when you make them at home, they're made with leftover Veal Parmesan (page 348), but they're so good that I often make them from scratch just to have the hero.

Makes 4 servings

1. To prepare the marinara sauce, chop all the tomatoes. In a saucepan, heat the olive oil over medium heat. Add the onion, garlic, and bay leaf and cook, stirring occasionally, until the onion is translucent, about 5 minutes. Add the tomatoes, oregano, and thyme. Cook, stirring occasionally, until the sauce thickens slightly, about 15 minutes. Stir in the parsley and season with salt and pepper. Taste, and if the sauce is bitter, add the sugar.

2. Season the veal with salt and pepper. Place the flour, egg, and bread crumbs in separate shallow dishes. Working with one piece of veal at a time, dredge the veal in the flour, egg, and bread crumbs.

3. In a 12-inch skillet, heat the olive oil over medium-high heat. Add 2 pieces of breaded veal and cook, turning once with tongs, until golden brown, about 3 minutes. Set aside. Cook the remaining veal.

4. Set a rack 10 inches from the broiler heating element. Preheat the oven to broil.

5. Split open the bread. Lay a piece of veal on the bottom half of a piece of bread and sprinkle one-quarter of the Parmesan cheese on top. Spoon one-quarter of the marinara sauce on top. Cover with one-quarter of the provolone cheese. Drizzle with a little olive oil. Press the sandwich together and set aside on a baking sheet. Continue with the remaining sandwiches. Place in the oven and broil until the cheese is golden and bubbly and the bread is starting to become crisp on the edges, about 8 minutes.

For the veal

4 veal scaloppine (about 1 pound), cut in half if desired

Salt and freshly ground black pepper to taste

½ cup all-purpose flour

1 large egg, beaten

1 cup dried bread crumbs

¼ cup extra-virgin olive oil, plus more for drizzling

1 loaf Italian bread or French batard, cut into 4 pieces, or 4 hero rolls

½ cup freshly grated Parmesan cheese (about 1½ ounces)

4 ounces provolone cheese, sliced

Grilled Cheese Sandwich on Black Bread with Liverwurst

8 ounces liverwurst, sliced

8 large slices black bread (pumpernickel)

4 teaspoons prepared horseradish

4 to 5 ounces Swiss (Emmenthaler) cheese, sliced

4 thin slices onion

4 teaspoons English mustard

2 tablespoons unsalted butter

I USUALLY LIKE to visit a German deli to buy a better-quality liverwurst when I make this. This preparation also adapts for a delightful and very easy hors d'oeuvre. Many supermarkets sell the hors d'oeuvre–size black bread. English mustard is much hotter than Dijon mustard. If you can't find it, stir together some dry mustard and water to the consistency you like.

Makes 4 servings

1. Lay a thick slice or slices of liverwurst to cover a slice of black bread. Sprinkle 1 teaspoon prepared horseradish on top. Cover with a slice or slices of Swiss cheese. Lay the sliced onion on top. Spread the second slice of black bread with hot English mustard and lay on top of the sandwich. Continue in this order with the other sandwiches.

2. In a large skillet, melt the butter over medium heat, then cook the sandwiches until the cheese has melted and both sides are golden brown, about 6 minutes. Serve hot.

Santa Barbara Chicken Sandwich

THIS SANDWICH appears on the menu of a number of res-taurants in Santa Barbara, California. I imagine it was invented in one restaurant, became popular, and the other restaurants started copying each other. It is deservedly popular and a very nice lunch sandwich. The key is using brioche buns, usually found in supermarkets with their own bakeries or Trader Joe's.

Makes 4 servings

2 boneless, skinless chicken breast halves, sliced in half to make 4 pieces

4 brioche buns or honey wheat buns, sliced open if they aren't already

4 tablespoons unsalted butter, at room temperature

Salt and freshly ground black pepper to taste

Green leaf or butter lettuce, as needed

Mayonnaise, as needed

3 ounces Monterey Jack cheese, sliced

8 slices bacon, cooked and broken in half

1 avocado, pitted, peeled, and very thinly sliced

4 thin slices from a large tomato

1. Preheat the oven to 350°F.

2. Place the chicken breast halves between 2 sheets of plastic wrap and pound with a mallet or the side of a cleaver until very thin. Cut the breast halves in half, if needed, to fit the size of the brioche bun.

3. Spread the insides of the brioche buns with 2 tablespoons of the butter. In a large skillet, cook the buttered brioche bun halves, cut side down, over medium heat until golden, about 4 minutes. Remove and set aside.

4. Increase the heat to medium-high and add the remaining 2 tablespoons butter to the skillet. Add the chicken and cook on one side until golden, about 2 minutes. Turn to the other side, season with salt and pepper, and cook for another 1 to 2 minutes. Remove the chicken.

5. Place some lettuce leaves on the bottom of each brioche bun. Spread a little mayonnaise on top and lay a chicken breast on top of the mayonnaise. Lay the cheese on top of the chicken, then lay the bacon, avocado, tomato slice, and another lettuce leaf spread with a little mayonnaise. Place the top half of each brioche bun on top and press down gently. Wrap in aluminum foil and place in the oven until the cheese melts, about 10 minutes. Serve hot.

Quesadillas, Enchiladas, and Burritos with Cheese

Mexican food, and especially the Mexican food that influences the cooking of the southwestern United States, is so often about cheese wrapped in tortillas. So I thought a chapter all its own was fitting for some of our favorite dishes. Here you will be asked to use a variety of Mexican cheeses, today easily found in the supermarket, made by American firms such as La Chona, Cacique, Kairoun Dairies, El Mexicano, and the Fud brand sold in Walmart. I do provide alternatives, too. Start with a vegetarian offering such as Quesadilla with Kabocha Squash and Roast Chiles (page 144), and you'll swear it contains meat, it is so flavorful. Never made a Chimichanga (page 147)? Don't know what it is? You'll learn here how to make this behemoth from Arizona-Sonoran cuisine.

HOMEMADE SALSA

Makes about 1 cup

1 large ripe tomato (about 8 ounces), finely chopped
1 tablespoon chopped red onion
2 fresh green serrano chiles, seeded and finely chopped
3 tablespoons finely chopped fresh cilantro (coriander leaves)
Salt to taste
Lime juice to taste

Combine all the ingredients and serve. Refrigerate any leftovers.

Quesadilla with Ham and Cheese

ALTHOUGH THIS QUESADILLA, called a *sincronizadas*, could be cut up and served as an appetizer, I prefer it quartered and served as a main course with salsa. It's excellent with rajas con queso (Poblano Chiles Strips in Cheese, page 286) on the side. When buying the ham, an ideal product to look for in the supermarket is a package containing two ¼-inch-thick slices of cooked ham, about 8 × 6 inches. The name *sincronizadas* comes from the fact that the two tortillas are identically sized—that is, synchronized.

*Makes 2 to 4 main-course servings
or 6 to 8 appetizers servings*

2 burrito-size flour tortillas (12 inches in diameter)

8 ounces cooked ham

2 cups shredded Mexican 4-cheese blend (8 ounces)

Homemade or store-bought salsa (see box)

1. Heat a 12-inch cast-iron skillet or a griddle over medium heat until very hot.

2. Place a tortilla in the ungreased skillet and spread the ham and cheese over the surface of the tortilla right to the edge. Cover with the second tortilla. Cook until the bottom is golden brown in spots. Turn with a large offset spatula and continue cooking the second side, pressing down gently, until the cheese has melted and the tortilla is hot but not breaking apart at the edges, about 10 minutes. Serve with salsa.

Quesadilla with Griddled Chicken, Chile, and Cheese

1 pound Italian long frying peppers or fresh poblano chiles

3 ounces fresh red jalapeño chiles or chiles de agua

12 ounces fresh New Mexico chiles (also called Anaheim or Hatch chiles)

1 pound boneless, skinless chicken breast halves

Vegetable oil or pork lard, as needed

Salt to taste

¼ cup finely chopped fresh cilantro (coriander leaf)

Freshly ground black pepper to taste

½ teaspoon ground cumin

1 fresh habanero chile, seeded and thinly slivered

4 burrito-size flour tortillas (12 inches in diameter)

6 ounces Monterey Jack cheese, shredded

6 ounces queso blanco, shredded

Sour cream, for garnish

(continued)

IN EARLY SEPTEMBER, the number of different chiles and peppers available at local markets is dazzling. One of my favorite uses for them is roasted with melted cheese. Although we think of quesadillas as snack food, they make a satisfying entrée when stuffed with some pan-seared chicken, too. I call for some specific chiles in this recipe, not all of which might be available to you, so you can use whatever is available as long as you have four different kinds. Chile nomenclature is confusing; for example, chiles and peppers are the same thing, peppers referring to chiles that are not piquant and chiles referring to the piquancy of the fruit. You will need two 12-inch diameter skillets for this recipe, or you can cook them in batches.

Makes 4 to 6 servings

1. Place a wire rack over stovetop burners and roast the Italian peppers, jalapeños, and New Mexico chiles until blistered black all over, turning with tongs. (Alternatively, you can grill the chiles.) Remove from the heat and place in a plastic bag to steam for 30 minutes. Remove from the bag and clean away the blistered skin, seeds, and stem, rubbing them off with paper towels. Cut the chiles into strips.

2. Meanwhile, heat a large cast-iron skillet over high heat. Place the chicken breasts between 2 sheets of plastic or wax paper and flatten by pounding with a mallet or the side of a cleaver until as thin as scaloppine, about ¼ inch thick. Brush a light film of oil or lard on the skillet, season the chicken with salt, place in the skillet, and cook until golden brown on both sides, turning once, about 4 minutes in all. Remove the chicken, slice into thin strips, then cut the strips in half. Toss the chicken with the cilantro, black pepper, and cumin. (If you've decided to grill the chiles, you can grill the chicken, too.)

3. Wipe the skillet clean with paper towels. Grease lightly with lard (preferably) or oil. Lay a tortilla down in the skillet and then arrange half the roasted chiles and habanero chile over the entire tortilla. Arrange half the chicken over the chiles. Season with salt if desired. Spread half the cheeses over the chicken and place a tortilla on top, pressing down a bit with a spatula. Turn the heat to medium and cook until the bottom of the tortilla turns golden brown, 3 to 4 minutes. Turn and cook until the cheeses have melted and are running, 3 to 4 minutes. Remove from the skillet and place on a cutting board. Repeat with the remaining tortillas and fillings. Quarter the quesadillas and arrange on a serving platter.

4. Prepare the salsa by tossing all the salsa ingredients in a bowl. Serve hot with the sour cream and salsa.

For the salsa

12 ounces ripe tomatoes, chopped

1 fresh green finger-type chile, or 2 fresh serrano chiles, chopped

3 tablespoons chopped red onion

Juice from ½ lime

2 tablespoons finely chopped fresh cilantro (coriander leaf)

½ tablespoon finely chopped fresh flat-leaf parsley

Salt and freshly ground black pepper to taste

Quesadilla with Kabocha Squash and Roast Chiles

4 fresh poblano chiles

4 fresh New Mexico chiles (also called Anaheim or Hatch chiles)

2 large fresh jalapeño chiles

3 Mexican spring onions or 8 scallions

1 medium tomato

4 large garlic cloves

One 2¾-pound kabocha squash

3 tablespoons extra-virgin olive oil

4 small fresh serrano chiles, chopped

¼ cup chopped fresh cilantro (coriander leaf)

¾ teaspoon ground cumin

¾ teaspoon ground dried epazote (optional) (page 145)

Salt and freshly ground black pepper to taste

6 flour tortillas (8 inches in diameter)

3 ounces queso añejo or Monterey Jack cheese, cut in thin slices

3 ounces queso quesadilla or queso blanco, cut in thin slices

1 cup crème fraîche or sour cream

THIS QUESADILLA is all about roasted chile and squash. It looks like an enchilada, but there is no sauce and, in fact, you could eat this with your hands. The variety of chiles provides a piquant flavor, and the squash provides some of the body you will like in a preparation that can be dinner. I call for Mexican spring onions because that's what my supermarket labels them as: They're just spring onions and it doesn't matter where they are from.   *Makes 6 side-dish servings or 3 main-course servings*

1. Preheat the oven to 425°F.

2. Place the poblano chiles, New Mexico chiles, jalapeños, onions, tomato, and garlic in a roasting pan and roast until the skins are blackened and/or blister off, about 20 minutes for the garlic and tomato, 40 minutes for the rest.

3. Meanwhile, place the whole kabocha squash in another roasting pan and fill with a little water. Roast this at the same time until easily pierced by a skewer, about 40 minutes. Remove the squash, cut in half, and remove the seeds. Scoop out one half and cut into slices. Save the other half of the squash for another purpose. Reduce the oven temperature to 350°F.

4. When all the vegetables are cool, remove their peels and seeds and cut into strips. Chop the onions. Transfer to a large skillet over medium-low heat with the squash, olive oil, and serrano chiles and begin to cook, stirring occasionally. Add the cilantro, cumin, epazote, and salt and pepper, stir, and cook until very hot, about 5 minutes.

5. Divide the chile and squash mixture into 6 portions and place on the tortillas. Divide the cheeses into 6 portions, reserving a little for sprinkling on top of the quesadillas, lay both cheeses on top of the stuffing, and roll up the tortillas. Arrange the rolled tortillas in a row in a large baking casserole. Sprinkle the top with the reserved cheese, cover with aluminum foil, and bake until bubbly, about 20 minutes. Serve with crème fraîche.

EPAZOTE

Epazote is an annual herb native to Central America and southern Mexico used in Mexican cooking. It has a pungent, musty flavor and is favored in stews and bean cookery in Mexico. It is not very common and will likely be found in a Mexican or Latino market.

Quesadilla with Potatoes and Chorizo Sausage

8 ounces red potatoes

8 ounces Mexican chorizo sausage, removed from the casing and crumbled

2 canned chipotle chiles in adobo, cut into strips

12 flour tortillas (8 inches in diameter)

8 ounces queso Oaxaca or hard mozzarella

4 tablespoons pork lard or vegetable oil

A QUESADILLA, at its simplest, is two tortillas sandwiching shredded cheese, fried in a skillet until melted. Once you master the basic one, the varieties are unlimited, and you can get as inventive as you want. *Makes 12 quesadillas to serve 6*

1. Bring a saucepan of water to a boil over medium heat with the potatoes, then cook until a skewer can glide easily into them, about 15 minutes after the water comes to a boil. Remove and drain, peel, and dice.

2. In a skillet over low heat, add the chorizo sausage and cook, stirring occasionally, until cooked through and the fat has rendered, about 10 minutes. Add the potatoes and chipotle chiles to the skillet, increase the heat to medium, and cook, shaking or stirring the potatoes so they don't stick too much, until the potato has browned just a little, about 5 minutes. Let cool.

3. Lay a tortilla on a surface in front of you and spoon some stuffing on one half. Layer some strips of cheese on top, fold the tortilla over, and press down gently.

4. In a large skillet, melt 1 tablespoon lard over medium-high heat, tilting the skillet to spread it around the entire pan, and cook the quesadilla on both sides until golden but not crisp, about 1 minute, turning only once. Set aside in a warm oven while you cook the remainder, using the remaining lard to cook them.

Chimichanga

THE MEXICAN STATES of Tamaulipas, Coahuila, Chihuahua, Sonora, and Baja California all heavily influence the cookery of the southwestern United States: southern California, New Mexico, Arizona, and southwestern Texas. The southern portion of Arizona was once part of Mexico, and Tucson, in particular, has cookery they call Arizona-Sonoran. The highlight of this style of cooking is the chimichanga, or "chimi." A chimichanga is a burrito prepared with a choice of meat, vegetables, and spices, deep-fried, and served on a bed of lettuce with cheese and mild sauce. They are large and overstuffed, and every restaurant and mom-and-pop eatery has its own version of this favorite dish. Although there are several competing stories about their origin, the strongest claim comes from the El Charro Café, the oldest Mexican restaurant in Tucson. The restaurant was started in 1922 and the original owner, Monica Flin, was said to have nearly blurted an expletive in the kitchen when a burrito flipped accidently into the deep fryer. However, in deference to the young nieces and nephews about, she changed the swear word to *chimichanga*, the Spanish equivalent of "thingamagig." You can serve them with the optional ingredients listed in the ingredient list and with rice and beans.

Serves 8

(continued)

1 tablespoon vegetable oil

3 pounds beef chuck roast, trimmed of fat and cut into 3 × 1-inch chunks

One 15-ounce can diced tomatoes

1½ cups beef or chicken broth

1 cup dry red wine

1 green bell pepper, chopped

1 red onion, finely chopped

One 4-ounce can diced green chiles

5 large garlic cloves, finely chopped

1 teaspoon dried oregano

Salt and freshly ground black pepper to taste

6 to 8 cups vegetable oil, for frying

16 burrito-size flour tortillas (12 inches in diameter)

One 1-pound package shredded Mexican 4-cheese blend or 8 ounces mild cheddar and 8 ounces Monterey Jack cheese, grated

2 cups shredded iceberg lettuce

2 cups chopped scallions

2 cups sour cream (optional)

2 cups guacamole (optional)

1. In a large flameproof casserole, heat the 1 tablespoon vegetable oil over medium-high heat. Add the beef chunks and cook, turning, until brown on all sides, about 8 minutes. Add the tomatoes, broth, wine, bell pepper, onion, can of green chiles, garlic, and oregano. Cover and simmer until the meat is very tender, about 3½ hours. Season with salt and pepper.

2. Remove the beef chunks, place on a cutting board, and shred the meat with forks. Place the shredded beef back into the pot with the juice and keep warm.

3. In a large skillet over medium-high heat, add the vegetable oil to a depth of at least 1½ inches and heat to at least 350°F. Heat 2 flour tortillas in the microwave for 35 seconds on low power; you want to heat the tortillas so they are soft enough to fold and so they won't break when folding.

4. Set the 2 tortillas on top of one another on a work surface and place some of the meat, using a slotted spoon and draining as much juice as possible, in the center of the tortilla. You might want to try a heaping serving spoonful first and see how much it is, making sure the sides of the burrito can be folded inwards over the meat. Top with a sprinkle of cheese. Make sure to reserve one-quarter of the cheese for sprinkling on top of the finished chimichangas. Fold two sides in and then roll the tortilla over tightly. If it doesn't want to stay together, use a toothpick to hold it together.

5. Test the temperature of the oil with a thermometer or flick some water droplets into the skillet. If it sizzles vigorously, the oil is ready for cooking. Gently place the chimichanga into the skillet, seam side down, using tongs. If you have too much liquid in the chimichanga, it may leak out and cause the oil to splatter. If at any time it starts to unravel, remove immediately and rewrap. Cook, turning once, until golden brown on all sides, 1 to 2 minutes. As you finish each one, place the cooked chimi on a paper towel–covered tray to drain and leave in a warm oven as you assemble and cook the rest. Continue cooking the remaining chimis. Arrange the chimichangas on a large serving platter and sprinkle shredded lettuce and scallions on top and the reserved cheese. Serve with the sour cream and guacamole.

Burrito with Skirt Steak, Roasted Chiles, and Monterey Jack

4 fresh poblano chiles

4 fresh New Mexico chiles
(also called Anaheim
or Hatch chiles)

3 tablespoons extra-
virgin olive oil

1 medium white
onion, thinly sliced

2 large garlic cloves,
finely chopped

1 fresh serrano chile,
finely chopped

1 canned chipotle chile
in adobo, chopped

¼ cup chopped fresh cilantro

1 teaspoon ground cumin

1 teaspoon ground dried
epazote (optional)

Salt and freshly ground
black pepper to taste

8 ounces Monterey Jack
cheese, shredded

1 pound skirt steak, sliced
in thin strips crosswise,
then cut in half

4 burrito-size flour tortillas
(12 inches in diameter)

1 ripe avocado, pitted,
peeled, and sliced

THIS BURRITO IS NOT your typical rice- and-bean-stuffed behemoth, but really more like a simple wrap stuffed with luscious and complementary flavors of pan-seared skirt steak, roasted poblano and Anaheim chiles, piquant chile adobo, and serrano chiles with onions and melted Monterey Jack cheese. This blend is harmonious, delicious, and slightly piquant.

Makes 4 servings

1. Preheat the oven to 425°F.

2. Place the chiles on a wire rack over a stovetop burner on high heat and roast, turning occasionally with tongs, until their skins blister and blacken on all sides. Remove the chiles and place in a paper or heavy plastic bag to steam for 20 minutes, which will make peeling them easier. When cool enough to handle, rub off as much blackened peel as you can and remove the seeds by rubbing with a paper towel (to avoid washing away flavorful juices) or by rinsing under running water (to remove more easily).

3. In a large skillet over medium heat, heat 2 tablespoons of the olive oil. Add the onion and cook, stirring, until softened, about 5 minutes. Add the garlic and serrano chile and cook, stirring, until the onions turn yellow, about 5 minutes. Add the roasted chiles, chipotle chile, cilantro, cumin, and epazote (if using) and season with salt and pepper. Cook, stirring, until softened, about 5 minutes. Add the cheese and cook, stirring, until it has melted.

4. Meanwhile, heat a cast-iron skillet or carbon-steel pan over high heat. Add the remaining olive oil, then add the skirt steak and cook, stirring constantly, until it loses its color, about 3 minutes. Cook for another 2 minutes, then transfer to the skillet with the chiles and stir to mix well.

5. Lay a tortilla in front of you and spread one-quarter of the steak-and-chile mixture just below the center line of the tortilla. Place the avocado slices on top and fold one end over once, then fold the two sides over and roll up tightly. Continue with the remainder and serve.

Enchiladas Verdes

9 cups water

1 pound (9 to 12) tomatillos, husked

3 small onions, quartered

8 large garlic cloves, crushed

8 fresh green serrano chiles

Leaves from 15 sprigs fresh cilantro (coriander leaf)

1¼ pounds whole bone-in chicken breast

1 teaspoon salt, plus more as needed

½ teaspoon dried thyme

2 bay leaves

¼ cup crème fraîche or sour cream

¼ cup vegetable oil, plus more as needed

12 corn tortillas

For the garnish

⅓ cup crumbled queso añejo or domestic (cow's milk) feta cheese or shredded mild white cheddar or Monterey Jack

¼ cup crème fraîche or sour cream

2 center slices of a medium onion, separated into rings

6 radishes, sliced or cut into roses

THE WORD *ENCHILADA* comes from the Spanish verb *enchilar*, which basically means to get chile all over something. Therefore, an enchilada is something "en-chilied." What this means is that you will dip the tortilla into the chile sauce. In this "green" version of enchilada, the green color comes from tomatillos and green chiles, while the red version, Enchilada Rojos (page 154), is made with tomatoes, red chiles, and chorizo sausage. The one technique that is a little tricky in this preparation is the quick pre-frying of the tortillas. The reason this is done, besides adding some nice flavor, is to make the tortillas softer for rolling and less likely to crack.

Makes 6 servings

1. Bring 6 cups of the water to a boil in a large saucepan and add the tomatillos, 1 small onion, 3 garlic cloves, and 4 serrano chiles. Reduce the heat to medium and simmer until the tomatillos are soft, about 30 minutes. Drain, reserving some of the cooking water, and transfer the vegetables to a blender. Add another small onion, 2 garlic cloves, the remaining chiles, and the cilantro to the blender. Blend, adding just enough of the reserved cooking water so the blades of the blender can twirl, until smooth, about 2 minutes. Place the tomatillo sauce in a skillet or saucepan with ½ teaspoon of the salt and heat over low heat, covered.

2. Place the chicken breast in a saucepan filled with the remaining 3 cups of water along with three-quarters of the remaining small onion, the remaining 3 garlic cloves, the remaining ½ teaspoon salt, the thyme, and bay leaves. Finely chop the reserved quarter of onion. Bring to just below a boil over high heat, and before the water starts bubbling, reduce the heat to medium and poach the chicken until firm, about 12 minutes. Let cool in the broth. Remove the chicken from the saucepan, pull the meat off the bones, discard the skin and bones, and shred the chicken into small pieces. Place the chicken in a skillet or saucepan and keep warm over low heat. Stir in the crème fraîche and the reserved chopped onion. Turn the heat off, and cover to keep warm.

3. In a cast-iron skillet, heat the vegetable oil over medium-high heat, then cook the tortillas one at a time until softened, about 3 seconds per side. Remove with tongs and set aside on paper towels to drain. Replenish the oil in the skillet if necessary to cook the remaining tortillas.4. Preheat the oven to 350°F.

5. Pour 1 cup of the tomatillo sauce on a dinner plate and lay a tortilla in the sauce. Fill the center with about 2 tablespoons of the chicken stuffing, then roll up and arrange in a baking dish. Continue filling and rolling the remaining tortillas. Pour the remaining sauce over the top of the enchiladas. Cover the baking dish with aluminum foil and bake until heated through, about 10 minutes. Remove from the oven, sprinkle with the cheese and crème fraîche, and garnish with the onion rings and radishes. Serve immediately.

Enchiladas Rojas

6 dried ancho chiles

1 cup boiling water

1 pound ripe tomatoes, cut in half, seeds squeezed out, and grated on the largest holes of a grater

2 small onions, 1 whole and peeled and 1 chopped

1 large garlic clove

1 tablespoon finely chopped fresh epazote leaves (optional)

1 teaspoon dried oregano

¼ teaspoon freshly ground cloves

¼ teaspoon ground cinnamon

1 teaspoon sugar

1 teaspoon salt

½ teaspoon freshly ground black pepper

¼ cup pork lard or vegetable oil, plus more as needed

1 cup crème fraîche or thick cream

1 pound Mexican chorizo sausage, removed from the casing and crumbled

1 cup grated queso añejo, grated queso enchilada, or crumbled domestic (cow's milk) feta cheese (about 3 ounces)

12 slightly stale flour tortillas (8 inches in diameter)

THESE "RED ENCHILADAS" can be made with corn tortillas as well. The green version, Enchiladas Verdes (page 152), is made with tomatillos. *Makes 6 servings*

1. Pull the stems off the ancho chiles and brush away the seeds. Tear into smaller pieces. Place in a bowl, pour the boiling water over the chiles, and let soak for 30 minutes.

2. Preheat the oven to 450°F.

3. Place the tomatoes, peeled onion, and garlic in a baking dish and roast until blackened a bit, about 15 minutes for the garlic, 25 minutes for the tomatoes, and 40 minutes for the onion. Remove from the oven and peel the tomato and garlic. Reduce the temperature of the oven to 350°F.

4. Place the soaking chiles with their water into a blender and blend for 10 seconds. Add the tomatoes, the roasted onion, the garlic, epazote (if using), oregano, cloves, cinnamon, sugar, salt, and black pepper and blend until completely smooth, about another 45 seconds.

5. In a 10-inch skillet, melt 1 tablespoon of the lard over medium heat, then pour in the contents of the blender and cook, stirring frequently, until bubbling and dense, about 5 minutes. Remove from the heat. Stir the crème fraîche into the skillet until blended. Cover the skillet and set aside. Thin the sauce if necessary with water.

6. In another 10-inch skillet (or the previous one, washed), melt 1 tablespoon of lard over medium heat, then cook the sausages until light brown and most of their fat has been rendered, about 5 minutes, stirring frequently. Remove the sausage from the skillet with a slotted spoon. Place the sausage in a bowl and blend with ¼ cup of the chile sauce and ⅓ cup of the cheese.

7. In a heavy skillet (a third skillet or the previous one, washed), melt the remaining 2 tablespoons lard over medium heat. Dip the tortillas in the tomato-chile sauce on both sides, then cook the tortillas, one at a time, until limp but not brown, about 1 minute per side, turning with tongs. Transfer to a plate as you cook each tortilla and place about ¼ cup of sausage mixture in the center. Fold about an inch of the right side of the tortilla over the filling, then roll up into a thick cylinder. Place the enchilada in a 13 × 10-inch baking dish. Replenish the lard or oil as you need to in order to cook the remaining tortillas, letting the lard melt and heat before cooking. Once the tortillas are all prepared, pour the remaining tomato-chile sauce over them, and sprinkle the top with the chopped onion and the remaining cheese. Bake until the cheese has melted and the enchiladas are light brown on top, about 15 minutes. Serve 2 enchiladas per person with some sauce spooned over them.

Spinach Enchiladas with Salsa Verde

1 cup sour cream

2 cups Salsa Verde (page 157)

20 corn tortillas (8 inches in diameter)

2 pounds fresh spinach, heavy stems removed and thinly sliced

4 cups shredded Monterey Jack cheese (about 12 ounces)

THEY KEY TO THIS DISH is having some salsa verde made. The recipe on page 157 will provide enough green sauce for this dish and several others. Spinach enchiladas are a great family dinner because they can be made in a casserole very quickly. If you like a more piquant taste, add some chopped green chiles to the spinach.

Makes 6 servings

1. Preheat the oven to 350°F.

2. In a bowl, stir together half of the sour cream and half of the salsa verde. Spread enough to lightly coat the bottom of two 12 × 9-inch baking casseroles. On each tortilla, spread a small amount of the remaining salsa and sour cream in the center. Lay a small handful of spinach over that and sprinkle with some of the cheese. Roll up, and place seam side down in the casseroles. Pour the remaining salsa over the top and sprinkle with the remaining cheese. Bake until the cheese on the enchiladas is browned and the contents are heated through, about 20 minutes.

SALSA VERDE

Use this mildly hot green sauce as a raw sauce for grilled meat, for dipping tortilla chips, or for enchiladas. It's versatile and delicious. You can heat the sauce, too, if you like.

Makes 6 cups

3 large fresh green poblano or New Mexico (Anaheim, Hatch) chiles
12 tomatillos (about 1¾ pounds), husks removed and quartered
1 medium white onion, coarsely chopped
1 fresh jalapeño chile, seeds removed and chopped
1 bunch fresh cilantro (coriander leaf), heavier stems removed and chopped
5 large garlic cloves, chopped
1 teaspoon salt
1 teaspoon extra-virgin olive oil
1 tablespoon fresh lime juice

1. Place the poblano chiles on a wire rack over a stovetop burner on medium-high heat until their skins blacken and blister all over, turning with tongs. Remove them and place in a paper bag or heavy plastic bag for 20 minutes, which will help steam off their skins. Once cool enough to handle, scrape and peel off the skin and remove the seeds by rubbing with a paper towel (to avoid washing away flavorful juices) or by rinsing under running water (to remove more easily). Cut into strips.

2. Put the tomatillos, onion, and jalapeño into a food processor and pulse 10 to 15 times. Add the remaining ingredients, including the chiles, and pulse until an ever-so-slightly chunky, not smooth, consistency. The sauce can be used immediately, but it will gain more flavor by sitting in the refrigerator overnight. Serve at room temperature.

Eggs and Cheese

This chapter could have hundreds of recipes, as the mixing of cheese and eggs, as in a cheese omelet, is common. I've limited the recipes in this chapter to a classic one (Eggs Mornay, page 166), a hearty one (Sausage and Cheese Scramble, page 161), and a couple of frittatas from around the Mediterranean.

Swiss Cheese–Egg Yolk Fritter

1 teaspoon unsalted butter

½ cup shredded Swiss (Emmenthaler) cheese (about 1½ ounces)

2 large egg yolks

Salt to taste

THIS SIMPLE LITTLE preparation is a wonderful snack when you've used an egg white for a recipe but not the yolk. It's a quick dish for one person, too; just halve the recipe. If making two fritters, though, make one at a time.   *Makes 2 servings*

In a 7-inch nonstick skillet, melt half the butter over medium heat. Add half of the cheese, which will soon start bubbling. Crack 1 egg yolk in the middle and shake the pan to distribute the egg yolk a bit. Season with salt. Turn in about 45 seconds. The fritter itself will be very sticky, so you won't be able to flip it with a spatula like a pancake; just pull one end up with a fork or the edge of the spatula and pull it over on itself and let it finish cooking until light golden, about another 10 seconds. Repeat with the remaining ingredients and serve immediately.

Sausage and Cheese Scramble

THIS IS MY HANGOVER breakfast preparation. It's spicy and gets you back on your feet quickly, and if it doesn't, at least it tastes great.

Makes 2 servings

2 teaspoons extra-virgin olive oil

8 ounces hot Italian or fresh andouille sausage, removed from the casing and crumbled

½ small onion, thinly sliced

1 small fresh serrano chile, seeded and finely chopped

2 ounces cream cheese, cut up into small pieces

4 large eggs, beaten

Salt and freshly ground black pepper to taste

In a large nonstick skillet, heat the olive oil over medium heat. Add the sausage, onion, and serrano chile and cook, breaking the sausage up with a plastic spatula as you stir, until the onion is softened and the sausage browned, about 5 minutes. Push all the ingredients to the center of the skillet, then add the cream cheese on top. Stir gently and, as the cream cheese starts to melt, pour in the eggs on top, season with salt and pepper, and let them set for a minute. Then start folding them over and into the sausage and cheese until everything is set and not runny. Serve hot.

Roasted Chile and Cheese Frittata

2 fresh poblano chiles

1 fresh New Mexico (also called Anaheim or Hatch chiles) chile

2 fresh red jalapeño chiles or any fresh red chile, seeded and chopped

2 fresh green serrano chiles, seeded and chopped

2 fresh red chiltepin (piquín) chiles or red Thai chiles, or 1 habanero chile

3 tablespoons extra-virgin olive oil

2 medium tomatoes, chopped (peeled, if desired)

2 ounces Monterey Jack cheese, shredded

2 ounces ricotta cheese (page 65)

2 ounces queso blanco, shredded

2 ounces Swiss (Emmenthaler) cheese, shredded

2 ounces Italian truffle cheese (see headnote) or provolone, shredded

8 large eggs

Salt to taste

Unsalted butter, for the casserole

Fresh flat-leaf parsley leaves, chopped, for garnish

THE INSPIRATION for this thick omelet is the Spanish tortilla, a cousin of the Italian frittata. It's thicker than a frittata, and it's baked. However, the distinguishing feature is that it is hot and cheesy: hot from mixed chiles and cheesy from mixed cheeses. There are several Italian cheeses called Italian truffle cheese, and they are a bit different. You can find them at Trader Joe's, where they call it just that, or on Internet sites such as www.gourmetfoodstore.com or www.dibruno.com, where it is sold as *sottocenere al tartufo*. Two other truffle cheeses, *perlagrigia* from the Venice region and *boschetto al tartufo bianchetto*, are sold at www.igourmet.com. *Makes 4 servings*

1. Preheat the oven to 350°F.

2. Place the chiles on a rack over a burner on high heat and roast until their skins blister black on all sides, turning occasionally with tongs. Remove the chiles and place in a paper or heavy plastic bag to steam for 20 minutes, which will make peeling them easier. When cool enough to handle, rub off as much blackened skin as you can and remove the seeds by rubbing with a paper towel (to avoid washing away flavorful juices) or by rinsing under running water (to remove more easily). Chop coarsely and set aside.

3. In a skillet, heat the olive oil over medium-high heat, then cook, stirring, all the chiles and the tomatoes until fragrant and a bit soft, about 5 minutes.

4. In a bowl, mix together the cheeses, chile mixture, and eggs and season with salt. Pour into a well-buttered 9-inch round baking casserole, preferably earthenware, and bake until it congeals and sets, or until a skewer pushed to the center in the middle comes out clean, about 45 minutes. Remove from the oven, place a larger heatproof plate over the casserole, and invert in one quick motion. Lift the casserole off, sprinkle with parsley, and serve hot or warm.

Sweet Bell Pepper and Manchego Frittata

4 green bell peppers

3 tablespoons extra-virgin olive oil

3 garlic cloves, 2 finely chopped and 1 crushed

1 tablespoon finely chopped fresh basil leaves

Salt and freshly ground black pepper to taste

1 tablespoon finely chopped pork fatback

3 small dried red chiles

6 large eggs

½ cup shredded manchego cheese (about 1½ ounces)

Paprika, for dusting

THIS FLAVORFUL FRITTATA is a great summer appetizer when sweet bell peppers are at their best. Look for fleshy bell peppers that feel heavy. If your skillet is not ovenproof, let the handle stick out of the oven as you broil. You can serve the frittata cut up into wedges or squares and offer them to guests either hot or at room temperature. This preparation is actually called a tortilla in Spain and is a cousin of the frittata.

Makes 4 servings

1. Set an oven rack 4 to 5 inches below the broiler heat element. Preheat the broiler.

2. Place the bell peppers on a rack over a burner on high heat and roast until their skins blister black on all sides, turning occasionally with tongs. Remove the peppers and place in a paper or heavy plastic bag to steam for 20 minutes, which will make peeling them easier. When cool enough to handle, rub off as much blackened skin as you can and remove the seeds by rubbing with a paper towel (to avoid washing away flavorful juices) or by rinsing under running water (to remove more easily). Cut into strips.

3. Place the peppers in a medium skillet with 2 tablespoons of the olive oil, the chopped garlic, and basil and season with salt and pepper. Turn the heat to medium and cook, stirring occasionally, until softened, about 20 minutes.

4. In a 10-inch ovenproof nonstick skillet (preferably), heat the remaining 1 tablespoon olive oil with the pork fatback, dried chiles, and crushed garlic over medium heat and cook, stirring, until the fatback is crispy, about 12 minutes. Remove the garlic when it begins to turn light brown. Remove and discard the dried chiles. Add the pepper strips.

5. Beat the eggs until frothy and pour into the skillet, shaking to distribute them. Sprinkle the cheese around and cook for 2 minutes. Place under the broiler until the top sets, 2 to 4 minutes. Remove from the oven and slide the frittata onto a serving platter. Dust lightly with paprika and serve cut into wedges.

Eggs Mornay

For the Mornay sauce

2 tablespoons unsalted butter

3 tablespoons all-purpose flour

1½ cups hot whole milk

Salt and freshly ground white pepper to taste

Pinch of ground nutmeg

¾ cup shredded Gruyère cheese (about 2 ounces)

Pinch of cayenne pepper

For the bread and eggs

1 tablespoon unsalted butter, plus more for greasing casserole

Four 5 × 3-inch slices white Italian or French country bread, crusts removed

4 large eggs

Paprika to taste

3 tablespoons freshly grated Parmesan cheese

1 tablespoon finely chopped fresh chives or flat-leaf parsley, for garnish

THERE'S NOTHING WRONG with old-fashioned, and eggs Mornay certainly are that. They may seem extravagant for a home-cooked Sunday breakfast, but they are neither hard nor time-consuming to make. A Mornay sauce is a béchamel sauce with cheese, and a béchamel sauce is a white sauce made with a roux of flour and milk. It probably was a restaurant invention in France in the nineteenth century. Eggs Mornay is a dish one finds in the cookbooks of famous French chef Auguste Escoffier, who adds a light sprinkle of bread crumbs on top and a slight glaze of butter under the broiler.   *Makes 4 servings*

1. Preheat the broiler.

2. Prepare the Mornay sauce. In a medium saucepan, melt the butter over medium heat, then stir in the flour to form a roux, cooking for 1 minute while stirring constantly. Remove the saucepan from the heat and whisk in the milk a little at a time until it is all blended. Sprinkle with salt and white pepper and the nutmeg. Return to the heat and cook, stirring almost constantly, until thickened, 5 to 8 minutes. Add the cheese and cayenne and stir until it has melted and is smooth.

3. To prepare the bread and eggs, in a large skillet, melt the 1 tablespoon butter over medium heat, and once it stops bubbling but before it turns brown, cook 2 slices of the bread on both sides until golden brown, 2 to 3 minutes. Transfer the pieces of bread to a lightly buttered medium baking casserole that will hold all 4 bread slices snugly. Cook the remaining 2 pieces of bread.

4. Bring a shallow saucepan of water to a boil, then start stirring in one direction to create a whirlpool. In rapid succession, crack the eggs and carefully and gently slip them into the swirling water. Once they are all in, give the water a gentle swirl with a wooden spoon and let cook until the whites, but not the yolks, solidify, about 2 minutes. Remove the eggs with a slotted spoon, let drain a bit on paper towels, then place 1 egg on each slice of bread. Cover the eggs and bread with some spoonfuls of the Mornay sauce and sprinkle with paprika and the Parmesan cheese. Place under the broiler until bubbling and dappled golden brown, about 1 minute. Remove and garnish with chives. Serve hot.

Eggs with Gruyère

2 large eggs

2 teaspoons heavy cream

Salt to taste

2 teaspoons unsalted butter

1 ounce Gruyère cheese, shredded

THIS IS A VERY EASY, and nice, way to make a broiler omelet. If you are making more than one, make them in batches. If your skillet is not ovenproof, carefully place the skillet under the broiler with the handle sticking out of the open oven door.

Makes 1 serving

1. Set an oven rack 2 to 3 inches below the broiler heat element. Preheat the broiler.

2. In a bowl, beat the eggs, cream, and salt with a wire whisk until frothy.

3. In a 7-inch nonstick skillet, melt the butter over medium-high heat, then pour in the eggs, sprinkle on the cheese, and cook, pushing the eggs to the center of the skillet, until the bottom is set, about 30 seconds. Place under the broiler only until the top is dry but not browned, about 1 minute. Slide the omelet off the skillet onto a plate, flipping one half over the other. Serve hot.

Cheese and
More Cheese

This chapter is called what it is because this is where you will find all the recipes where cheese is the unequivocal star of the dish. Here you will encounter a wider range of possible cheeses to use in your cooking than in the other chapters. Many of them are best ordered from various Web sites, a method I use frequently these days. Web site addresses are provided where necessary. You'll find the authentic Fondue Neuchâteloise (page 188) with not only the recipe but also a full accounting of the protocol of eating a fondue as if you were in Switzerland. Simple recipes such as Fried Halloumi Cheese (page 173) from the Middle East are easy to try, and I'll bet you've never tried the Greek meze called Bouyourdi (page 178), a dish of melted cheeses with tomatoes and chiles. If you've ever been intimidated by a cheese soufflé, the recipe on page 182 will guide you with all the tips and techniques that restaurant chefs use to make a soufflé perfectly.

Fried Breakfast Cheese with Honey

8 ounces Trader Joe's Frying Cheese, cut into small cubes

Honey, strawberry, raspberry, cloudberry, or lingonberry jam, for serving

THE ONLY PLACE I'VE SEEN the baked cheese used in this preparation is at Trader Joe's, so if you've got one near you, try this. It's made with a reindeer's milk cheese from Finland called *juustoleipa* (pronounced hoo-stoh-LEE-pah), meaning "bread cheese" because the cheese is eaten as if it were bread. Trader Joe's has contracted for it to be made with cow's milk. This preparation is delicious because the baking process affected by the application of heat, whether microwaved or fried, caramelizes the natural sugars in the cheese and forms a crust on the top. Have it with honey or jams such as cloudberry, lingonberry, strawberry, or raspberry and piping hot black coffee. The method in this recipe calls for a microwave, but typically you fry the cheese in a nonstick skillet for a couple of minutes per side. *Makes 2 servings*

Place the cheese on a plate and microwave on high power until glossy and ready to burst, 20 to 30 seconds. Serve with your choice of condiments.

Breaded and Fried Tomme Vaudoise

TOMME VAUDOISE is a soft, small round of cow's milk cheese from the Vaud canton and the Geneva region of Switzerland that melts well. It has a rather thin rind covered with white or red mold and is creamy in consistency. This preparation is typical of the region and has a pleasant milky and buttery flavor. You can also try using sections of Camembert or Brie cheese or any soft cow's milk cheese made in small rounds. Serve with rye bread. Tomme Vaudoise can be purchased at www.artisanalcheese.com.

Makes 4 servings

4 Tomme Vaudoise cheeses

1 large egg, beaten

Dried bread crumbs, as needed

6 tablespoons clarified butter (see box)

½ teaspoon ground cumin

Freshly ground black pepper to taste

1. Dip the rounds of cheese in the egg, then dredge in the bread crumbs on all sides.

2. In a skillet, melt the butter over medium heat, then cook the cheese until golden brown on both sides, 3 to 4 minutes. Serve hot with a sprinkling of ground cumin and pepper.

CLARIFIED BUTTER

Clarified butter is butter that has had its milk solids removed. Cooks do this because the butter won't burn as readily at higher temperatures. There are two ways to clarify butter. Melt some butter in a small butter warmer or saucepan, then collect all the foam on top and remove. Pour the melted butter slowly into another container, making sure none of the milky substance gets poured too. Alternatively, melt the butter and pour through a strainer with multiple layers of cheesecloth into another container.

Boiled Czech Cheese

8 ounces farmer's
cheese, sliced

½ teaspoon salt

½ teaspoon caraway seeds

½ teaspoon paprika

8 tablespoons (1 stick)
unsalted butter

1 large egg yolk,
lightly beaten

SOME YEARS AGO IN PRAGUE, I encountered this preparation on many restaurant menus. It was usually offered as an appetizer (one would eat it with crackers and beer), and I could never resist it. It occurred to me on one outing that this could be made at home rather easily. It's called *sýr vařený*—that is, literally, "boiled cheese." *Makes 4 servings*

1. Place the cheese in layers in a ceramic bowl, sprinkling each layer with salt, caraway seeds, and paprika. Cover with plastic wrap and let stand in a cool place, but not the refrigerator, for 3 days. (A basement would be ideal, or, lacking a basement, the refrigerator top shelf set to 58°F.)

2. In a saucepan, melt the butter over medium heat, then add the cheese. Stir constantly until the cheese is melted and creamy, about 5 minutes. Add the egg yolk and mix well. Pour into two 3-inch molds and chill. Slice to serve.

Fried Halloumi Cheese

HALLOUMI CHEESE is a salted raw sheep's milk cheese sometimes mixed with goat's milk, made traditionally in Cyprus but loved throughout the Middle East. Formed into 6 × 4 × 1-inch blocks, they are cooked in hot whey, after which they are salted, folded over on themselves, and submerged in brine. The cheese is soaked in water before using to remove salt. Supermarkets are carrying halloumi cheese more frequently, and you can always find it in Middle Eastern markets. When eating, I like to dip the fried cheese in some olive oil and *labna* (strained yogurt). This recipe can also be made with Syrian white cheese or Mexican queso blanco, in which case you do not need to soak it in water.

Makes 4 servings

2 tablespoons clarified butter (see box, page 171), unsalted butter, or extra-virgin olive oil

8 ounces halloumi cheese, soaked in water to cover for 8 to 24 hours, drained, and sliced into ½-inch-thick, 2-inch squares

In a large nonstick skillet, melt the clarified butter over medium-high heat. When it begins to bubble, add the cheese slices. Cook until their bottoms are golden brown, 2 to 3 minutes, then turn with a spatula. Cook for another 2 to 3 minutes, and serve.

Fried Feta Cheese and Black Olives

6 ounces feta cheese, in one piece

2 tablespoons extra-virgin olive oil

12 imported black olives, pitted

1 teaspoon dried oregano

1 lemon, quartered

Romaine lettuce leaves or pita bread chips, for serving

THE FAMOUS FETA CHEESE of Greece is a brined cheese made from sheep's milk. Feta is enjoyed elsewhere too, but I think the Greek and Bulgarian feta cheeses are the best. In this recipe, feta cheese is soaked to remove more salt and then fried with black olives and oregano. Serve it on a small plate as a part of a meze. Make sure the feta cheese is not crumbled.

Makes 4 servings

1. Soak the feta cheese in cold water for 2 hours to remove some of the salt. Drain and dry by patting with paper towels. Break the cheese into bite-size pieces, but make sure the pieces are not smaller than bite size.

2. In a skillet, heat the olive oil over medium heat, then add the pieces of feta cheese, olives, and oregano. Cook until the feta cheese starts to melt, then remove the skillet from the heat, transfer its contents to a serving platter or individual plates with a wedge of lemon, and serve immediately, picking up pieces of cheese with the lettuce leaves as a wrapper or placing them on top of pita bread chips.

MAKING YOUR OWN CHEESE

The biggest limitation I found when I made my first cheese was the storage and equipment requirements. I had to jury-rig most everything. However, the satisfaction of holding your very own homemade wheel of cheese is worth the effort.

This is what I did. I poured 2 gallons of whole pasteurized organic milk, 1 pint of organic heavy cream, and 1 tablespoon of plain whole yogurt in a pot and left it for 25 minutes. I removed 6 cups of milk and set it aside and put the pot of milk on top of another pot for a double boiler. I heated the milk to 110° F. Then I added the reserved milk which brought the temperature to 90° F. At this point I used 40 drops of liquid vegetable rennet in ¾ cup water and added it to the milk. I let it sit 25 minutes until it coagulated. The resulting milk was thickened slightly but still very liquidy, which I cut into ½-inch squares using a knife, although one barely sees the cross marks. I let it rest 5 minutes to release the whey. I used an 8-inch whisk to break up the curds, stirring with a figure-8 motion for 4 minutes. I let it sit 3 minutes and did this three more times, taking about 15 minutes, and stirring all the time. In my first attempt the curds were about an ⅛ inch big and should have been ¼ inch. I heated the curds to 90° F (and they should not be heated more than 92° F), stirring, about 5 minutes. I removed the pot from the heat and stirred for 10 minutes.

With a fine-mesh skimmer I lifted the curds from the whey and poured them into cheesecloth-lined perforated plastic molds set on a rack in a roasting pan. I leveled it off, covered it with wax paper, and left it for 24 hours at 72°, removing the cheesecloth and turning it two times in that period.

In the next step I removed the cheese from its mold and placed it on a metal grate. (I used the grate that came with my oval roaster.) I rubbed 1 teaspoon salt over the top and sides of the cheese with my fingertips and set the cheese on the top shelf of my refrigerator, which was at 58° F. After 24 hours, I turned the cheese, salted the untreated surface, and left it for another 24 hours in the refrigerator.

I filled the large oval roaster two-thirds with water and rested the metal grate on top of a bowl that would hold it above the water. I placed the salted cheese on top of the grate, placed the cover on, and placed it on the refrigerator's top shelf at 58°, undisturbed for 3 days.

After the 3 days were up I turned the cheese once a day for 8 weeks, washing the grate each time. Each time I turned the cheese I dampened the top of the cheese with a little salted water, using a paper towel or cloth. Soon a white smear of rind developed. Once it was pinkish, the cheese could be eaten or left to mature longer. (If you mature longer, damp it with vinegar every day and turn it once a day. The black spots are okay; only if you see blue spots is that bacterial growth.)

Grilled Feta Cheese in Grape Leaves

1 pound feta cheese
(preferably Greek or
Bulgarian and preferably
in one piece)

32 grape leaves
packed in brine

Six or eight 10-inch
wooden skewers

Extra-virgin olive
oil, for drizzling

1 lemon, cut into
8 to 10 wedges

THIS TURKISH MEZE, called *yaprak sarmasi*, is an interesting preparation that's perfect as an appetizer when you have the grill going. Remove the grape leaves from the jar and rinse the brine off, then wrap the cheese up carefully and skewer. The whole dish can be prepared ahead of time, wrapped and skewered, and kept in the refrigerator until needed. Grape leaves are sold in jars; you'll need the largest size.

Makes 8 to 10 servings

1. Soak the feta cheese overnight in water. Drain and cut into ½-ounce rectangular pieces.

2. Prepare a hot charcoal fire or preheat a gas grill on high for 15 minutes.

3. Rinse the brined grape leaves and arrange them in front of you with the underside of each leaf (the duller green side) facing upward. Place a rectangle of cheese on each leaf, just above where the stem is, and fold over once in the direction away from you. Fold the side leaf flaps over and continue rolling the leaf. Arrange 2 skewers parallel to each other, about ½ inch apart, and double-skewer the wrapped cheese onto them, putting 8 to 10 bundles on each set of skewers.

4. Drizzle some olive oil over the leaves and grill until the leaves get crispy black in places and the cheese seems to be melting, 5 to 10 minutes, turning once. Serve immediately with lemon wedges.

Saganaki

THE GREEK MEZE SAGANAKI, which is nothing but fried cheese, is one of my favorite dishes, and when in Greece I always order it. Traditionally, it is made in a saganaki, a small two-handled frying pan that gives its name to the dish. Serve some Kalamata olives and lemon wedges on the side. Moreover, you can't forget a glass of ouzo to wash it down. You can order the kefalotyri cheese from www.igourmet.com or www.christosmarket.com. *Makes 3 or 4 servings*

8 ounces kefalotyri cheese, cut into wedges 3 × 2 × ¼ inch

All-purpose flour, for dredging

½ cup extra-virgin olive oil

Freshly ground black pepper to taste

Lemon wedges, for garnish

1. Soak the cheese in water for 30 minutes. Pat dry with paper towels and dredge in flour, tapping off any excess.

2. In a small cast-iron skillet, heat the olive oil over medium heat until it begins to smoke. Add the pieces of cheese and cook until golden brown, about 2½ minutes in all, turning only once and scraping them up with a metal spatula. Sprinkle with pepper and serve with lemon wedges.

VARIATION: Place under the broiler until bubbling.

GRILLED CHEESE

It may seem impossible to grill cheese, but there are some cheeses and methods that work well. In the Italian region of Apulia, *caciocavallo alla spiedo* is a preparation made with 6-month-old caciocavallo cheese stuck on a skewer with chunks of bread and grilled with a little olive oil. Some Arab cheeses such as halloumi can be grilled as can several highly dense, low-moisture cheeses.

Bouyourdi

2 tablespoons extra-virgin olive oil

1¼ pounds ripe tomatoes, peeled

6 ounces Greek or Bulgarian feta cheese

6 ounces Gouda cheese

6 ounces kasseri cheese

6 ounces kefalotyri or kashkaval cheese

1 large fresh green serrano chile, seeds and membrane removed and sliced into very thin rings

BOUYOURDI IS A DISH of melted cheese with tomatoes and chiles served as a meze in Greece. I had it in Navplion, at an ouzerie called Ouzerie Epi Skinis. An ouzerie is an eating establishment that serves a good choice of ouzos along with various foods. There are many different recipes, some including mushrooms, for example, but this one is how they do it at Epi Skinis. Uniquely, they use four cheeses (two is more common): feta, Gouda, kasseri, and kefalotyri. Gouda is not a Greek cheese, so I asked twice about it, and they assured me they used Gouda. A Greek cookbook author friend of mine was horrified, but such is the European Union; after all, they eat feta in Holland and the Dutch aren't offended. One can make it in one big casserole, in the little pans called *saganaki*, or in individual ovenproof ramekins. Tomatoes and chile always go into a bouyourdi. In Turkish, *bouyourdi* is a nineteenth-century term referring to a general passport or written order. Possibly this dish got its name from the irreverent Greeks, then occupied by the Ottoman Turks, who decided that the odious "passport" needed in their own country should just be eaten! The cheeses called for can be ordered from www.igourmet.com or www.christosmarket.com. *Makes 8 servings*

1. Preheat the oven to 350°F.

2. Oil eight 4-inch diameter ovenproof ramekins with 1 table-spoon of the olive oil. Cut eight ¼-inch-thick slices from the tomatoes and chop the remainder. Place a tomato slice on the bottom of each ramekin. Cut the cheeses into 8 slices each. Place the feta cheese on top of the sliced tomato. Sprinkle some chopped tomato and chopped chile over the feta. Layer the Gouda, kasseri, and kefalotyri cheeses, interspersing with chopped tomato and chile, in that order. Drizzle the remaining tablespoon of olive oil on top and bake until all the cheeses melt, 25 minutes. Serve hot.

Cheese Crisps

Extra-virgin olive oil, as needed

1 pound montasio, Asagio, or Parmigiano-Reggiano cheese

THIS NOW VERY WELL-KNOWN antipasto is nothing more than a crisp-fried cheese wafer made in a small pan with grated cheese. Although popularly made by many chefs in their restaurants, its roots are found in the frico of the northeastern region of Italy known as Friuli-Venezia Giulia. Even though it's simple, it's a bit tricky to make. Of course, once you've made one successfully, it does seem so easy. The cheese used for making it is a 3-month-old montasio, a cow's milk cheese with a buttery, creamy taste that melts very well. The difficult part of making a crisp frico, called by the locals *frico croccante*, is knowing when to remove the wafer from the pan. If it cooks too long and becomes golden brown, it will be bitter. Montasio cheese can sometimes be found in Whole Foods markets but can also ordered from www.pastacheese.com or www.igourmet.com. You can try using freshly grated Parmesan cheese (preferably Parmigiano-Reggiano cheese), grating from a large, not-dried-out chunk.

Makes 30 crisps

Rub some olive oil on a paper towel, then use the paper towel to grease a 7-inch nonstick skillet. Alternatively, you can use a spray can of oil. Turn the heat to medium and once the skillet is hot, begin grating the cheese over the skillet until the bottom is covered with cheese in a single layer. Turn the heat to low and cook until very light golden, 1 to 2 minutes, then begin to peel the wafer up in one piece using a rubber spatula, and flip to the other side for 30 seconds. Remove the wafer from the skillet and serve at room temperature.

VARIATION: If you want to stuff them, place each frico over a clean, empty 6-ounce tomato paste can or wine corks and fold the sides down to form a cup or a flower. Let cool before removing and filling. They can be stuffed with cheese mousse or smoked salmon mousse.

Cheese Soufflé

4 tablespoons unsalted butter, plus more for the dish

¼ cup freshly and finely grated Parmesan cheese (preferably Parmigiano-Reggiano cheese)

¼ cup all-purpose flour

1½ cups hot milk

¼ teaspoon sweet paprika

¾ teaspoon salt

⅛ teaspoon freshly ground white pepper

Pinch of ground nutmeg

6 large eggs, at room temperature, separated

2 cups packed shredded Gruyère cheese or mixed Gruyère and Swiss (Emmenthaler) cheese (about 8 ounces)

½ teaspoon cream of tartar

SOUFFLÉS HAVE THE REPUTATION of being the most difficult of culinary preparations and far beyond every cook but an accomplished one. This isn't true and it is true. A soufflé is tricky; however, anyone can master a soufflé at least by the second try and by following a good recipe closely.

I've written this recipe in the hope you can get it on the first try. The first trick is the beating of the egg whites. The bowl you whisk them in and the egg beater should be clean, and to play it extra cautious, splash some distilled vinegar into the bowl, then dry thoroughly with paper towels. The trace residue of the vinegar will help stabilize the whites. Also, there must be absolutely no egg yolk, not even a drop, in the whites. You will also have a perfect soufflé if you incorporate the egg whites carefully into the sauce by folding them in gently in batches. This will make your soufflé light and fluffy. Never beat vigorously, stir, or whip. Soufflés are also infamous for collapsing and looking a bit pathetic. You can avoid this, too. When you remove the collar from the soufflé (explained below), the puff should hold up. If it starts collapsing, very quickly reseal the foil collar and bake for another 5 minutes. However, even if the soufflé collapses, it does not change the taste one iota. I learned how to make cheese soufflés when I was about 15 years old using my mom's *Better Homes and Garden New Cook Book* published in 1953. The seasoning ideas come from Julia Child's cookbooks.

Makes 4 servings

1. Preheat the oven to 400°F.

2. Butter the bottom and sides of an 8 × 3-inch round baking or soufflé dish. Place the Parmesan cheese in the dish, and shake and roll the cheese so it covers the bottom and sides of the dish.

3. In a saucepan, melt the 4 tablespoons butter over medium heat, then add the flour to form a roux and cook, stirring constantly with a whisk, for 2 minutes. Remove the saucepan from the heat and slowly pour in the hot milk, whisking constantly. Return the saucepan to medium heat and boil, stirring with a wooden spoon or whisk until it thickens, about 2½ minutes. Whisk in the paprika, salt, pepper, and nutmeg. Remove from the heat. Whisk in the egg yolks one at a time, whisking constantly as you do.

4. In a copper bowl (preferably), beat the egg whites with the cream of tartar with a hand whisk or hand-crank beater until they are stiff and form peaks when the beater is removed. Stir and fold one-quarter of the beaten egg whites into the white sauce. Add the white sauce to the remaining egg whites. This is a critical part of the soufflé. Run a rubber spatula to the bottom of the bowl with the egg whites, sprinkle in some Gruyère cheese, and lift straight up and fold toward your other hand holding the rim of the bowl. Give the bowl a quarter turn and fold again with another sprinkle of cheese. Repeat this until most of the whites and sauce and cheese are mixed, but don't overmix or you'll kill the bubbles and the soufflé won't rise. Pour the mixture, using a rubber spatula, into the soufflé dish. For a dramatic effect, make a collar for the baking dish by wrapping the baking dish in a long sheet of heavy-duty aluminum foil (or two sheets of regular foil) or parchment paper so that it rises 3 inches above the lip of the baking dish. Secure the foil or paper with masking tape or crimp it. *(continued)*

5. Bake the soufflé in the bottom third of the oven until it puffs up 3 inches above the baking dish and the top is golden brown, about 30 minutes. Do not open the oven door while it bakes. To test for doneness, stick a metal skewer into the center of the soufflé; if it comes out slightly wet, the center will be creamy and less stable, and if it comes out dry, the soufflé will be stable but drier. Remove from the oven, remove the collar, and bring to the table. You can keep the puff standing by plunging a fork and spoon directly into the center crust and tearing the center apart. Serve hot and immediately.

SOUFFLÉ TIPS

The beating of the egg whites, the only thing that causes a soufflé to rise and be fluffy, requires your close attention. The bowl you beat them in must be clean. If you have an unlined copper bowl, that would be ideal. Lacking that, any bowl or even a large glass measuring cup is fine. The bowl must be absolutely clean and dry. The fluffiest result will come from beating with a large balloon whisk by hand. A hand beater is fine and quicker. An electric mixer or beater is satisfactory, but make sure you don't overbeat, meaning that the whites should not form very stiff peaks that are dry. The egg whites must not contain a molecule of yolk; otherwise they will not rise properly, so exercise care when you separate them. The egg whites should be at room temperature. The béchamel sauce you will fold the whites into must be dense but not so heavy that the whites break down when folded in. The temperature of the sauce should be warm, not cool. The batter when poured into the soufflé dish should come to within an inch of the rim. You can fill it to the rim and attach an aluminum foil collar around the dish for a spectacular effect of the soufflé rising above the rim. A soufflé will collapse very quickly once it's out of the oven, so one always makes guests wait for the soufflé and never the reverse.

Raclette

LONG AGO, THE FAMOUS Swiss cheese specialty raclette was served at outdoor festivals in the mountains of Valais. We don't know how long ago it was first made, but we do know that there is a dish of potatoes smothered in a rich melted raclette cheese known as *bratchäs*. The first written mention of this melted cheese called *bratkäse* or *bratchäs* comes from a monastery in the Swiss cantons Obwalden and Nidwalden in the Middle Ages, indicating it was eaten as early as 1291. Today, it is mainly served in the *carnotzets*, or converted cellars of restaurants in Switzerland.

The traditional Swiss raclette is an unforgettable eating experience and so enjoyable when done properly with family and friends around an open fireplace. Modern "raclette heaters" are now sold, which are merely hot plates for melting already cut cheese, which takes away the raw primal fun of the original. A true raclette requires a quarter or half wheel of Bagnes or Conches (Valais) cheese. These are all full-fat cow's milk cheeses now sold under the general rubic "raclette cheese." The half wheel of cheese is held before the roaring fire, and as the cheese melts it is scraped (*raclette* comes from the French word meaning "to scrape," *racler*) onto individual plates along with boiled baby potatoes in their skins, cornichons, and pearl onions. While guests wait for their scraped cheese, they may peel their potatoes and drink cold Swiss wines such as Fendant, Lavaux, or La Côte, all of which could be replaced with a good sauvignon blanc. Tea is also traditional. *(continued)*

One 5-pound half wheel raclette cheese

2 pounds boiled small potatoes (about an inch in diameter)

4 cups pickled pearl onions

4 cups cornichon pickles

This recipe is written for those who wish to experience an authentic and traditional raclette as it's made in front of a live fire. If you don't have a fireplace hearth in your home, this can be reproduced by building a fire in the well of your outdoor grill in warm or cold weather. My instructions are somewhat involved because I assume you do not have any special equipment. The raclette heaters now sold for home use are much, much easier, but they take the fun out of the true raclette because they are merely cheese melters. You can buy the 5-pound half wheels of raclette cheese at www.igourmet.com or www.gourmet-food.com. *Makes 6 servings*

1. Build a fire in your fireplace and add logs until there is a good amount of coals. You could also build a fire outdoors in your grill firebox, leaving the grilling grate off.

2. I must presume you have not bought a $500 raclette holder for this task, so you will need to follow these instructions to jury-rig the implements and tools to melt the cheese. Approach this with good cheer. The hardest thing is holding an unwieldy and heavy wheel of cheese with an outstretched arm surrounded by high heat with spring-loaded tongs for up to a minute while the cheese melts. These instructions will guide you in doing this, but remember that this isn't exactly easy, and it's supposed to be fun. It's advisable to have someone with a great sense of humor to help you, especially when your arm gets tired.

3. Set a tall pot upside down in front of the fire to act as a kind of table (or use a sturdy small table). Place a large plate on top of the pot. You also need long spring-loaded tongs and something to scrape the melted cheese, such as a 10-inch chef knife with a firm blade or even a cake server. You will also need another knife to scrape off any cheese that might adhere to the first scraper. Have several clean kitchen towels drenched in cold water to wrap around the hand holding the tongs closest to the fire (it gets hot!). Finally, have a large two-pronged fork and an extra plate available to retrieve and place the wheel of cheese in case you drop it into the fire and need to remove it to the kitchen for washing. This happens!

4. Wrap your hand and wrist in one of the wet towels. Grasp the wheel of cheese firmly with the tongs at the end of the cheese farthest from the fire. Test that your grip is secure. Hold the cut side of the cheese wheel in front of the fire and let it start melting. Once you see some dripping, remove the wheel to the plate on top of the pot and scrape off the melted cheese. Have an assistant transfer the cheese to a diner's individual plate. Return the wheel to the fire and melt some more. Serve with the accompaniments.

Fondue Neuchâteloise

For the binding

¼ cup white wine (see Note)

2 tablespoons kirsch

1 tablespoon cornstarch

For the fondue

1 large garlic clove,
cut in half

1 pound Gruyère cheese,
cut in ¼-inch cubes

1 pound Swiss
(Emmenthaler) cheese,
cut in ¼-inch cubes

1 pound Appenzeller
cheese, cut in ¼-inch cubes

Pinch of ground nutmeg

Pinch of freshly ground
black pepper

2⅓ cups white wine
(see Note)

1½ to 2 loaves day-old
crusty French baguette
loaf (about 1½ pounds),
cut in 1-inch cubes

FONDUE IS ONE OF the most elemental foods known. It is nothing but melted cheese for dipping stale bread. For most of my adult life, many people in the United States thought of fondue as gastronomically corny, and this was especially true in the last quarter of the twentieth century, when it was so dated that the only fondue set was the one in the attic. For Alpine denizens, especially those who live in the Berneralpen of Switzerland, and those of us who lived in Switzerland, like me, fondue is simply one of the greatest preparations ever invented. Generally, the only thing served with a fondue is a side salad made with a nice vinaigrette. *Makes 6 servings*

1. For the binding, in a very small bowl, mix the wine, kirsch, and cornstarch until well blended.

2. For the fondue, rub the inside of the caquelon (the fondue pot) with the cut side of the garlic clove, rubbing all over. Put the cheeses in the pot with the nutmeg and pepper. Pour the white wine over the cheese and turn the heat to medium. Start to heat, stirring constantly in a figure-8 motion. Once the cheese has melted, add the kirsch mixture and stir in until well blended.

3. Transfer to a tabletop burner and serve with the bread, keeping the cheese hot but under a boil, adjusting the heat if necessary. Start eating immediately, being careful you don't burn your mouth.

NOTE: Swiss Neuchâtel white wine is recommended. Other Swiss white wines that you can use are Fendant from Valais, the lake districts of Biel and Murten, or the Zurich region; or wines from Lake Geneva (La Côte) such as Aigle, Dêzaley, or St. Saphorin. A slightly sour sparkling white wine could also be used. Generally the wine should have a high acidity. Chablis or riesling make the most sense if you can't find the Swiss wines called for.

ON PREPARING AN AUTHENTIC SWISS FONDUE

I literally grew up on fondue. In fact, the recipe on page 192 is founded upon the one handed down to me by my mom and dad, who took us to Switzerland on vacation when we lived in France from 1954 to 1958. Later, during the winter of 1970 while living in Switzerland as a student, it was in an Alpine chalet in Sion that the pure joy of eating fondue on a cold winter's night was forever planted in my mind.

Fondue is a typical meal of the *vignerons*, the vineyard workers in the Berneralpen. Fondue is always prepared with the help of guests, never beforehand. The guests are assigned various tasks such as cutting the bread, dicing the cheese, and rubbing the caquelon (the ceramic fondue pot) with garlic, and of course, someone has to open and pour the wine, for conversation is helped along with a little wine.

As for the equipment needed, you must have a fondue set, which consists of the caquelon, long two-pronged forks, small plates, a burner stand, and Sterno for fuel. The fondue pot is traditionally always made of ceramic, though enameled cast iron may be used. The metal fondue pots you may see are actually for heating oil for beef fondue, the metal being more appropriate for heating the frying oil than ceramic. Because everyone wants to eat, and it's hard enough getting people to wait their turn and be able to reach the fondue pot without standing, the ideal number, and maximum number, of people at a one-pot fondue party is six. The cheese that goes into a fondue Neuchâteloise is pretty much circumscribed to the ones called for in the recipe, although you will find different cheeses used in other Swiss, French, and Italian Alpine regions.

The first guest—at home the guest of honor and at a restaurant the eldest—skewers a piece of bread securely and dips it into the fondue, stirring in a figure-8 pattern and not a circle. He or she removes the fork from the fondue pot, twirling the fork to capture the cheese, and eats, being careful not to burn the lips on any hot metal. The process is repeated around the table, one at a time: Diners should never stick their forks into the fondue while someone else is doing so.

Now, besides the all-important commodious conversation, there are some rituals that fondue eaters should observe. If a man drops his bread into the fondue, he must fish it out and then lose his turn or, if in a restaurant, buy the next round of wine. If a woman drops hers, she must kiss each man at the table, whether at home or at a restaurant. All eating stops while the man or woman is doing this, but drinking may continue. After each round, namely after each of the six people has had a bite, everyone toasts the fondue itself with a shot of kirsch. This shot is about a large thimble full. The basic rule of thumb is 5 to 7 ounces of cheese, total, per person and ⅜ cup of white wine per person in the fondue itself.

White wine should always be drunk with fondue because it assists in the digestion of all that cheese, which will otherwise, after all, as the old wives' tale goes, congeal again uncomfortably in your stomach. For people who don't drink alcohol, a sparking apple cider is also good to drink, as is tea, which acts in the same way as the wine.

Fondue Française

1 large garlic clove,
cut in half

1 cup dry white wine,
such as sauvignon blanc

8 ounces Vacherin
Fribourgeois cheese,
rind removed, cut
into ¼-inch dice

8 ounces Swiss
(Emmenthaler) cheese,
rind removed, cut
into ¼-inch dice

2 tablespoons kirsch

Freshly ground black
pepper to taste

1 French baguette
loaf, cut into cubes

THIS RECIPE COMES FROM my mother, written in her hand on a note card around 1954 when we lived in Paris, where my father was stationed with the U.S. Air Force. Two of my parents' best friends were Paul and François Trancart. Paul gave this recipe to my mom, and 60 years later my 92-year-old mother still exchanges Christmas cards with Paul. Vacherin Fribourgeois is an essential cheese for this fondue, and it can be found on the Internet at www.artisanalcheese.com, www.formaggiokitchen.com, or www.idealcheese.com.

Makes 4 servings

Rub the inside of a ceramic or enameled cast-iron fondue pot with the cut garlic clove. Add the white wine and heat over medium heat. Add the cheeses and cook, stirring constantly in a figure-8 motion, until melted and smooth, about 20 minutes. Add the kirsch and black pepper and continue stirring. Transfer to a table-top burner and serve with the bread, keeping the cheese hot but under a boil, adjusting the heat if necessary.

Fondue Moitié-Moitié Fribourgeois

THIS FONDUE from Fribourg, Switzerland, means "half and half" not only because it uses half Gruyère cheese and half vacherin cheese, but also because it refers to the fact that Fribourg is where German and French Switzerland meet, and one will see half the street signs in French and the other half in German. Vacherin Fribourgeois is an essential cheese for this fondue and can be found on the Internet at www.artisanalcheese.com, www.formaggiokitchen.com, or www.idealcheese.com.

Makes 6 servings

Rub the inside of a ceramic or enameled cast-iron fondue pot with the cut garlic clove. Add the Gruyère cheese, all but 2 tablespoons of the wine, and the lemon juice and heat over medium heat, stirring constantly in a figure-8 motion, until melted and smooth, about 20 minutes. Mix the cornstarch with the remaining wine and stir into the cheese to thicken it. Add the vacherin and kirsch to the pot and continue to cook until melted and smooth. Transfer to a tabletop burner and serve with the bread, keeping the cheese hot but under a boil, adjusting the heat if necessary.

1 large garlic clove, cut in half

12 ounces Gruyère cheese, grated

1 cup dry white wine, such as sauvignon blanc

1½ teaspoons fresh lemon juice

1 tablespoon cornstarch

12 ounces Vacherin Fribourgeois cheese, grated

2 tablespoons kirsch

1 French baguette loaf, cut into cubes

Roquefort Fondue

4 tablespoons
unsalted butter

1 cup dry white wine

2 tablespoons brandy

1 pound Roquefort cheese

8 ounces Brie cheese, cubed

½ teaspoon ground celery
seeds or celery salt

½ teaspoon ground nutmeg

½ teaspoon freshly
ground black pepper

16 Bacon-Onion
Rolls (page 195)

EVEN THOUGH Roquefort cheese is one of the most famous of French cheeses, Roquefort fondue probably was not invented in Roquefort-sur-Soulzon, its home. In this strongly flavored fondue with its blue-green tinge, bread is not dunked in the fondue, as is traditional. Rather, one must make bacon-onion rolls, and the fondue is spooned over them. It's extravagant and delicious. Because of how strong the taste is, I recommend serving this preparation as an appetizer or first course in small bowls. Sweet wines, port, and sauternes are usually recommended as a wine accompaniment to Roquefort cheese, but for this fondue I prefer a Bordeaux.

Makes 8 appetizer servings or 16 hors d'oeuvres servings

In a ceramic or enameled cast-iron fondue pot, melt the butter with the wine and brandy over medium-low heat. Add the cheeses and heat gently until they melt, making sure the mixture never boils and stirring constantly in a figure-8 motion. The rind of the Brie will float in little chunks, but leave them in. Stir in the ground celery seed, nutmeg, and pepper. Transfer to a tabletop burner. Let each diner take a bacon-onion roll, place it in a small bowl, and ladle the fondue over the top.

Bacon-Onion Rolls

THESE DELICIOUS ROLLS are used with the Roquefort Fondue, but one taste of them will have you making them all the time.

Makes 16 rolls

2½ cups all-purpose flour

1 tablespoon sugar

One ¼-ounce package (2¼ teaspoons) active dry yeast

½ teaspoon salt

⅔ cup whole milk

4 tablespoons unsalted butter

6 slices thick-cut bacon

¾ cup chopped onion

1. In a large bowl or the bowl of an electric mixer, combine 2 cups of the flour, the sugar, yeast, and salt. Mix well.

2. In a small saucepan, heat the milk with the butter over medium heat until the butter is melted. Let the milk and butter cool to 100°F. Add the milk to the dry ingredients. Beat until a dough forms. Turn out onto a floured work surface and knead, adding more of the remaining flour if necessary, until smooth and elastic, about 8 minutes. Alternatively, knead with the dough hook of an electric mixer on medium speed for 4 minutes.

3. Place in a greased bowl, turning the dough so it is greased all over, and cover with a damp kitchen towel. Let rise in a warm place (such as a turned-off oven) until doubled in size, about 2 hours.

4. Meanwhile, in a skillet over low heat, cook the bacon until crisp. Remove the bacon, leaving the fat in the pan. Add the onion to the bacon fat and cook over medium-low heat, stirring, until golden, about 5 minutes. Remove from the heat and crumble the bacon into the onion. Remove and discard about 3 tablespoons of bacon fat from the pan by tilting it.

5. Punch down the dough. On a floured surface, roll the dough into a 15 × 9-inch rectangle. Spread the bacon-onion mixture to within an inch of the edge and roll up like a jelly roll from the long side. Seal the ends and cut the log into 1-inch slices. Place the slices, cut side up, on a buttered 13 × 10-inch baking sheet, cover with a damp cloth, and let rise for 30 minutes.

6. Meanwhile, preheat the oven to 400°F.

7. Bake until golden brown, about 20 minutes.

Neuchâtel Ramekin

½ (8 ounces)
Short Dough recipe
(page 77)

All-purpose flour, as needed

8 ounces Gruyère
cheese, shredded

2 large eggs

1 cup whole milk

IN ENGLISH, a ramekin is a small individual-size baking dish, but in the canton of Neuchâtel in Switzerland, it's also the name of a Gruyère cheese, egg, and milk pie. Typically they are served as appetizers, but you can also make this as one large flan.

Makes 8 appetizer servings

1. Preheat the oven to 425°F.

2. Roll out the dough until very thin, dusting with flour as needed. Cut out eight 6-inch disks, then lay and press them into eight 3-inch ramekins and trim off excess pastry. Gather excess bits, form into a ball, and reroll if necessary. Refrigerate for 1 hour.

3. In a bowl, mix the Gruyère with the eggs and milk. Fill the ramekins half full. Bake until set and dappled golden brown, 25 to 30 minutes. Serve hot.

Cajun Fondue

IN LOUISIANA, they call this late-night favorite simply "cheese" (*fromage*). You'll be hard-pressed not to eat this cross between fondue and a quiche all by yourself. If not for late night, it also is a great appetizer. Eat it with pieces of French bread.

Makes 6 servings

2 large eggs

4½ cups shredded Swiss (Emmenthaler) cheese (about 1 pound)

1 cup half-and-half

½ teaspoon cayenne pepper

½ teaspoon salt

¼ teaspoon sweet paprika

1. Preheat the oven to 350°F.

2. In a bowl, beat the eggs, then stir in the cheese, half-and-half, cayenne, salt, and paprika. Pour into an 8 × 3½-inch casserole or soufflé pan and bake until it has set and is slightly golden on top, about 20 minutes. Serve hot.

Pasta with Cheese

What would a chapter on pasta and cheese be without Macaroni and Cheese? Well, it's here, on page 200, and so are 39 other exciting recipes. Some are classics like Spaghetti alla Carbonara (page 223), with several provisos reminding you that it's a wee bit trickier than you think. There are a lot more than just tons of Italian pasta recipes in this chapter, although those predominate as the Italians are the masters, but you'll be delighted with the unusual Swiss Macaroni and Cheese with Potatoes and Fresh Applesauce (page 206). There's lasagne such as Rich Green Lasagne with Fondue (page 245), and Maccheroni ai Quattro Formaggi (page 212), and Cannelloni Sorrento (page 227) for you to enjoy.

Macaroni and Cheese

3 tablespoons unsalted butter

3 tablespoons finely chopped onion

½ garlic clove, finely chopped

3 tablespoons all-purpose flour

3½ cups whole milk

1 pound elbow macaroni

1 pound mild white or orange cheddar cheese, shredded

2 tablespoons Dijon mustard

¾ teaspoon salt, plus more for the pasta water

2 tablespoons dried bread crumbs

I FIRST PUBLISHED THIS RECIPE in my book *Bake Until Bubbly: The Ultimate Casserole Cookbook* but include it here because it's the quintessential American pasta-and-cheese dish, and I like the recipe and the story. It was a popular dish before 1937, when the Kraft Foods Company first put it into a box.

There can be no doubt that its ultimate origins are Italian. The first written recipe for macaroni and cheese is found in a thirteenth-century Italian cookery manuscript. As for the American macaroni and cheese, there are two stories about its origin. In the first, it is thought that it had its beginnings at a New England church supper. In southeastern Connecticut it was known long ago as macaroni pudding. In the second, and more famous story it is said that it was introduced by Thomas Jefferson to Virginia after his sojourn in Italy in 1787. Jefferson, who was quite enamored of Italian culture, had a pasta machine brought back from Italy. After Jefferson's wife died, his daughter Mary Randolph became the hostess of his house, and she is credited with inventing the dish using macaroni and Parmesan cheese. Later, the Parmesan was replaced with cheddar cheese.

I still find a plate of macaroni and cheese to be a satisfying dish. Some cooks add bread crumbs to the top of the casserole, and I like that au gratin finish, too. The key to this dish is the cheese, so it will be wise to choose a high-quality cheddar cheese such as Vermont Shelburne Farm cheddar. Do not used an aged cheddar. *Makes 4 to 6 servings*

1. Preheat the oven to 400°F.

2. In a saucepan, melt the butter over medium heat, then add the onion and garlic and cook, stirring, until translucent, about 3 minutes. Add the flour to form a roux, stirring for about 1 minute. Remove the saucepan from the heat and whisk in the milk. Return to the heat and simmer over low heat, stirring, until smooth but still liquidy, about 15 minutes. Add the cheese, 1 cup or a handful at a time, stirring frequently, until it melts. Then add the mustard and salt and stir until well blended.

3. Meanwhile, bring a large pot of abundantly salted water to a rolling boil. Add the pasta and cook until half cooked (harder than al dente; follow the package instructions). Drain the pasta and transfer to a large bowl. Pour the cheese sauce over the pasta and stir and toss a bit. Transfer the macaroni to a buttered 10-inch diameter casserole at least 3 inches deep. Sprinkle the bread crumbs on top and bake until the top begins to turns golden and the sauce is bubbly, about 25 minutes. Let rest for 10 minutes, then serve.

Homemade Egg Noodles
with Cottage Cheese

For the noodles

3 cups all-purpose flour

2 large eggs

¼ cup water and
more as needed

½ teaspoon salt

For the sauce

4 ounces thick-cut bacon

¼ cup salt

2 tablespoons pork lard

8 ounces sour cream

8 ounces cottage cheese,
drained in a strainer,
uncovered, for 8 hours

1 tablespoon chopped
fresh dill

THE ITALIANS are not the only people in love with pasta. In Hungary, a fresh noodle dish with cottage cheese, sour cream, and crispy bacon called *túrós csusza* is made, and it will go right into your repertoire. It's the kind of dish that calls for homemade noodles. They are made with flour and eggs and rolled thin, then pinched off into coin-size pieces before cooking. But you can buy wide egg noodles instead and it will still be terrific.

Makes 4 servings

1. For the noodles, in a bowl, mix the flour, eggs, water, and salt. Form into a ball and then knead for about 8 minutes. If it is crumbly and too dry, add water only by wetting your hands until you can form a ball. Wrap in plastic wrap and let stand for 1 hour. Roll the dough out quite thin, using a pasta rolling machine. Flour a board or counter surface, pinch off coin-size pieces of dough, and scatter them on top of the flour-strewn counter to dry, making sure they don't touch each other; otherwise they may stick together. Let dry for 2 hours.

2. In a skillet large enough to hold all the noodles, cook the bacon over low heat until crisp, about 25 minutes. Remove from the skillet, crumble coarsely, and set aside. Reserve the bacon fat in the skillet.

3. Bring 4 quarts of water to a rolling boil over high heat and salt abundantly using 3 of the 4 tablespoons of salt and then tasting the water and using the last tablespoon if necessary. Add the lard, then add the noodles in handfuls. Cook over high heat, stirring frequently so the noodles don't stick, until cooked, about 6 minutes, but check before then. Drain without rinsing.

4. Mix the drained noodles with the bacon fat in the skillet. Add the sour cream, cottage cheese, and dill and toss well. Add the bacon and toss again. Serve warm, just above room temperature.

Cottage Cheese Dumplings

1¾ pounds cottage cheese

⅔ cup all-purpose flour

4 large eggs, separated

2½ cups (about 6 ounces) fresh bread crumbs

1 teaspoon salt, plus more for the pasta water

½ cup (4 ounces) pork lard (preferably) or butter

1 cup sour cream

THESE DELICIOUS Hungarian dumplings are made with bread and cheese, and I love to serve them with some kind of pork dish such as pan-seared chops or pork stew with paprika. You may hesitate about using a half cup of pork lard as called for in the recipe, but if you want the amazing authentic Hungarian taste, I highly recommend using it. Remember, you're serving 6 people and not eating that much by yourself!

Makes 6 servings

1. Push the cottage cheese through a sieve or food mill or blend in a food processor. In a bowl, mix the cottage cheese, flour, egg yolks, 1¼ cups of the bread crumbs, and the salt. Separately, beat the egg whites until stiff. Fold the egg whites gently into the mixture.

2. Bring 2 large pots of lightly salted water to a boil over high heat. Reduce the heat to medium so the water is bubbling gently. Shape the dumplings into the size of a lime with floured hands so they don't stick, then drop them into the water, half in one pot and half in the other, and cook until spongy and solid, about 15 minutes. Remove with a skimmer, drain well, and set aside until they are all cooked.

3. In a large skillet, melt the lard over medium-high heat. Roll the dumplings in the remaining bread crumbs, then cook in the lard until golden brown on all sides, 5 to 6 minutes. Serve with the sour cream.

Spaghetti with Cheese au Gratin

THIS IS A SUBTLE DISH, where a very light tomato sauce is made first and then tossed with some spaghetti before going into a baking pan to be covered by a soft pecorino cheese from Sardinia known as Fiore Sardo or pecorino Sardo. Although Fiore Sardo cheese can't always be found, many Italian markets and better supermarkets carry other young, semihard pecorinos, also called table or eating pecorinos (as opposed to grating pecorino). You can also buy it on the Internet at www.markys.com or www.dibruno.com.

Makes 4 servings

½ cup extra-virgin olive oil

2 garlic cloves, finely chopped

3 tablespoons finely chopped fresh flat-leaf parsley

10 large fresh basil leaves, finely chopped

1 pound ripe tomatoes, peeled, seeded, and chopped

Salt and freshly ground black pepper to taste

12 ounces spaghetti

4 ounces Fiore Sardo cheese or soft table pecorino cheese, thinly sliced

1. In a large casserole or skillet, add the olive oil, garlic, parsley, and basil over low heat and cook until you begin to hear some sizzling, about 5 minutes. Add the tomatoes, season with salt and pepper, and stir. Increase the heat to high and cook until much of the liquid has evaporated, 4 to 6 minutes.

2. Preheat the oven to 350°F.

3. Meanwhile, bring a large pot of water to a vigorous boil over high heat, salt abundantly, and add the pasta. Cook, stirring occasionally, until al dente. Drain well. Toss the tomato sauce with the pasta and place in a 12 × 9-inch baking casserole. Arrange the cheese on top and bake until it melts, about 5 minutes. Serve immediately.

Swiss Macaroni and Cheese with Potatoes and Fresh Applesauce

For the onions

3 tablespoons unsalted butter

2 large onions, chopped

Salt to taste

For the pasta

8 ounces Yukon Gold potatoes, peeled and diced

8 ounces ziti or rigatoni

Unsalted butter, for greasing the casserole

6 ounces Appenzeller or Gruyère cheese, grated

¾ cup heavy cream

For the applesauce

2 tablespoons unsalted butter

1½ pounds Granny Smith apples, peeled, cored, and sliced

1 tablespoon sugar

¼ cup apple juice

I FIRST ENCOUNTERED many Swiss specialties when I was a year-abroad college student in Basel in the early 1970s. *Älpermagronen mit ankestückli* is truly a Swiss Alpine farmer's comfort food from the canton of Unterwald. It is a rib-sticking dish of potato and macaroni and cheese served with, of all things, freshly made applesauce called *ankestückli*. Don't think you can open a jar of applesauce for this dish; you must make the fresh applesauce and you'll make the dish spectacular.

Makes 6 servings

1. Preheat the oven to 425°F.

2. In a large skillet, melt the butter over medium-low heat, then add the onions and cook, stirring, for 10 minutes. Reduce the heat to low and cook, stirring, until golden, another 15 minutes. Season lightly with salt and set aside.

3. Bring a large pot of water to a boil over high heat, then add the potatoes and cook until half-cooked, about 3 minutes. Add the pasta and cook until al dente, at which time the potatoes should be soft, too. Drain well.

4. Transfer half the pasta and potatoes to a lightly buttered 9 × 2-inch round baking casserole and sprinkle with half the cheese. Cover with the remaining pasta and potatoes and the remaining cheese. Pour the cream over the cheese and bake until the cheese melts and the dish is bubbling, about 20 minutes.

5. Meanwhile, prepare the applesauce. In a large skillet, melt the butter over medium heat. Add the apples and cook, stirring, for 2 minutes. Sprinkle the sugar over them, and reduce the heat to medium-low. Add the apple juice and cook gently until all the liquid is absorbed, about 15 minutes. Mash the apples slightly with a fork or leave whole. Keep warm.

6. Remove the casserole from the oven and spoon the onions over the top. Serve with the fresh applesauce on the side.

Fettuccine with Fontina Fondue

4 ounces Fontina Val
d'Aosta cheese, diced

2 tablespoons
unsalted butter

2 tablespoons heavy cream

1 garlic clove, crushed

Salt, as needed

8 ounces fettuccine

2 large egg yolks

Freshly ground black
pepper to taste

THIS NOT-OFTEN-SEEN RECIPE is one from the Piedmont region of northern Italy and has the same creamy, mellow, stick-to-your-ribs taste as any fondue from the Alps. In this recipe, the local fontina from the Val d'Aosta is used. When shopping for the fontina, which is after all the critical part of the dish, search for this Fontina Val d'Aosta, which is the best of the various fontina cheeses sold. Never use a non-Italian fontina. The dish can be served as a first or main course with a rosé. If you would like to make the canapés suggested in the box below, then double the ingredients used in step 1.

Makes 2 servings

LEFTOVER FONDUE

Leftover Piedmontese fonduta—which is what the cheese sauce used in step 1 of the Fettuccine with Fontina Fondue (above) is—makes for a wonderful canapé. Slice day-old white bread into 2½ × 1½-inch triangles. Cook them in equal amounts of butter and olive oil until golden. Let cool, then spread with a film of soft butter. Cook some bacon until crisp and break into the same size as the bread. Spoon a little leftover fondue on top of the bread and top with a piece of bacon. Place all the triangles on a baking tray and put into a 375°F oven for 2 to 3 minutes. Serve hot with a little Dijon mustard.

1. Bring some water to a boil in the bottom portion of a double boiler over high heat. Put the cheese, butter, cream, and garlic in the top portion of the double boiler. (Use some of the rind of the cheese, which adds a nice texture, but only if using Fontina Val d'Aosta, not an inferior fontina.) Reduce to low heat and stir gently in a figure-8 motion until the cheese is melted and smooth.

2. Meanwhile, bring 5 quarts of water to a rolling boil over high heat, salt abundantly, then add the pasta. Cook over high heat, stirring occasionally so the pasta doesn't stick together, until al dente. Drain without rinsing.

3. Meanwhile, raise the heat to high under the double boiler. Quickly beat in the egg yolks, one at a time, until the sauce is creamy. Season with salt and pepper. Transfer the pasta to a serving bowl, toss with the sauce, and serve.

Fresh Fettuccine with Mascarpone Sauce

2 large egg yolks

3 tablespoons extra-virgin olive oil

½ cup mascarpone cheese

Salt and freshly ground black pepper to taste

12 ounces fresh fettuccine

½ cup freshly grated Parmesan cheese (preferably Parmigiano-Reggiano cheese)

THIS DELIGHTFULLY simple preparation is creamy, cheesy, and delicious. In Italy, this dish fits into a class of pasta preparations called *spaghetatta*, which are lighter or simple pasta dishes one might have later in the evening at home, perhaps after the theater.

Makes 4 servings

1. In a bowl, place the egg yolks and slowly beat in the olive oil in a very thin stream, beating all the time as you would while making a mayonnaise. Stir in the mascarpone a little at a time and season with salt and pepper.

2. Bring 6 quarts of water to a rolling boil over high heat, salt abundantly, then add the pasta. Cook over high heat, stirring occasionally so the pasta doesn't stick, until al dente. Drain without rinsing.

3. Transfer the pasta to a serving bowl or platter and cover with the sauce. Toss well and sprinkle with Parmesan cheese. Serve immediately.

Perciatelli with Three Cheeses

THE CHEWY THICK SPAGHETTI with the hole in the middle is called either perciatelli or bucatini. In this preparation, the heat of the pasta will melt the cheeses in a few seconds and just enough to blend the flavors even further. A dusting of cayenne provides a nice bite and a pretty contrast to the creamy color of the cheeses. Perciatelli is usually found sold in Italian markets, on Italian-food Web sites, and in the grocery section of www.amazon.com. In supermarkets, it's not that common except in the northeastern United States. *Makes 2 servings*

Salt, as needed

8 ounces perciatelli (bucatini)

½ cup freshly grated Parmesan cheese (preferably Parmigiano-Reggiano cheese)

3 ounces mascarpone cheese

2 ounces Gorgonzola cheese, crumbled

3 tablespoons finely chopped fresh flat-leaf parsley

3 tablespoons extra-virgin olive oil

⅛ teaspoon freshly ground black pepper

Pinch of cayenne pepper

1. Bring 5 quarts of water to a rolling boil over high heat, salt abundantly, then add the pasta. Cook over high heat, stirring occasionally so the pasta doesn't stick, until al dente. Drain without rinsing.

2. Meanwhile, in a bowl, mix the Parmesan, mascarpone, Gorgonzola, parsley, olive oil, black pepper, and cayenne. Add to the pasta, toss well, and serve.

Maccheroni ai Quattro Formaggi

4 tablespoons
unsalted butter

2 tablespoons all-
purpose flour

1 cup half-and-half

2 ounces fresh mozzarella
cheese, julienned

2 ounces Gruyère
cheese, julienned

2 ounces Fontina Val
d'Aosta cheese, julienned

2 ounces mild imported
provolone (preferably)
or young Asiago
cheese, julienned

Salt, as needed

12 ounces macaroni, such
as cut ziti or elbow

2 teaspoons freshly ground
black pepper, or to taste

Freshly grated Parmesan
cheese (preferably
Parmigiano-Reggiano
cheese), for sprinkling

I'M USING THE ITALIAN NAME for this famous pasta dish because *quattro formaggi* sounds so much more appetizing than "four cheeses." This recipe is the classic one that every cook will do a riff on, including me, as you'll see in some of the other recipes in this chapter. Just remember that what you're actually making is a Mornay sauce; you're not just dumping cheese into the pasta. A Mornay sauce is a béchamel sauce with cheese, and béchamel is nothing but white sauce. To julienne something is to cut it into matchstick shapes. You may purchase young (called fresh) Asagio cheese at www.pastacheese.com.

Makes 4 servings

1. Preheat a 12 × 9-inch or 11-inch round baking casserole in a 150°F oven.

2. In a small saucepan, melt half the butter over medium heat, then stir in the flour to form a roux and cook, stirring, for 1 minute. Remove the saucepan from the heat and slowly pour in the half-and-half, stirring constantly. Bring to a boil over high heat, then reduce to medium and cook, stirring, until dense, about 5 minutes. Remove from the heat, add the cheeses, and stir until melted. Keep warm.

3. Meanwhile, bring 6 quarts of water to a rolling boil over high heat, salt abundantly, then add the pasta. Cook over high heat, stirring occasionally so the pasta doesn't stick, until al dente. Drain without rinsing.

4. Transfer the macaroni to the preheated baking casserole and sprinkle with black pepper and the remaining butter. Mix well. Pour the cheese sauce over the macaroni and toss. Correct the salt if necessary. Serve immediately with the Parmesan on the side.

Spaghetti with Seven Cheeses

SINCE YOU MAY NOT FIND the cheeses I call for in this recipe, just remember that some should be mild and soft and the others should be strong, like blue cheese. Use only cow's milk cheeses. The flavors of this dish are wonderfully perfumed, and it is a very memorable pasta. Because there is so much cheese, you will want to follow this pasta with a light salad or a very simple white meat, grilled or pan-seared, such as chicken breast. All the cheeses called for can also be bought at www.igourmet.com.

Makes 4 to 6 servings

2 tablespoons unsalted butter

1 tablespoon extra-virgin olive oil

¾ cup chopped pancetta (about 2 ounces)

2 ounces Taleggio cheese

2 ounces Bel Paese cheese

2 ounces Gorgonzola cheese

2 ounces Fontina Val d'Aosta cheese

2 ounces mascarpone cheese

2 ounces smoked ricotta (preferably) or ricotta cheese (page 65)

1 ounce Parmesan cheese (preferably Parmigiano-Reggiano cheese), freshly grated

¾ cup sparkling white wine (such as Asti Spumante)

1 garlic clove, crushed

Freshly ground white pepper to taste

Salt, for the pasta water

1 pound spaghetti

1 tablespoon finely chopped fresh flat-leaf parsley

1. In a large skillet, melt the butter over medium heat. Add the olive oil and pancetta and cook, stirring, until the pancetta begins to brown, about 5 minutes. Take the skillet off the heat and remove all but 1 tablespoon of the cooking fats.

2. Add the seven cheeses, sparkling wine, garlic, and pepper to the skillet and stir in a figure-8 motion until all the cheese melts and is smooth. Continue cooking until it begins to bubble slightly; if the cheese is already bubbling too much, reduce the heat.

3. Meanwhile, bring 6 quarts of water to a rolling boil over high heat, salt abundantly, then add the pasta. Cook over high heat, stirring occasionally so the pasta doesn't stick, until al dente. Drain without rinsing. Transfer the pasta to a bowl or platter, pour the sauce over the pasta and toss, sprinkle with the parsley, and serve.

Cavatelli with Creamy Cheese Fondue

8 ounces ricotta
cheese (page 65)

½ cup mascarpone cheese

¼ cup freshly grated
pecorino cheese, plus
more to taste

2 thin slices prosciutto (less
than ½ ounce), chopped

3 tablespoons dry
Marsala wine

2 tablespoons heavy cream

1 tablespoon extra-
virgin olive oil

Salt and freshly ground
black pepper to taste

1 pound cavatelli

CAVATELLI are a special little pasta popular in southern Italy and Sicily. Essentially, cavatelli are orecchiette that have been rolled up. They look like small cowry shells. In the Francis Ford Coppola movie *The Godfather, Part III*, there is one erotically charged scene where Vinny Mancini (Andy Garcia) instructs Mary Corleone (Sofia Coppola) in making gnocchi in a slow, methodical way that is also gastronomically instructive. The method is almost the same for cavatelli. In this preparation, the various cheeses are blended in a double boiler for a satisfying first course.

Makes 4 servings

1. Bring some water to a boil in the bottom of a double boiler. In the top part of the double boiler, melt the ricotta, mascarpone, and pecorino with the prosciutto, Marsala wine, cream, olive oil, salt, and pepper, stirring in a figure-8 motion.

2. Meanwhile, bring 6 quarts of water to a rolling boil over high heat, salt abundantly, then add the pasta. Cook over high heat, stirring occasionally so the pasta doesn't stick, until al dente. Drain. Transfer the pasta to a bowl or platter. Once the cheeses have melted and blended well, pour over the pasta and toss with more pecorino to taste.

Pasta Cas e Ova

THIS NEAPOLITAN PASTA dish is an easy and quick way to prepare short pasta. It's dressed with pecorino cheese and Parmesan cheese and sometimes contains lamb. However, since I don't make it often, I like to make it special by making my own gnocchetti sardi, which is a pasta slightly smaller than the otherwise identical cavatelli. *Cas e ova* is Neapolitan dialect for *cacio e uova*, "cheese and eggs." When making it without lamb, use Parmesan and pecorino, and when making it with lamb, use only pecorino.

Makes 4 servings

2 large eggs

¼ cup finely chopped fresh flat-leaf parsley

Salt and freshly ground black pepper to taste

1 pound short pasta, such as elbow macaroni, ditalini, cavatelli, or gnocchetti sardi

4 tablespoons unsalted butter, melted

2 ounces pecorino cheese, freshly grated

2 ounces Parmesan cheese (preferably Parmigiano-Reggiano cheese), freshly grated

1. In a bowl, beat the eggs with the parsley, salt, and pepper until foamy.

2. Bring 6 quarts of water to a rolling boil over high heat, salt abundantly, then add the pasta. Cook over high heat, stirring occasionally so the pasta doesn't stick, until al dente. Drain without rinsing. Transfer the pasta to a serving bowl and toss with the egg mixture, butter, and cheeses. Toss until the cheese melts, then serve.

VARIATION: Preheat a cast-iron or carbon-steel skillet over high heat until very hot. Toss 12 ounces diced lamb sirloin with 2 teaspoons olive oil and ¼ teaspoon salt. Cook, tossing or stirring, until golden brown on all sides, about 4 minutes. Remove and toss with the pasta, cheese, and eggs.

Orecchiette with Ricotta

1 teaspoon salt, plus more for the pasta water

1 pound orecchiette

¾ cup pasta cooking water, or more as needed

1 pound ricotta cheese

2 ounces (¼ cup) melted pork lard (preferably homemade from fresh pork fat) or unsalted butter

1 teaspoon freshly ground black pepper

ORECCHIETTE is a kind of pasta from the Apulia region of southern Italy. It means "little ear" and is in the shape of a concave disk. In Apulia, most people still make it themselves, but it is available in stores. You can also make this dish with rigatoni. Your guests will marvel at the simple yet rustic taste, and they'll ask you questions, and the answer is threefold: the best fresh ricotta (homemade if need be), melted pork lard, and the pasta cooking water. That's where "rustic" comes from.

Makes 6 servings

Bring a large pot of water to a rolling boil, salt abundantly, and add the pasta. Cook over high heat, stirring occasionally so the pasta doesn't stick together, and just before the pasta is al dente, remove 1 cup of the pasta cooking water. In a bowl, beat the ricotta vigorously with ¾ cup of the pasta cooking water until it is fluid and smooth. Beat in the lard, 1 teaspoon salt, and pepper. Add more water if necessary. Drain the pasta when cooked a little softer than al dente. Toss with the ricotta mixture and serve hot.

Macaroni with Ricotta

IF YOU READ A PASTA RECIPE in a medieval Italian cookery manuscript, you will notice that this recipe is very similar. During the Renaissance, macaroni was often cooked in broth as well as water and then usually flavored with cheeses such as ricotta, pecorino, caciocavallo, provola, and Parmigiano and spices, cinnamon and saffron being the most common.

Makes 4 to 6 servings

12 ounces ricotta cheese (preferably from ewe's milk; see page 65 for homemade)

1 tablespoon sugar

⅛ to ¼ teaspoon ground cinnamon

Salt, as needed

1 pound short macaroni, such as elbow macaroni, mezze ziti, tubetti, or ditali

¼ cup milk (optional)

1. In a bowl, stir the ricotta, sugar, cinnamon, and salt together.

2. Bring a large pot of abundantly salted water to a boil and add the pasta. Cook over high heat, stirring occasionally so the pasta doesn't stick together, until al dente. Save ¼ cup of the cooking water if not using the milk and drain the pasta. Blend the ricotta with the milk or cooking water, beating with a fork. Toss the pasta with the ricotta mixture and serve immediately.

Spaghetti with Ricotta and Parmesan

Salt, as needed

12 ounces spaghetti

6 tablespoons homemade ricotta cheese (see page 65)

6 tablespoons freshly grated Parmesan cheese (preferably Parmigiano-Reggiano cheese)

¼ cup dry white wine

2 tablespoons extra-virgin olive oil

⅛ teaspoon red chile flakes

Freshly ground black pepper to taste

IN THIS QUICKLY PREPARED DISH, you will toss all the ingredients together and let the heat of the cooked pasta do all the work. The resulting sauce has a creamy, cheesy texture that is thinned with wine. It's ideally served with a salad or steamed vegetable. *Makes 4 servings*

1. Bring 6 quarts of water to a rolling boil over high heat, salt abundantly, then add the pasta. Cook over high heat, stirring occasionally so the pasta doesn't stick together, until al dente. Drain without rinsing.

2. Meanwhile, in a large bowl, mix the ricotta, Parmesan, white wine, olive oil, red chile flakes, and salt and pepper to taste. Transfer the pasta to the bowl, toss with the sauce, and serve.

Linguine with Ricotta and Tomatoes

THIS IS A RAW SAUCE preparation. That means it is easy. You mix the ingredients and toss them with the hot cooked pasta, which melts the cheeses slightly and heats the tomato so the full flavors permeate the whole dish.   *Makes 4 servings*

Salt, as needed

12 ounces linguine

8 ounces ricotta cheese

¼ cup freshly grated Parmesan cheese (preferably Parmigiano-Reggiano cheese)

¼ cup mascarpone cheese

5 ripe plum tomatoes, cut into thin wedges

2 tablespoons extra-virgin olive oil

Freshly ground black pepper to taste

1. Bring 6 quarts of water to a rolling boil over high heat, salt abundantly, then add the pasta. Cook over high heat, stirring occasionally so the pasta doesn't stick together, until al dente. Drain without rinsing.

2. Place the ricotta, Parmesan, mascarpone, tomatoes, and olive oil in a serving bowl. Season with salt and pepper. Transfer the cooked pasta to the bowl, toss several times so everything is mixed, and serve.

Fettuccine with Pink Sauce

12 ounces ripe tomatoes,
cut in half, seeds squeezed
out, and grated down to
the peel on the largest
holes of a standing grater

4 tablespoons
unsalted butter

2 large garlic cloves, crushed

6 tablespoons crème fraîche

3 tablespoons heavy cream

Salt and freshly ground
black pepper to taste

8 ounces fresh or
dried fettuccine

1½ cups freshly grated
Parmesan cheese
(preferably Parmigiano-
Reggiano cheese)

THIS PASTA PREPARATION is so called because the crème fraîche and cream turn the red tomato sauce pink. It's really wonderful with fresh homemade fettuccine, but any fettuccine, dried or fresh, will work in this recipe. I use the leftovers with a few eggs to make a great frittata for lunch the next day.

Makes 4 servings

1. Pass the grated tomatoes through a strainer or food mill so you have only the juice of the tomato.

2. In a skillet large enough to hold the pasta, melt the butter over medium heat with the garlic cloves, and when the garlic is sizzling, add the tomato juice and cook for 5 minutes. Then add the crème fraîche, cream, and season with salt and pepper. Continue cooking until the crème fraîche is blended.

3. Meanwhile, bring 6 quarts of water to a rolling boil over high heat, salt abundantly, then add the pasta. Cook over high heat, stirring occasionally so the pasta doesn't stick together, until a little harder than al dente. Drain without rinsing.

4. Transfer the pasta to the sauce and cook until all the liquid of the sauce has been absorbed by the pasta, stirring and tossing almost constantly. Add the cheese, toss again, and serve.

Homemade Fresh Fettuccine with Homemade Ricotta Cheese

THIS PREPARATION, because of its simplicity, will only be notable if you make it with homemade fresh fettuccine and homemade ricotta cheese (page 65). Since that might not be possible, you can use store-bought fresh fettuccine and buy the ricotta cheese fresh at an Italian market, where you can find higher-quality ricotta cheese than you can in the supermarket. If you use commercially made supermarket ricotta cheese and dried fettuccine, there will be absolutely nothing notable about this recipe, but you may still like it. *Makes 4 servings*

5 tablespoons unsalted butter

1 pound homemade ricotta cheese (see page 65), pushed through a sieve

¼ cup finely chopped fresh flat-leaf parsley

Salt and freshly ground black pepper to taste

1 pound fresh homemade (preferably) or store-bought fettuccine

Freshly grated Parmesan cheese (preferably Parmigiano-Reggiano cheese), for garnish

1. In a large flameproof casserole, melt the butter over medium heat, then add the ricotta cheese and mix well so that it becomes smoother. Season with the parsley, salt, and pepper.

2. Meanwhile, bring 6 quarts of water to a rolling boil over high heat, salt abundantly, then add the pasta. Cook over high heat, stirring occasionally so the pasta doesn't stick, until al dente. Drain without rinsing, but save some of the cooking water.

3. Add enough pasta cooking water (about ⅔ cup) to the ricotta cheese to thin it like a sauce. Add the pasta, toss well, and sprinkle with pepper. Serve with Parmesan cheese on the side.

SPAGHETTI ALLA CARBONARA

The whole story of the origin of this famous dish of Rome and its place in *cucina romana* is vague. The origin of carbonara is much discussed, yet no one really knows. There are several competing theories, but all are anecdotal.

First, although thought of as a typical Roman dish, the name is said to come from a dish made in the Apennine mountains of the Abruzzo by woodcutters who made charcoal for fuel. They would cook the dish over a hardwood charcoal fire and use penne rather than spaghetti because it was easier to toss with the eggs and cheese.

Second, the obvious one, is that given the meaning of *alla carbonara*, "coal worker's style," the dish was a meal eaten by coal workers, or the abundant use of coarsely ground black pepper resembles coal flakes.

Another story suggests that food shortages after the liberation of Rome in 1944 were so severe that Allied troops distributed military rations consisting of powdered eggs and bacon, which the local populace used with water to season the easily stored dried pasta. There is also a theory that in the Ciociaria area, in the region of Lazio about halfway between Rome and Benevento, pasta was seasoned in a Neapolitan style with eggs, lard, and pecorino cheese. During the German occupation of Rome during the World War II, many middle-class families dispersed from Rome into this region to escape the oppressiveness of the occupation and may have learned about this dish. After the war, Roman cuisine became very popular throughout Italy and this dish, now transformed into carbonara, became a prime example.

Yet another story suggests that the famous restaurant in the Campo dei Fiori in Rome, La Carbonara, was named after its specialty. Although the restaurant has been open since the early part of the twentieth century, and does in fact have carbonara on its menu, the restaurant itself denies any such connection and tells us that the name came about for other reasons. A highly unlikely story told in *Il nuovo cucchiaio d'argento* (translated recently into English as *The Silver Spoon*) is that the dish was originally made with black squid ink and therefore acquired its name because it was as black as coal. The simplest story, and therefore the most likely, is that the dish had always existed at the family level and in local osterie before traditional Roman cuisine got its stamp of fame.

Spaghetti alla Carbonara

THIS FAMOUS PREPARATION is famously destroyed by many an overenthusiastic cook. Keep all the proportions sensible so that the final plate will be a nicely flavored and attractive dish of delicately twirled pasta melded with eggs, cheese, and bacon and not a thick, creamy mass of slopped-together spaghetti. Traditionally, spaghetti alla carbonara is not made with bacon but with guanciale, salted and cured pig's jowl, which tastes a bit stronger and saltier than the more commonly found and used pancetta. One could use salted pork or blanched bacon, too, but guanciale can be ordered via the grocery section of www.amazon.com, www.zingermans.com, and www.salumeriaitaliana.com, and it is occasionally seen at some Whole Foods markets.

Remember that "creamy" Italian dishes such as this one and fettuccine Alfredo or risotto never contain cream. Their "creaminess" comes from eggs. The method used in this recipe to incorporate the eggs I learned from my son Ali, who lived in Bologna for a year and who learned it from his Italian roommate, who was Roman. One of his roommates separated all the eggs first, beating the whites until frothy and then adding the whites into the pasta, beating furiously, and then the yolks. Ali says, "beating in the eggs is crucial, and make sure you don't drain the pasta too much. Also we used to add a little red chile flakes even though it's not traditional." The rule of thumb for the eggs is one per person.

Makes 4 servings

(continued)

1 tablespoon extra-virgin olive oil

4½ ounces guanciale or pancetta, cut into thin, ½-inch strips

2 large garlic cloves, crushed

4 large eggs

¾ cup freshly grated Parmesan cheese (preferably Parmigiano-Reggiano cheese)

¾ cup freshly grated pecorino cheese

Salt, as needed

1 pound spaghetti

1 teaspoon freshly ground black pepper

1. In a large, heavy, flameproof casserole, heat the oil with the guanciale and garlic over medium-low heat, then cook, stirring almost constantly so nothing sticks, until the guanciale is almost crispy but not quite and has rendered much of its fat, 8 to 10 minutes. Remove the casserole from the heat, leave the guanciale in the casserole, but remove and discard the garlic cloves.

2. Separate 2 of the eggs into 2 bowls, beating the whites until frothy but not stiff. Add half of the cheeses to the egg whites.

3. Meanwhile, bring 6 quarts of water to a rolling boil over high heat, salt abundantly, then add the pasta. Cook over high heat, stirring occasionally so the pasta doesn't stick, until al dente. Saving the cooking water, drain the pasta without rinsing and transfer to the casserole.

4. Toss the guanciale and spaghetti together over low heat. Stir in the frothy egg whites while beating furiously to mix well. Add the 2 egg yolks and do the same. Now stir in the 2 remaining eggs, stirring vigorously. Add 2 or 3 ladlefuls of the pasta cooking water (about 1 cup) to make the sauce thinner. Toss in half of the remaining cheeses. Serve in individual serving bowls with the remaining cheeses.

Lasagnette with Mascarpone Cheese

LASAGNETTE IS A FLAT PASTA about ¾ inch wide with a ruffled edge and is usually found in Italian markets. Cooks like this pasta because of its chewy texture and full body. If you can't find it, buy some no-boil (instant) lasagne and soak it in boiling water until softened, then cut lengthwise into ¾-inch strips. This preparation is creamy, cheesy, and delicious.

Makes 4 servings

12 ounces lasagnette or no-boil lasagne

2 large egg yolks

3 tablespoons extra-virgin olive oil

½ cup mascarpone cheese

Salt and freshly ground black pepper to taste

½ cup freshly grated Parmesan cheese (preferably Parmigiano-Reggiano cheese)

1. If you have not found lasagnette in the store, prepare the no-boil lasagne by boiling it until pliable, about 2 minutes. Drain and cut into ¾-inch-wide strips.

2. In a bowl, place the egg yolks and slowly beat in the olive oil in a very thin stream, beating all the time as you would for making a mayonnaise. Stir in the mascarpone a little at a time and season with salt and pepper.

3. Bring 6 quarts of water to a rolling boil over high heat, salt abundantly, then add the pasta. Cook over high heat, stirring occasionally so the pasta doesn't stick, until al dente. Drain without rinsing and transfer to a serving bowl or platter and cover with the sauce. Toss well and sprinkle on the Parmesan cheese.

Baked Rigatoni with Broccoli

Salt, as needed

8 ounces rigatoni

1¼ pounds broccoli, stems and florets separated

3 tablespoons unsalted butter, plus more for greasing the casserole

3 tablespoons all-purpose flour

2 cups hot whole milk

¾ cup freshly grated Parmesan cheese

Freshly ground black pepper to taste

¼ teaspoon cayenne pepper

8 ounces mozzarella cheese, diced

¼ cup dried bread crumbs

Extra-virgin olive oil, for greasing and drizzling

THIS RECIPE IS A FAVORITE in our family because not only does it taste good but it is also easy on the cook. You can cook the broccoli and rigatoni in the same water and prepare the whole casserole hours before you bake it. *Makes 4 servings*

1. Preheat the oven to 400°F.

2. Bring 6 quarts of water to a rolling boil over high heat, salt abundantly, then add the rigatoni and cook for 6 minutes. Add the broccoli stems to the pot with the pasta, cook for 2 minutes, then add the broccoli florets, and cook until tender, about 5 minutes longer. Never cook broccoli more than 7 minutes. Drain and transfer the pasta and broccoli to a bowl.

3. Meanwhile, in a saucepan, melt the butter over medium heat, then add the flour to form a roux and cook, stirring, for 2 minutes. Remove the saucepan from the heat and pour the milk in slowly, stirring or whisking all the time. Return to the burner, add the Parmesan cheese, and cook until thicker, about 10 minutes. Season with salt, pepper, and the cayenne.

4. Add the mozzarella and half of the white sauce to the bowl with the rigatoni and toss. Butter a 10-inch baking casserole, add the rigatoni, and spread out evenly. Spoon the remaining white sauce on top, sprinkle with the bread crumbs, drizzle with a little olive oil, and bake until golden and crispy on top, about 20 minutes.

Cannelloni Sorrento

CANNELLONI ARE SHEETS of pasta dough rolled up and stuffed with a filling and are typical in the Naples region. Once Italian immigrants began settling in America, they came to call them manicotti, and that's the name I grew up on when we had them in New York. In the old days, home cooks made their own cannelloni, but today they are store-bought dried and pre-shaped. The word *cannelloni* derives from the Italian word for cane, as in bamboo cane or sugar cane. *Manicotti* derives from the Italian word for "muff"—that is, a hand-warmer. The first mention of cannelloni is in an Italian domestic vocabulary from 1851, but they probably existed before then. This preparation is called *cannelloni alla sorrentina* or *cannelloni alla partenopea*, Partenopea being the ancient name for Naples. In fact, it is truly a gem of Neapolitan cooking, a rich and baroque dish that has been an Italian family favorite for years. They also made their ragù with a larded piece of beef or pork. Few people have larded a piece of meat, so I will devote a little bit of attention to this process. Beef is larded when it is tough and lacking the kind of fat and connective tissue that makes for a tasty morsel. Normally, long cooking will make it tender, but in some cases one wants the beef to take on more flavor. This recipe is such a case. The ragù is an important element in this recipe, and you can enrich it by using beef broth whenever water is called for. This recipe is an all-day affair, so it's best to relax, put on some music, and occupy yourself on a cold miserable day with some lovely aromas and taste. *Makes 6 to 8 servings*

For larding the beef

One 3½-ounce slice prosciutto, cut into strips

One 2-ounce slice pancetta, cut into strips

10 sprigs fresh flat-leaf parsley

One 3-pound piece beef chuck

Freshly ground black pepper to taste

For the ragù

¼ cup extra-virgin olive oil

¼ cup pork lard or unsalted butter

1 medium onion, chopped

3⅓ ounces pancetta, chopped

1 large garlic clove, finely chopped

2 cups tomato purée

1¼ cups dry red wine

¼ cup tomato paste

Water, as needed

Salt to taste

(continued)

For the stuffing

12 ounces ricotta
cheese (page 65)

2 large eggs

1¼ cups freshly grated
Parmesan cheese
(3½ ounces)

Salt and freshly ground
black pepper to taste

¼ cup finely chopped
fresh flat-leaf parsley

2½ ounces prosciutto,
chopped

8 ounces fresh
mozzarella, diced

20 manicotti or
cannelloni shells

For the béchamel

3 tablespoons
unsalted butter

3 tablespoons all-
purpose flour

2 cups hot milk

Salt and freshly ground
white pepper to taste

Pinch of ground nutmeg

1¾ cups freshly grated
Parmesan cheese
(about 5 ounces)

1. There are two ways one can lard a piece of beef. The first requires a larding needle. As so few people have a larding needle, I will provide alternative directions in a moment. Open the larding needle and secure to it strips of prosciutto, pancetta, and parsley. Make an incision in the beef with a long skewer or filleting knife, pushing all the way through so that the larding needle will not meet any resistance. Push the larding needle into the hole made by the skewer and push all the way through the beef, repeating the process in about 4 different places. Once the larding needle has punctured the entire piece of beef, the catch will release and the fat strips will stay in place inside the beef.

If you do not have a larding needle, you can use one of two methods: First, make very long, deep incisions in the beef using a narrow filleting knife and widen the hole using the handle end of a wooden stirring spoon and then stuff the strips of pancetta, prosciutto, and parsley into the holes, using the handle end of the wooden spoon or your finger to push them in. Or second, make 4 long slashes through the beef, stuff them with the strips of pancetta, prosciutto, and parsley, then close them up and tie off with 4 separate lengths of kitchen twine to reform the beef to its original shape. Sprinkle the meat with pepper.

2. For the ragù, in a large flameproof casserole, heat the olive oil over medium-low heat with the pork lard. Add the onion, pancetta, and garlic, and once the lard melts, add the beef. Once the beef has browned, turning once or twice, and the onions are softened, about 30 minutes, add the tomato purée and half the wine, stir, reduce the heat to low, partially cover, and simmer for 2 hours.

3. Add 2 tablespoons tomato paste mixed with ¼ cup water to the casserole. Continue cooking, stirring occasionally, until the sauce is quite dark, about 1 hour. Add the remaining 2 tablespoons tomato paste mixed with ¼ cup water and continue cooking for another 2 hours. Add the remaining red wine and cook for

2 hours. The beef will be completely tender and the ragù thick. If it is too thick, add a little water. Season with salt. Remove the beef, which you can serve as a second course.

4. Meanwhile, for the stuffing, in a bowl, mix together the ricotta and eggs with a fork until smooth. Add the Parmesan cheese and season with salt and pepper. Stir in the parsley. Add the prosciutto and mozzarella and mix well.

5. Bring 6 quarts of water to a rolling boil over high heat, salt abundantly, then add the cannelloni. Cook over high heat, stirring occasionally so the pasta doesn't stick, until half cooked, about 4 minutes. Drain and immediately plunge into a bowl of ice cold water and leave them there until you stuff them.

6. Preheat the oven to 350°F.

7. Spread some ragù on the bottom of two 12 × 9-inch baking casseroles. Stuff the cheese stuffing into a large pastry bag fitted with a ½-inch nozzle and squeeze into the cannelloni. Lay the cannelloni in the casserole in one layer and cover with spoonfuls of ragù.

8. To prepare the béchamel sauce, in a medium saucepan, melt the butter over medium heat, then stir in the flour to form a roux, cooking for 1 minute while stirring. Remove the saucepan from the heat and whisk in the milk a little at a time until it is all blended. Sprinkle with salt and pepper and the nutmeg. Return to the heat and cook, stirring almost constantly, until thick, 10 minutes. Stir in the Parmesan cheese and cook until the cheese melts, about 3 minutes. Spoon the béchamel sauce over the ragù on top of the cannelloni.

9. Bake the cannelloni until bubbling and lightly browned on top, 40 to 45 minutes. Remove from the oven and serve hot.

Cannelloni with Meat and Swiss Chard

6 tablespoons extra-virgin olive oil

12 ounces finely chopped (not ground) beef sirloin (such as rib eye)

3 large garlic cloves, finely chopped

One 28-ounce can whole plum tomatoes, chopped, liquid saved

1 sprig fresh basil

1 bay leaf

1 teaspoon sugar

Salt and freshly ground black pepper to taste

22 to 24 manicotti or cannelloni shells (about 12 ounces)

1 pound Swiss chard leaves

½ cup chopped fresh flat-leaf parsley

3 tablespoons unsalted butter

3 tablespoons all-purpose flour

1½ cups whole milk

3 cups freshly grated Parmesan (preferably, Parmigiano-Reggiano) cheese (about 5 ounces)

THE CORSICAN NAME of this dish, *pienu di canniloni*, means "stuffed cannelloni"; cannelloni is a pasta made from a flour-and-egg dough that's formed into large tubes and sold commercially in supermarkets as manicotti. Although Corsica is a province of France, the Italian culinary influence is greater there than the French influence. *Makes 6 servings*

1. In a skillet, heat 3 tablespoons of the olive oil over high heat, then cook the beef, stirring occasionally, until it turns color, 2 to 3 minutes. Transfer to a large bowl.

2. In the same skillet, heat the remaining 3 tablespoons olive oil over medium-high heat with 2 of the garlic cloves. When it begins to sizzle, add the tomatoes and their liquid, the basil, bay leaf, and sugar. Reduce the heat to medium and cook, stirring, until denser, about 20 minutes. Season with salt and pepper.

3. Meanwhile, preheat the oven to 350°F.

4. Bring a large pot of abundantly salted water to a vigorous boil, then drop the manicotti in and cook until almost al dente, stirring occasionally to keep them separate. Drain without discarding the water. Keep the parboiled manicotti in a bowl of cold water until needed.

5. Let the pasta water return to a boil over high heat, then add the Swiss chard and cook until it wilts, about 5 minutes. Drain very well, squeezing out as much liquid as possible. Chop the Swiss chard with the parsley and the remaining garlic clove and mix with the beef.

6. In a saucepan, melt the butter over medium heat, then add the flour to form a roux and cook, stirring, for 2 minutes. Remove the saucepan from the heat and add the milk gradually, whisking it in until blended. Return the saucepan to the heat and cook over medium-low heat, stirring occasionally, until it thickens, about 15 minutes. Stir into the meat and Swiss chard.

7. Arrange the manicotti shells in paper towels or a clean kitchen towel to dry a bit. Stuff each shell with the stuffing and arrange in two oiled 12 × 9-inch baking casseroles. Spoon the tomato sauce over each casserole, then sprinkle on the cheese and bake until the cheese is dappled black, about 25 minutes.

Fettuccine with Lamb and Greek Cheese

12 ounces boneless lamb ribs or leg

Salt, as needed

8 ounces fettuccine

3 tablespoons extra-virgin olive oil

3 large garlic cloves, finely chopped

Freshly ground black pepper to taste

4 ounces kefalotyri or kasseri cheese, grated

¼ cup finely chopped fresh mint

ALTHOUGH THIS IS A TYPICAL Greek family dinner that uses leftover roast lamb, I like it so much that I just go ahead and make it whenever I have the hankering for a luscious and easy dinner. Kefalotyri cheese is a hard sheep's milk cheese that grates and melts well. It's hard to find in this country, so I buy mine at www.igourmet.com or www.christosmarket.com. Two other Greek cheeses, kasseri and mizithra, can also be used, and they are often found in supermarkets these days and certainly in Greek grocery stores. If you can't find any of them, use ricotta salata or young pecorino.   *Makes 4 servings*

1. Preheat a large cast-iron skillet over high heat for 10 minutes.

2. Add the lamb and cook, turning once, until crispy dark golden brown on both sides, 8 minutes in all. Reduce the heat to low and cook the lamb until rare, 4 to 5 minutes. Transfer the meat to a cutting board and let rest for 5 minutes. Slice into julienne strips.

3. Meanwhile, bring 6 quarts of water to a rolling boil over high heat, salt abundantly, then add the pasta. Cook over high heat, stirring occasionally so the pasta doesn't stick, until al dente. Drain without rinsing.

4. Meanwhile, in the cast-iron skillet you used before, heat the olive oil over medium heat with the garlic, and once it's been sizzling for a few seconds, add the lamb and cook for 1 minute. Season with salt and pepper. Then add the pasta and cook for 2 minutes while tossing. Add the cheese and mint and toss again until well coated. Serve hot.

Tossed Lasagne with Chile and Cheese

YOU CAN USE ANY THREE CHEESES you want in this dish and not necessarily the ones I call for, though the taste will change. This dish requires thin lasagne noodles, sometimes called no-boil or instant lasagne, that you will break in half to have squares. The chiles are blistered and then tossed with the pasta and the cheeses with some of the pasta cooking water, which will create the sauce to make the cheese blend well. This is a preparation that disappears quickly and is loved by those who like the piquancy of mild and hot chiles.

Makes 4 to 6 servings

2 fresh poblano chiles

2 fresh New Mexico (also called Anaheim or Hatch) chiles or Italian long (frying) peppers

3 fresh jalapeño chiles

1 fresh habanero chile

Salt, as needed

8 ounces no-boil thin lasagne, broken in half

4 tablespoons unsalted butter

1½ cups shredded raclette cheese (about 4 ounces)

1½ cups shredded provolone cheese (about 4 ounces)

1½ cups shredded kasseri cheese (about 4 ounces)

Freshly ground black pepper to taste

1. Place the chiles on a wire rack over a burner on high heat and roast until their skins blister black on all sides, turning occasionally with tongs. Remove the chiles and place in a paper or heavy plastic bag to steam for 20 minutes, which will make peeling them easier. When cool enough to handle, rub off as much blackened peel as you can (except for the habanero, which does not need to be peeled) and remove the seeds by rubbing with a paper towel (to avoid washing away flavorful juices) or by rinsing under running water (to remove more easily). The chiles can also be roasted on a grill. Cut the chiles into thin strips.

2. Bring 6 quarts of water to a rolling boil over high heat, salt abundantly, then add the pasta. Cook over high heat, stirring occasionally so the pasta doesn't stick, until al dente. Drain without rinsing, saving ¾ cup of the cooking water.

3. Add the butter to the empty pasta pot (take out the strainer insert if it has one) and melt over medium heat. Add the lasagne squares, cheeses, chiles, black pepper, and cooking water and cook, tossing and stirring constantly, until the cheese melts and blends and become saucy. Serve immediately.

Spaghetti with Fresh Chiles

Salt, as needed

12 ounces spaghetti

¼ cup extra-virgin olive oil

2 fresh green jalapeño chiles, seeded and finely chopped

2 fresh green serrano chiles, seeded and finely chopped

4 fresh red finger-type chiles, seeded and finely chopped

2 large garlic cloves, finely chopped

2 tablespoons unsalted butter

1½ cups freshly grated Parmesan cheese (about 3 ounces)

THIS CHILE-LOVER'S DISH is what they call a *spaghettata* in Italian cuisine, a simple and quick pasta dish that can be whipped up at the last minute late at night when you've come back from the theater or a movie and are a little hungry, although this recipe is not an Italian one per se; it's more typical of a California dish. Ideally, you'll want to use piquant chiles that are both red and green, but use what's available.

Makes 4 servings

1. Bring 5 quarts of water to a rolling boil over high heat, salt abundantly, then add the pasta. Cook over high heat, stirring occasionally so the pasta doesn't stick, until al dente. Drain without rinsing.

2. Meanwhile, in a skillet, heat the olive oil with the chiles and garlic over medium-high heat and cook until it has been sizzling for 2 minutes. Turn the heat off and add the pasta, tossing well. Add the butter and cheese and toss until they melt. Serve hot.

TOMATO SAUCE

This basic tomato sauce can be used whenever a recipe calls for tomato sauce. Normally, I make three times the amount called for in this recipe. Although fresh, vine-ripened tomatoes are best, canned whole or crushed tomatoes, tomato paste, and tomato purée are fine to use when tomatoes are not in season—just not the canned "tomato sauce." Cooks seem to make a simple tomato sauce in two ways, with onions or without and with chopped garlic or whole. It's your choice.

Makes 3 cups

¼ cup extra-virgin olive oil
3 large garlic cloves, finely chopped or lightly crushed
1 medium onion, finely chopped (optional)
2 pounds ripe plum tomatoes, cut in half, seeds squeezed out, and grated
    against the largest holes of a box grater down to the peel
6 large fresh basil leaves
Salt and freshly ground black pepper to taste

In a deep saucepan, heat the olive oil over medium-high heat. Add the garlic and cook until it begins to sizzle in less than a minute, or, if using lightly crushed garlic, until it begins to turn light brown, about 1 minute. Remove and discard the crushed garlic, but leave the chopped garlic, and add the onion, if using. Cook the onion, stirring frequently, until translucent, 5 to 6 minutes. Add the tomatoes and basil, and season with salt and pepper. Cook until dense, 15 to 25 minutes, uncovered, reducing the heat if it is sputtering too much. Stir occasionally with a long wooden spoon so the bottom doesn't burn, and add small amounts of water if necessary.

Spinach Pasta Roll with Ricotta

For the pasta

3 cups all-purpose flour

3 large eggs

1 teaspoon salt

For the stuffing

2 pounds spinach

1 pound ricotta
cheese (page 65)

Salt and freshly ground
black pepper to taste

For serving

3 cups Tomato
Sauce (page 235)

2 cups freshly grated
pecorino cheese

ALTHOUGH THIS RECIPE INVOLVES a bit of preparation, you will not only impress guests but if you're lucky will also have leftovers, which make a great lunch. This recipe, called *rotolo di spinaci e ricotta*, is one from Miramontes restaurant in Fonni, in the Nuoro province of Sardinia.

Makes 6 servings

1. For the pasta, pour the flour onto a work surface. Make a well in the middle, forming the walls like the lip of a volcano crater. Break the eggs into the well and sprinkle with the salt. Break the yolks with your fingers and begin to incorporate the eggs with the flour, a little at a time, with your fingers, drawing more flour from the inside wall of the well. Make sure you don't break through the wall; otherwise the eggs will run. Scrape any dough off your fingers and knead it into the dough.

2. Once the flour and eggs are combined and you can form it into a ball, knead for about 8 minutes, until you can form a smooth ball. As you press down while kneading, use the ball to pick up any clumps of dough. Knead for at least 3 minutes before you decide you need more liquid. If the ball of dough is not forming you can add some water. Do so by wetting your hands only, as many times as you need. If the dough is too wet, meaning if there is any sign of stickiness, dust with flour. Continue kneading, pressing down with the full force of both palms, until a smooth ball is formed. Wrap the dough in wax paper or plastic wrap and leave for 30 minutes to 1 hour at room temperature.

3. For the stuffing, steam the spinach with the water adhering to it from its last rinsing in a large pot over medium-high heat, covered, until it wilts, about 5 minutes. Remove and drain well in a colander, squeezing excess water out by pressing with the back of a wooden spoon. Squeeze more water out of the spinach once it has cooled by squeezing like a snowball. Chop and toss in a bowl with the ricotta and eggs. Season with salt and pepper.

4. On a wide, clear and uncluttered surface, roll the pasta out with a rolling pin until it is a thin 24 × 14-inch sheet. Place the spinach mixture in the center and spread it with a spatula to cover the whole sheet, but not too near the edges. Roll the pasta sheet up as tightly as you can and place it on a large section of cheesecloth. Wrap up in the cheesecloth and tie off the ends and two places in the middle.

5. Bring a large pot of water to a rolling boil over high heat, salt abundantly, and slide the cheesecloth-wrapped rolled pasta into the water and boil for 35 minutes. Remove from the water, remove the cheesecloth, and slice the rolled pasta. Serve with tomato sauce and pecorino cheese.

Cheese Ravioli with Broccoli and Gorgonzola Sauce

Salt, as needed

10 ounces cheese ravioli

6 ounces broccoli crowns, florets separated

1½ tablespoons unsalted butter

2½ ounces Gorgonzola cheese

5 tablespoons crème fraîche

Freshly ground black pepper to taste

1½ ounces freshly and finely grated Parmesan cheese

YOU CAN BUY STORE-BOUGHT ravioli for this preparation, although making your own is such a nice treat. The preparation is quite simple, as you will cook the broccoli and ravioli together and in the meantime heat the cheese sauce ingredients together until they melt. The broccoli crown is that part of a whole broccoli without the stem. See page 239 for making your own ravioli.

Makes 3 servings

1. Bring a large pot of water to a vigorous boil over high heat, salt abundantly, then add the ravioli and broccoli together and cook until tender, 6 to 7 minutes. Drain without rinsing and toss with the butter.

2. Meanwhile, in a small skillet or saucepan, heat the Gorgonzola cheese and crème fraîche. Season with salt and black pepper and cook until smooth. Toss with the cooked ravioli and Parmesan cheese and serve hot.

Homemade Cheese Ravioli with Butter and Sage

MANY YEARS AGO my youngest son, Seri, fell in love with homemade ravioli and insists on it for his birthday every year. Although this magnificent ravioli dish was actually thought up by Seri for his fifteenth birthday, I recognized it as a dish from the Abruzzo region of Italy. In Italian, I suppose it would be called by the fancy name *ravioli di ricotta e scamorza Abruzzeze con burro promufato alla salvia e con parmigiano*, which means "ravioli stuffed with fresh ricotta and scamorza with sage-infused butter and Parmigiano cheese." The dish is also called *ravioli all'Aquilana* or *gravioli*, and it can be drizzled with some juices from a roasting lamb and a sprinkle of ground red chile. For this recipe, I cooked some broccoli florets with the ravioli. This recipe is for a big party of friends or family. It's labor-intensive but fun. You will need a hand-crank or electric pasta roller and, preferably, a ravioli mold.

Makes about 160 ravioli (about 5 pounds) to serve 12

1. To prepare the ravioli dough, pour the flour onto a surface. Make a well in the middle, piling up the flour around it so that it resembles the walls of a volcanic crater. Crack the eggs into the well and sprinkle with the olive oil and salt. Incorporate the eggs with the flour by breaking the yolks with your fingers a little at a time, drawing more flour from the inside wall of the well. Make sure you don't break through the wall; otherwise the eggs might run. Scrape any dough off your fingers and knead it into the dough. *(continued)*

For the ravioli

8 cups unbleached all-purpose flour

8 large eggs

2 tablespoons extra-virgin olive oil

2 teaspoons salt

For the stuffing

2 pounds ricotta cheese (page 65)

8 ounces scamorza cheese, finely diced

2 large eggs

¼ teaspoon freshly ground nutmeg

2 teaspoons salt

For the dressing

6 tablespoons unsalted butter

12 large fresh sage leaves, chopped

2 pounds broccoli, florets only

Freshly grated Parmesan cheese (preferably Parmigiano-Reggiano cheese), for serving

2. Once the flour and eggs are combined and you can form the dough into a ball, knead for 8 to 10 minutes. Do not add water unless the dough is impossible to form into a ball after a minute or two of trying. As you press down while kneading, use the ball to pick up any loose clumps of dough. Don't add any liquid until you've kneaded the ball for at least 3 minutes. If the dough is too dry at this point and you must add water to help it bind, do so only by wetting your hands, as many times as you need. If the dough is too wet—meaning if there is any sign of stickiness—dust with flour. Continue kneading, pressing down with the full force of both palms, until a smooth ball is formed. Wrap the dough in wax paper or plastic wrap and leave for 1 hour at room temperature.

3. Unwrap the ball of dough and dust with flour. Place on a floured surface, pressing down with your palms to flatten. With a rolling pin, roll the pasta out until it is about 12 inches in diameter and cut into thirds. Roll each third with the rolling pin until it is thin enough to fit into the widest setting of a pasta-rolling machine. Roll once at the widest setting. Close the setting one notch and roll again. Gather the sheet of pasta and fold in thirds and roll through the roller so you have a nice rectangle. Continue ratcheting down the setting until the dough reaches the thinnest setting. Dust the dough on both sides with flour at the slightest sign of stickiness. If necessary, continue to dust with flour as you roll through narrower and narrower settings; otherwise the dough will become hopelessly stuck together. By this time you will have a very long, thin ribbon of pliable dough that looks and even feels like a velvety chamois cloth. You can use it at this stage for lasagne if you want.

Cut the ribbon of pasta into lengths that will fit over the ravioli-maker, if using one, always dusting with flour at any sign of stickiness. Or lay a length of thin pasta dough on the counter with another equal length nearby.

4. For the stuffing, in a large bowl, mix together the ricotta, scamorza, eggs, nutmeg, and salt until well blended.

5. Arrange a sheet of pasta over an indented ravioli mold and press the dough down into the wells. Place teaspoonfuls of the stuffing in the ravioli. Lay a sheet of pasta over the stuffing and, with a roller, press down hard to seal the two sheets. Carefully turn the ravioli maker upside down and peel the ravioli out, arranging them on a large floured baking sheet while you continue the preparation. Place the tray in the freezer while you continue preparing the remaining ravioli. As the ravioli freeze—and make sure they are completely frozen before storing—transfer them to a gallon-size plastic zip-top bag and keep frozen unless you intend on cooking them that day. If the latter, let the ravioli dry on a large kitchen or dining room table covered with a sheet or tablecloth, making sure they don't overlap. (The reason to transfer the frozen ravioli from the tray to the freezer bag is to free up space in your freezer.)

If you don't have a ravioli mold, lay a sheet of pasta down on a surface and place teaspoon-size dollops of stuffing side by side (assuming the sheet of pasta from your machine is at least 4 inches wide) all along its length. Drape the other equal-size sheet of pasta over the bottom sheet and carefully press down so that you can cut through them easily. Using a pastry wheel, cut the ravioli into individual pieces. Dust with flour and arrange on a baking tray in the refrigerator until needed.

6. In a small saucepan, melt the butter with the sage over low heat.

7. Meanwhile, bring a large pot of abundantly salted water to a vigorous boil and add the frozen ravioli. After the water returns to a boil, add the broccoli and cook until the ravioli have puffed up and are floating on the surface, 8 to 10 minutes. Drain well and toss with the melted sage butter and Parmesan cheese. Serve with more Parmesan to be passed at the table.

Tortellini with Bleu d'Auvergne Sauce

Salt, as needed

Two 9-ounce packages fresh cheese tortellini

2 tablespoons unsalted butter

6 ounces Bleu d'Auvergne cheese

3 ounces mascarpone cheese

2 tablespoons finely chopped fresh flat-leaf parsley

Freshly grated Parmesan cheese, if desired, for serving

THIS IS A VERY SIMPLE RECIPE with the Roquefort-like cheese from France called Bleu d'Auvergne. Many supermarkets carry it under the President label. Bleu d'Auvergne is a recent cheese, invented in the mid-nineteenth century, so the story goes, when a farmer from the Auvergne sprinkled mold from rye bread on his milk curd and then pierced the curd with a needle. This allowed the air through, and the curd developed blue veins. The smell is strong and the taste is pastoral and pungent. In this recipe, it is calmed down with a little mascarpone cheese for a delightful pasta dish. Store-bought cheese tortellini is fine to use. *Makes 4 servings*

1. Bring 6 quarts of water to a rolling boil over high heat, salt abundantly using 4 to 6 tablespoons salt, then add the tortellini. Cook over high heat, stirring occasionally so the tortellini doesn't stick, until tender, about 8 minutes.

2. Meanwhile, in a large skillet, melt the butter over low heat with the blue cheese, mascarpone, and parsley. Before the cheeses are melted, drain and transfer the cooked tortellini to the skillet with whatever water adheres to them and simmer gently until all the cheeses have melted, about 4 minutes. Serve with Parmesan, if desired.

Lasagne with Mozzarella

THIS LASAGNE is a popular dish among housewives in Naples, as it's easy to make. It's a *lasagne in bianco*, an all-white free-form lasagne made with fresh mozzarella and freshly grated Parmigiano-Reggiano cheese. It can be made spicier by a liberal hand with the black pepper. It has a pizza equivalent, *pizza bianca*, made without tomatoes. ***Makes 4 to 6 servings***

Salt, as needed

1 pound lasagne

8 tablespoons (1 stick) unsalted butter

8 salted anchovy fillets, rinsed

8 ounces fresh mozzarella cheese, cut into tiny dice

Freshly ground black pepper to taste

½ cup freshly grated Parmesan cheese (preferably Parmigiano-Reggiano cheese)

1. Bring a large pot of water to a rolling boil. Salt abundantly and drop the lasagne in gradually, stirring to keep the sheets from sticking to each other. Drain the lasagne when al dente and pat dry with paper towels before using.

2. Meanwhile, melt the butter in a large skillet over medium heat and add the anchovies. Mash the anchovies with the back of a wooden spoon, and once they have melted, reduce the heat to very low.

3. Add the lasagne to the skillet, tossing gently but well. Add the mozzarella, making sure it doesn't clump, and continue tossing. When the mozzarella begins to get stringy, season with pepper to taste and sprinkle with the Parmesan cheese. Continue tossing gently. Transfer to a serving platter, sprinkle with a bit more black pepper, and serve.

Green Lasagne with Four Cheeses

4 cups thick Béchamel Sauce (page 53)

¼ cup grated or finely chopped Fontina Val d'Aosta cheese (about 1 ounce)

¼ cup finely diced fresh mozzarella cheese (about 1 ounce)

¼ cup freshly grated pecorino cheese (about 1 ounce)

6 tablespoons freshly grated Parmesan cheese (preferably Parmigiano-Reggiano cheese)

1 large garlic clove, lightly crushed

Salt, as needed

1 pound spinach (green) lasagne

3 tablespoons unsalted butter

THIS PRETTY green and white lasagne, called *lasagne verde con quattro formaggi* in Italian, is made with a white béchamel sauce instead of tomatoes, and with four cheeses: fontina, mozzarella, pecorino, and Parmesan. If using no-boil (instant) lasagne, skip step 2.

Makes 6 servings

1. Put the béchamel sauce in a large saucepan, then stir into it the fontina, mozzarella, pecorino, 4 tablespoons of the Parmesan, and the garlic. Continue stirring over medium-low heat until the cheeses are blended. Remove and discard the garlic if desired.

2. Preheat the oven to 400°F.

3. Bring a large pot of water to a rolling boil. Salt abundantly and drop the lasagne in gradually. Drain when al dente and transfer to a pot of cold water until needed. Dry the lasagne with paper towels before using.

4. Butter a deep lasagne pan or a large baking casserole. Spread a layer of lasagne sheets on the bottom and then spoon over some sauce. Make 4 layers in all, finishing with a layer of sauce. Dot the top with the remaining butter, sprinkle the remaining Parmesan cheese on top, and bake until light golden brown, 30 to 35 minutes.

Rich Green Lasagne with Fondue

THIS SIMPLE RECIPE from the Piedmont region of Italy is, basically, fondue on lasagne. Fondue is popular not only in Switzerland but also in Alpine Italy, where they use Fontina Val d'Aosta for an amazing dressing for pasta as well as for a traditional bread-dunked fondue. To make your own green lasagne, follow steps 1 and 2 and the first paragraph of step 3 on pages 239–240, adding 8 ounces of cooked chopped spinach in step 1.

Makes 4 servings

1 cup whole milk

5 ounces fresh mozzarella cheese, diced

5 ounces Fontina Val d'Aosta cheese, diced

¼ cup heavy cream

Salt and freshly ground black pepper to taste

1 pound spinach (green) lasagne

3 tablespoons unsalted butter, melted

1. Preheat the oven to 400°F.

2. In a double boiler, heat the milk over medium-high heat. Add the cheeses and stir in a figure-8 motion until melted. Add the cream and continue stirring until the fondue is denser, about 5 minutes. Season with salt and pepper.

3. Bring a large pot of water to a rolling boil. Salt abundantly and drop the lasagne in gradually, stirring to keep it from sticking. Drain the lasagne when al dente and pat dry with paper towels. Toss the lasagne with the butter and cover the bottom of a buttered lasagne pan with a layer of lasagne. Pour some sauce on top and then add more lasagne, making 3 layers in all, finishing with a layer of sauce. Bake the lasagne, uncovered, until golden brown, 20 to 25 minutes.

Lasagne with Ricotta

¼ cup extra-virgin olive oil

1 large garlic clove, crushed

8 ounces mild Italian sausage, removed from the casing and crumbled

4 ounces pork tenderloin, very finely chopped

½ cup dry red wine

4 tablespoons tomato paste

½ cup tepid water

Salt and freshly ground black pepper to taste

12 large fresh basil leaves

1 pound lasagne

1 cup ricotta cheese (page 65)

6 tablespoons hot milk

Olive oil, for greasing the pan

1 cup freshly grated pecorino cheese

1 cup freshly grated Parmesan cheese (preferably Parmigiano-Reggiano cheese)

BECAUSE THE STAR of this rich and delicious lasagne is the ricotta cheese, I suggest only fresh ricotta, which you can make yourself or buy at a good Italian market. Supermarket-style ricotta cheese doesn't have the required consistency and taste to make this dish spectacular. See page 65 for how to make your own ricotta cheese. *Makes 6 to 8 servings*

1. In a large skillet, heat the olive oil over medium heat, then add the garlic clove and cook until it begins to turn light brown. Remove and discard the garlic. Add the sausage meat to the skillet and cook, breaking it up with a wooden spoon, for about 4 minutes. Add the pork tenderloin and continue cooking for another 4 minutes, stirring occasionally.

2. Pour in the red wine and cook until it is almost evaporated, about 12 minutes. Dilute the tomato paste with the tepid water and stir into the pan. Reduce the heat to low, season with salt and pepper, cover, and cook until the sauce is thick, about 20 minutes. Turn the heat off and stir in the basil.

3. Preheat the oven to 350°F.

4. Bring a large pot of water to a rolling boil. Salt abundantly and drop the lasagne in gradually. Drain when half cooked and transfer to a pot of cold water until needed. Dry the lasagne with paper towels before using. (Skip this step if using homemade fresh lasagne or no-boil lasagne, in which case you'll simply layer the fresh or no-boil lasagne without any precooking.)

5. Stir the ricotta and hot milk together until the mixture is smooth and creamy. Oil a lasagne pan and cover the bottom with a layer of lasagne. Cover with a layer of ricotta and then a sprinkle of pecorino and Parmesan. Spoon some meat sauce over the grated cheese and continue in this order, finishing with a layer of lasagne. Spoon some meat sauce on top. Cover with a tented piece of aluminum foil and bake for 30 minutes. Serve hot or let cool, cover tightly, and freeze or refrigerate.

Lasagne with Walnuts and Three Cheeses

Salt, as needed

1 pound lasagne
ricce or lasagne

4 ounces Gorgonzola cheese,
at room temperature

4 ounces mascarpone cheese,
at room temperature

⅔ cup freshly grated
Parmesan cheese

1 cup finely ground walnuts

ALTHOUGH THIS IS A RICH and extremely satisfying preparation, it is usually served as a pasta first course followed by something lighter. It's exceedingly simple to make, although it's important to save a little of the pasta cooking water to use to thin the sauce if required. Typically, a ruffle-edged lasagne called *lasagne ricce* is used. *Makes 4 to 6 servings*

1. Bring 6 quarts of water to a rolling boil over high heat in a large pot. Salt abundantly and drop the pasta in gradually. Stir as it cooks so the lasagne does not stick together. Drain the lasagne when al dente, reserving some of the pasta cooking water.

2. Meanwhile, beat together the Gorgonzola, mascarpone, Parmesan, and walnuts in a large bowl. Toss the pasta with the cheese and nut mixture, adding some pasta water to make it saucier. Serve hot.

Macaroni and Cheese Pie

AROUND THE TOWN of Modica in Sicily's rugged interior, housewives typically make this simple, all-homemade baked macaroni preparation called *pasticcio di ricotta* for Christmas dinner. Sicilian homes to this day have resisted processed foods, and one will find more homemade foods, such as the macaroni, sausage, and ricotta cheese used in this recipe, than in the rest of Italy. If you have an extrusion pasta machine and sausage-stuffing equipment, then I highly recommend you give homemade a try. If that amount of work doesn't appeal to you, then use store-bought fresh tubular macaroni or, lacking that, dried macaroni or ziti. *Makes 6 servings*

Salt, as needed

1 pound fresh macaroni or fresh ziti

3 tablespoons extra-virgin olive oil

1 pound mild Italian sausage, removed from the casing and crumbled

1 pound homemade ricotta cheese (page 65)

Freshly ground black pepper to taste

1. Preheat the oven to 350°F.

2. Bring a large pot of water to a rolling boil, salt abundantly, and add the pasta. Cook the macaroni until half cooked. Drain and toss with 2 tablespoons of the olive oil.

3. In a medium skillet, heat the remaining tablespoon olive oil and brown the sausage over medium-high heat until it loses its pink color, about 7 minutes, breaking the meat up further with a wooden spoon. Remove the sausage with a slotted spoon, squeezing out all fat with the back of the wooden spoon, and toss with the macaroni. Toss again with the ricotta and pepper.

4. Transfer the macaroni to a lightly greased earthenware (preferably) or other baking casserole. Bake until slightly crispy looking on some edges of the pasta, 20 minutes and serve.

Buckwheat Fettuccine with Savoy Cabbage and Taleggio Cheese

4 tablespoons unsalted butter

4 large fresh sage leaves

Salt, as needed

3 medium potatoes, peeled and cut into small dice

6 leaves savoy cabbage, shredded into ¼-inch-wide strips

1 pound buckwheat pasta

6 ounces Taleggio cheese, sliced

Freshly ground black pepper to taste

THIS DISH called *pizzoccheri della Valtellina*, is well known in the northern provinces of Lombardy but rarely seen outside them. So to find it served in a restaurant in Santa Monica, California, made me both joyous and very suspicious. The Locanda del Lago, though, prepared it superbly, and one can easily make this earthy, rib-sticking dish at home. Commercially made buckwheat pasta is a bit thick for my tastes, making it too pasty. I prefer homemade, although that is more work. The *pizzoccheri* is actually a fettuccine-like pasta made from buckwheat flour. You are likely to use the commercial product—found in Italian markets usually—and it will need to cook for 10 minutes. Some cooks add beets to this dish or make it with fontina cheese. The final preparation should be creamy, and that is accomplished with water and not cream, so follow the instructions. If you can't find buckwheat pasta you can use whole wheat pasta.

Makes 6 servings

1. In a small butter warmer or saucepan, melt the butter with the sage and keep warm. You can do this quickly in a microwave, too.

2. Bring a large pot of abundantly salted water to a rolling boil, then add the potatoes and cabbage and cook until al dente, about 4 minutes. Add the pasta and cook until it is al dente, about 10 minutes for commercial buckwheat pasta and 3 to 4 minutes for homemade rolled thin. Drain the pasta mixture without rinsing.

3. In a deep platter or baking dish, arrange a layer of cooked pasta mixture, then layer half of the Taleggio cheese on top with a sprinkle of the sage-flavored butter and a little black pepper. Add another layer of pasta and finally the last layer of Taleggio, butter, and black pepper. Let sit for about 3 minutes and then serve. If it is not "creamy," add ¼ to ½ cup water and toss.

Molded "Cheesed" Pasta

½ cup plus 2 tablespoons extra-virgin olive oil

3 pounds ripe tomatoes, peeled, seeded, and chopped

2 large garlic cloves, crushed

½ cup finely chopped fresh basil leaves

6 cups olive oil, for frying

3 pounds eggplant, sliced ⅜ inch thick

8 ounces ground beef

½ cup dry white wine

Salt, as needed

1¼ pounds macaroni

½ cup dried bread crumbs

1 cup very finely diced pecorino or caciocavallo cheese (about 3 ounces)

Freshly ground black pepper to taste

2 large eggs, hard-boiled, shelled, and sliced

8 ounces fresh mozzarella cheese, sliced

1 ounce soppressata or any other salami, chopped

1 ounce mortadella, chopped

Freshly grated pecorino cheese, for sprinkling

THIS CLASSIC BAKED PASTA DISH from Sicily is a preparation for a special occasion. Called *pasta 'ncaciata*, or "cheesed pasta," it's beautiful with a golden cheese crust of pecorino. There are variations on this theme, and one could find in place of the eggplant a variety of other ingredients such as broccoli, fennel sausage, red wine, pine nuts, and red chile flakes in other cooks' versions. Many people no longer bother with step 2 because eggplant grown in the United States rarely contains bitter liquid any more.

Makes 6 to 8 servings

1. In a large nonreactive casserole or skillet, heat ¼ cup of the extra-virgin olive oil over medium heat, then add the tomatoes, garlic cloves, and 2 tablespoons of the basil and cook, stirring, until the mixture is somewhat denser, about 20 minutes. Remove and discard the garlic. Remove and reserve ½ cup of tomato sauce for step 6.

2. Heat the frying oil in a deep-fryer or an 8-inch saucepan fitted with a basket insert to 360°F. Fry the eggplant slices in batches until brown, 3 to 4 minutes per side. Remove and drain on paper towels.

3. In a medium skillet, heat another ¼ cup of the extra-virgin olive oil over medium-high heat, then add the ground beef and cook, breaking it up with a wooden spoon or fork, until browned, 4 to 5 minutes. Pour in the wine and cook until it evaporates. Stir in ¼ cup of the tomato sauce from the casserole.

4. Preheat the oven to 400°F.

5. Meanwhile, bring a large pot of water to a rolling boil, salt abundantly, and add the macaroni. Drain when just past half cooked and toss with the tomato sauce in the casserole.

6. Coat a large and deep baking casserole with the remaining 2 tablespoons extra-virgin olive oil and sprinkle with the bread crumbs, shaking them around the pan so it is evenly covered. Pour in half of the sauced macaroni, then one-third of the diced pecorino, then all of the cooked beef, pepper to taste, half the fried eggplant, another one-third of the pecorino, the remaining 6 tablespoons basil, the sliced eggs, mozzarella, salami, mortadella, and the last one-third of the pecorino. Make a last layer of the remaining macaroni and eggplant. Spread the top with the ½ cup reserved tomato sauce and sprinkle grated pecorino on top. Bake until the cheese on top is golden brown, 30 to 40 minutes. Let it rest for 10 minutes and then serve.

Rice and Polenta
with Cheese

We don't often think of cheese with rice, but remember that nearly every risotto has cheese in it. Still the Risotto con Fonduta (page 259) is something else entirely, with its melted fontina cheese puddled in the middle of the rice. Polenta is also made with cheese in a variety of cultures, and the Swiss Polenta Casserole recipe on page 265 will be an enlightening favorite. When you decide on a real celebratory meal, you must make the Tummàla (page 260), a magnificent Sicilian feast preparation; although a Christmas specialty, Sicilian cooks prepare it for all sorts of grand celebrations. It's involved, but you will mightily pleased with the result.

Chenna Pulao

2 tablespoons clarified
butter (ghee; page 171)

2 ounces queso blanco,
queso ranchero, or
paneer cheese

2 cloves

Seeds from
2 cardamom pods

One 1-inch cinnamon stick

1 bay leaf

1¼ cups long-grain rice
(such as basmati), rinsed
or soaked in water for
30 minutes and drained well

Pinch of saffron soaked
in 2 teaspoons milk

1 teaspoon salt

2 cups hot water

THIS RICE DISH is Bengali-style basmati rice cooked with cottage cheese, called *chenna* in Bengali. Although recipe writers often translate *chenna* as "cottage cheese," a better cheese to use in this dish is the paneer cheese sold in markets such as Whole Foods or the Mexican queso blanco sold in supermarkets or Syrian white cheese sold in Middle Eastern markets. It's important that the cheese used is a non-melting cheese. It's the perfect accompaniment to Chicken Coconut Curry with Paneer Cheese (page 362). *Makes 4 servings*

1. In a heavy saucepan with a heavy lid, melt the clarified butter over medium heat. Add the cheese, cloves, cardamom seeds, cinnamon stick, and bay leaf and cook, stirring, until the cheese is golden, about 3 minutes.

2. Add the rice and cook, stirring, until it starts to stick, about 2 minutes. Add the saffron and milk, salt, and water. Bring to a boil over high heat, then reduce the heat to medium, cover, and cook until the rice is tender and the water is absorbed. Serve hot. (Alternatively, once the water comes to a boil, turn off the heat, cover the rice with paper towels and the lid, and let sit until the liquid is absorbed, about 1 hour.)

Baked Rice with Three Cheeses

IN THE NORTHERN ITALIAN region of Piedmont, foods are richer than in more southerly Italy and rely on the produce of the mountain pastures, such as wonderful cow's milk cheeses. Given the Piedmont's proximity to Alpine Switzerland, it's not surprising to find such cheeses being used in cooked dishes. This preparation is called *risotto ai tre formaggi* (risotto with three cheeses), which is a bit unusual because it's not cooked in the risotto method but is basically a rice casserole made with three cheeses: Fontina Val d'Aosta, Parmesan, and Gruyère. Your supermarket deli will sell the smoked tongue needed for the recipe. You could also use headcheese instead of tongue.

Makes 4 servings

Salt, as needed

2 cups short-grain rice, such as Arborio

7 tablespoons unsalted butter

3 ounces Parmesan cheese (preferably Parmigiano-Reggiano cheese), 2 ounces grated, 1 ounce shaved

2 ounces Gruyère cheese, sliced

3 ounces smoked tongue, chopped

2 ounces Fontina Val d'Aosta cheese, sliced

1. Preheat the oven to 350°F.

2. Bring a saucepan of water to a boil with some salt, add the rice, and cook until al dente, about 10 minutes. Drain and toss with 6 tablespoons of the butter and the grated Parmesan.

3. In a large nonstick skillet, cook the rice, tossing constantly, for 2 minutes over medium heat. Butter a 9-inch baking casserole or a terrine with the remaining butter and spoon a layer of rice on the bottom, then a layer of the sliced Gruyère, shaved Parmesan, and the smoked tongue. Cover with the remaining rice. Layer the fontina on top. Bake until the cheese is melted and the rice soft, 15 to 20 minutes. Serve immediately.

Rice and Mozzarella

1½ cups water

2 tablespoons extra-virgin olive oil

1 cup medium- or short-grain rice

1 teaspoon salt

8 ounces fresh mozzarella cheese, cut into small dice

½ cup freshly grated Parmesan cheese (preferably Parmigiano-Reggiano cheese)

Freshly ground black pepper to taste

THIS DISH IS JUST hot rice and cheese, with the heat of the rice melting the mozzarella. The preparation is as simple as it gets, and with a little Parmesan cheese and black pepper you're finished. The dish is typically served as a first course, but if you decide to use it as an accompaniment I'd keep that simple, too—for example, a pan-seared chicken breast or pork chop.

Makes 4 small servings

1. In a heavy-bottomed saucepan, bring the water and olive oil to a boil over high heat. Pour in the rice, add the salt, stir, and let return to a boil. Reduce the heat to low, cover, and cook, without stirring, until the liquid is absorbed, about 12 minutes. Let the rice sit covered with the heat off for 10 minutes.

2. Meanwhile, spread the mozzarella on individual plates and spoon the rice over. Sprinkle with the Parmesan cheese and serve with freshly ground black pepper at the table.

Risotto con Fonduta

RISOTTA WITH FONDUE was invented accidently, so the legend goes, by Cavour's cook. Cavour, one of the leading figures of Italian unification in the mid-nineteenth century, was from the Piedmont, and the cook was trying to make a base for a soufflé when this fonduta, or fondue made with fontina cheese, was stirred into the risotto instead. The tricky part of this recipe is having the rice and fonduta finish at the same time. The rice you can slow down by lowering the heat, but the sauce should be used as soon as it melts. *Makes 4 servings*

1 tablespoon extra-virgin olive oil

2 tablespoons unsalted butter

2 cups Arborio rice

1 large garlic clove, finely chopped

1 bay leaf

½ cup dry white wine

5 cups hot or boiling beef broth

8 ounces Fontina Val d'Aosta cheese, diced

½ cup lukewarm milk

1 tablespoon all-purpose flour

1 large egg yolk, beaten

Salt and freshly ground white pepper to taste

1. In a saucepan, heat the oil with the butter over medium heat. Once the butter has melted, add the rice, garlic, and bay leaf and cook, stirring constantly, for 3 minutes. Add the wine, stir, and let it evaporate.

2. Pour 1 cup of broth into the rice and cook, stirring, until it is almost absorbed. Continue adding ½-cup increments of broth to the rice while stirring frequently until all the broth is absorbed, 20 to 30 minutes. You may not need all the broth, but if you need more than called for, use water.

3. Fill the bottom part of a double boiler with water and bring to a boil, then reduce the heat until the water is barely bubbling. Put the fontina, milk, and flour in the top part, set over the bottom part, and cook, stirring constantly, until the cheese has melted and is smooth. Add the egg yolk and mix well. Season with salt and pepper. Transfer the cooked rice to a round platter and make a well in the middle. Pour the fondue into the well and serve hot.

Tummàla

One 3-pound chicken

2 medium onions,
cut into eighths

2 celery stalks, cut
into chunks

4 ripe tomatoes, peeled,
seeded, and quartered

5 fresh flat-leaf parsley sprigs

10 black peppercorns

½ cup fresh bread crumbs

3 tablespoons milk

12 ounces ground veal

12 ounces pecorino
pepato cheese, grated

1 large garlic clove,
finely chopped

6 tablespoons finely chopped
fresh flat-leaf parsley

Salt to taste

¼ teaspoon freshly
ground black pepper

7 large eggs (2 hard-boiled,
shelled, and sliced)

2 tablespoons lard or
unsalted butter

1 medium onion, chopped

8 ounces mild Italian
sausage, sliced ½ inch thick

4 ounces pork rind,
cut into thin strips

2 tablespoons tomato paste

(continued)

TUMMÀLA IS A MAGNIFICENT Sicilian feast preparation, and although a Christmas specialty, Sicilian cooks prepare it for many grand celebrations. It's a dish from *cucina arabo-sicula*, the folkloric expression of a vestigial Arab culinary sensibility found in contemporary Sicily, some 800 years after the last of the Arab-Sicilian population disappeared. At the very least, we know that the Arabs introduced rice to the island in the ninth or tenth century.

The name is a bit of a mystery. It seems as if *tummàla* might derive from the Italian *timballo* and French *timbale*, a kind of molded dish like a kettledrum. On the other hand, some food historians argue that the name derives from either Muhammed Ibn al-Thumna, the eleventh-century emir of Catania, or from *tummala*, the supposed Arabic name for a certain kind of earthenware plate. In olden days, unborn chicken eggs were used in the preparation. As for the cheeses—pecorino pepato, caciocavallo, and fresh mozzarella—they can be found in Italian markets, gourmet cheese shops, better supermarkets, or on the Internet at sites such as at www.murrayscheese.com. Pecorino pepato is young pecorino cheese made with peppercorns thrown into the curd. I call for fresh mozzarella in place of fresh tuma, because Sicilian tuma made with sheep's milk is not available in this country as far as I know. Some Sicilian-style 3- to-6-month-old tuma is sold in Italian markets, and a firm in California also makes it. Caciocavallo is a spun-curd cow's milk cheese and can be replaced with provolone. Finally, don't let the list of ingredients intimidate you. Great length, in this case, does not mean great difficulty.

Makes 8 to 10 servings

2½ cups short-grain rice, such as Arborio, soaked in tepid water to cover for 30 minutes or rinsed well in a strainer, drained

Unsalted butter, for greasing the baking dish

1 cup dried bread crumbs

8 ounces fresh mozzarella cheese, sliced

4 ounces caciocavallo cheese, thinly sliced

4 ounces pecorino cheese, freshly grated

1. In a large stockpot that will fit the chicken comfortably, place the chicken with its gizzards, the onions, celery stalks, tomatoes, parsley, and peppercorns. Cover with cold water and bring to a near boil over high heat. As soon as the water looks like it is about to boil, reduce immediately to a simmer and cook the chicken until the meat falls off the bone when pushed with a fork, about 2 hours. The water should only be shimmering on top; don't let the water bubble, as it toughens the chicken.

2. Meanwhile, prepare the veal croquettes. In a bowl, soak the fresh bread crumbs in the milk. If the mixture looks soggy, squeeze the milk out. Add the veal, half of the pecorino pepato, the garlic, 2 tablespoons of the chopped parsley, ½ teaspoon salt, and the pepper. Lightly beat 1 large egg and add to the mixture. Mix well with a fork or your hands. Form croquettes the size and shape of your thumb. Cover and set aside in the refrigerator.

3. Drain the chicken, saving all the broth and transferring it to a smaller pot. Remove and discard all the skin and bones from the chicken and cut the meat into small pieces.

4. In a large skillet, melt 1 tablespoon lard over medium heat. Add the chopped onion and cook, stirring, until golden, about 8 minutes. Remove from the pan. Add the remaining lard to the pan, let it melt and get hot, then cook the veal croquettes until they are browned on all sides. Add the sausage and the pork rind and cook for 10 minutes. Add the sautéed onion, the remaining
(continued)

4 tablespoons parsley, and the tomato paste diluted in 1 cup hot water. Cook over low heat for 10 minutes. Set aside.

5. Preheat the oven to 350°F.

6. Bring the chicken broth to a boil over high heat and reduce by one-third. Pour 2½ cups broth into a heavy saucepan, bring to a boil, and add the rice and about 1½ teaspoons salt. Cook, covered and without stirring, until al dente, about 15 minutes. Pour about ¾ cup of broth into the veal-sausage mixture.

7. Drain the rice, if necessary, and mix it with the remaining pecorino pepato.

8. Butter a deep baking dish or casserole and spread 1 cup of dry bread crumbs on the bottom, shaking vigorously to spread them thin so that they coat the bottom of the baking dish.

9. Spread the rice on top of the bread crumbs, about ¾ inch thick. Spread three-quarters of the chicken and half of the veal croquette and sausage mixture on top of the rice. Make a layer with the hard-boiled egg. Layer the mozzarella cheese on top of the eggs. Cover with the remaining veal and sauce. Spread on a layer of the caciocavallo cheese. Mix the remaining chicken with the remaining rice and spread it on top.

10. Beat the remaining 4 large eggs lightly and combine with the pecorino cheese. Season with salt and pepper. Pour the mixture evenly over the top. Bake until the top has a nice golden crust, about 1 hour. Check from time to time to be sure it doesn't dry out. The tummàla can be served directly from the baking dish with the pan sauces or with tomato sauce.

Buckwheat Porridge with Milk and Cheese

BUCKWHEAT IS A GRASS categorized as a cereal that first began having some popularity in northern Italy by the fifteenth century. It is known as *grano saraceno* (Saracen grain) in Italian, leading one to believe that its origins might be with the Arabs. However, in the Middle Ages such ascriptions may have meant either that that is where people believed it to have come from or that any dark food, in this case a grain that looks like chocolate when cooked as a porridge, is swarthy like the Saracens (Arabs). This polenta or porridge, called *polenta in fiur*, is made with buckwheat and milk and is a popular dish from Valtellina, a valley in Lombardy next to Switzerland. Serve this buckwheat polenta with braised short ribs and you will have a memorable meal.

Makes 4 servings

3½ cups whole milk

½ cup heavy cream

1½ teaspoons salt

1 cup buckwheat flour

2 teaspoons fine corn flour

3 tablespoons unsalted butter

2½ ounces Taleggio cheese, diced

1. In the bottom part of a double boiler, pour enough water to reach and cover the bottom of the top part. Bring to a boil, and then reduce the heat so the water is just under a bubble.

2. Combine the milk and cream in the top part of the double boiler, and set it directly over another burner over medium heat, not on top of the bottom part of the double boiler. Make sure the mixture doesn't boil. Add the salt.

3. Using a wooden spoon, stir the milk in the top part of the double boiler until you have created a whirlpool. Now quickly pour the buckwheat and corn flour into the center of the whirlpool in a continuous steady stream, not too fast, not too slow.

(continued)

Do not stop stirring. Continue to stir at a slower pace once the buckwheat is in the pot. Reduce the heat to low and stir for 3 to 5 minutes while the polenta bubbles slightly; it will thicken.

4. Place a lid on top and place the top half of the double boiler on the bottom half. Cook for 40 minutes, stirring frequently. Add the butter and cheese and cook, stirring, until they have melted, about 8 minutes. Serve hot.

Swiss Polenta Casserole

POLENTA MADE FROM CORNMEAL is a staple food in the Swiss canton of Ticino, and this rich and substantial dish is a favorite way of preparing it. The dish can also be varied by using raclette cheese instead of Gruyère and breading and deep-frying the polenta croquettes instead of frying them.

Makes 4 servings

1 cup fine or medium cornmeal

3 cups water

2 tablespoons unsalted butter, plus more for greasing the casserole

1½ cups grated Gruyère cheese (about 5 ounces)

1 teaspoon salt

¼ teaspoon paprika

½ cup heavy cream

1. In a bowl, blend the polenta and 1 cup of the water, stirring until smooth.

2. In a saucepan, bring the remaining 2 cups of water to a boil over high heat. Gradually stir in the cornmeal mixture. Reduce the heat to low and cook, stirring frequently, until thick and smooth or until the mixture clears the sides of the saucepan, about 5 minutes.

3. Beat in the butter, ½ cup of the grated cheese, salt, and paprika. Spread this mixture in a small 10 × 7-inch baking casserole to a depth of 1 inch. Refrigerate until solid.

4. Preheat the oven to 350°F.

5. Butter a 9-inch square baking casserole. Cut the cornmeal mixture into fingers and place them in the casserole. Pour the cream over the polenta. Sprinkle with the remaining cheese and bake until the top is lightly browned, 20 minutes.

Polenta Cooked in Milk with Cheese

2 cups water

2 cups milk

1½ teaspoons salt

1 cup fine or medium cornmeal

1½ ounces Fontina Val d'Aosta cheese, diced

1½ ounces Asiago or Swiss (Emmenthaler) cheese, diced

2 tablespoons unsalted butter, melted

Freshly grated Parmesan cheese (preferably Parmigiano-Reggiano cheese), for sprinkling

Coarsely and freshly ground black pepper to taste

THIS RICH AND CREAMY POLENTA, made in the Italian regions of Piedmont and Val d'Aosta, is made with water or milk, depending on the town. In the Piedmontese towns of Novara and Vercello, cooks use milk, Fontina Val d'Aosta cheese, and Toma di Celle cheese. I've used Asiago and Piave cheese and that was quite good, too. This polenta is best as an accompaniment to beef stew cooked in red wine. You can try looking for these cheeses at www.murrayscheese.com or www.dibruno.com. *Makes 4 servings*

1. In the bottom half of a double boiler, pour enough water to reach and cover the bottom of the top part. Bring this water to a boil and then reduce the heat so the water is just under a bubble.

2. Combine the 2 cups water and the milk in the top part of the double boiler, and set it directly over another burner over medium heat, not on top of the bottom part of the double boiler. Add the salt.

3. Using a wooden spoon, stir the liquid in the top part of the double boiler until you have created a whirlpool. Now quickly pour the cornmeal into the center of the whirlpool in a continuous steady stream, not too fast, not too slow. Do not stop stirring. Continue to stir at a slower pace once the cornmeal is in the pot.

Reduce the heat to low and stir for 3 to 5 minutes while the polenta bubbles slightly; it will thicken.

4. Place the lid on top and place the top half of the double boiler on the bottom half. Cook for 1½ hours, stirring every 30 minutes. Add the fontina and Asiago cheeses and continue cooking, stirring, for another 10 minutes. Serve with a drizzle of butter and the Parmesan cheese and black pepper.

Soft Polenta and
Black Bean Ragoût

For the polenta

4 cups water

1½ teaspoons salt

1 cup fine or medium cornmeal

For the black bean ragoût

2 quarts water

1 bouquet garni, tied in cheesecloth, consisting of 5 sprigs fresh flat-leaf parsley, 5 sprigs fresh thyme, 5 sprigs fresh tarragon, 1 bay leaf, and 10 black peppercorns

1 cup dried black beans

2 tablespoons extra-virgin olive oil

2 large garlic cloves, finely chopped

1 teaspoon ground fennel seeds

For serving

1¾ cups freshly grated pecorino cheese (about 6 ounces)

2 tablespoons unsalted butter

AS YOU EAT SOFT POLENTA right out of the pot, it will slowly solidify. That phenomenon is one of the delightful textural changes you may enjoy in this preparation. An ideal accompaniment is grilled or roast, or even braised, lamb on top, cooked so the juices spill all over the polenta. If you grill or roast the lamb, use about 2 pounds lamb shoulder, rub it with a tablespoon of ground fennel seeds, salt, and pepper, and grill slowly (indirectly) or roast slowly (about 300°F) for 3 hours.

Makes 4 servings

1. For the polenta, in the bottom half of a double boiler, pour enough water to reach and cover the bottom of the top part. Bring this water to a boil over high heat, then reduce the heat so the water is just under a bubble.

2. Add the 4 cups water to the top part of the double boiler, and set it directly over another burner over medium heat, not on top of the bottom part of the double boiler. Bring to a boil and add the salt.

3. Using a wooden spoon, stir the water in the top part of the double boiler until you have created a whirlpool. Now quickly pour the cornmeal into the center of the whirlpool in a continuous steady stream, not too fast, not too slow. Do not stop stirring. Continue to stir at a slower pace once the cornmeal is in the pot. Reduce the heat to low and stir for 3 to 5 minutes while the polenta bubbles slightly; it will thicken.

4. Place the lid on the top and fit the top half of the double boiler on the bottom half. Cook over low heat for 1½ hours, stirring every 30 minutes.

5. While the polenta is cooking, for the black bean ragoût, bring the 2 quarts water to a boil in a large saucepan, add the bouquet garni, then add the black beans and cook until tender, about 1¼ hours. Drain, saving 1 cup of the cooking water, and transfer to a skillet with the olive oil, garlic, and fennel seeds. Cook over medium-high heat until the garlic is sizzling, then reduce the heat to low, add ½ cup of the reserved cooking water, and simmer until saucy and soft. Keep warm while you finish the polenta.

6. Spread the soft polenta on a platter, sprinkle most of the cheese over the polenta, and drop the butter in slivers over it, too. Ladle the beans over the polenta, sprinkle the remaining cheese on top, and serve.

Vegetables with Cheese

The recipes in this chapter have a variety of uses. They can be made as appetizers, side dishes, vegetarian dinners, or antipasti. There are some easy American classics like Cauliflower Casserole (page 282), with its cheddar cheese, and spicy hot Black Beans with Habanero Chile (page 276), which calls for a convenient bag of shredded Mexican four-cheese blend. The Stuffed Jalapeños with Chorizo Sausage (page 296) is simple to prepare as well, and for lovers of hot food, it's a winner. Mushrooms Stuffed with Gruyère Cheese (page 312) are the perfect little party appetizers. On a cold day you'll swoon over one of the most delicious dishes in this chapter, the Potato, Bacon, and Gruyère Casserole (page 313); what could be more perfect than that combination? Finally, let me say that I think the Eggplant Parmesan recipe on page 301 is simply the best you'll ever taste. Try it.

Artichokes Stuffed with Mozzarella

4 medium-large artichokes (about 2½ pounds in all)

8 ounces fresh mozzarella cheese, chopped

2 tablespoons freshly grated Parmesan cheese (preferably Parmigiano-Reggiano cheese)

1 large egg, lightly beaten

¼ cup finely chopped fresh flat-leaf parsley

Salt and freshly ground black pepper to taste

6 tablespoons dried bread crumbs

4 salted anchovy fillets, rinsed and finely chopped

¼ cup extra-virgin olive oil

1 lemon, cut into 6 to 8 wedges

THE ARTICHOKES in this preparation from southern Italy look rather majestic with their bracts pushed apart and stuffed with the mozzarella. It makes an impressive dish to serve guests as an antipasto. Although there is some preparation involved in this recipe, you can make it easier on yourself by parboiling the artichoke foundations before you stuff them. This will make it a manageable task, but at the expense of the prettiness of the dish. Be careful not to use more cheese than I recommend, because you do not want to overwhelm the artichokes. Serve as a first course, and let all the diners pick at will at the artichokes centered on the table. *Makes 6 to 8 servings*

1. Trim the stem and top third of the artichokes. Snip off the pointy tips of the bracts (leaves) with kitchen scissors and boil the whole artichokes until there is a slight resistance to a skewer piercing into their centers, about 40 minutes. Drain, and when cool enough to handle, remove the central hairy choke and inner bracts using a paring knife and a teaspoon. Leave the outer bracts attached to the foundation.

2. Preheat the oven to 375°F.

3. In a bowl, mix together the mozzarella, Parmesan, egg, and parsley and season with salt and pepper. Spoon this stuffing into the center of the artichokes and with your fingers spread the bracts apart and push some stuffing down there, too.

4. In a small bowl, mix the bread crumbs with the anchovies and then sprinkle this over the stuffing of the artichokes. Drizzle the olive oil over all the artichokes.

5. Arrange the artichokes in a baking pan and add a few cups of water to the pan. Cover with aluminum foil and bake for 25 minutes. Remove the foil and bake until the bread crumbs are golden, about 20 minutes. Serve with lemon wedges.

PORK CARNITAS

Crisp on the outside, succulent on the inside, this pork dish is made from the thick meaty cut called pork country ribs. Carnitas can be eaten wrapped in tortillas with guacamole or with black beans (page 275). Place the pork country ribs in a large flameproof baking casserole and season with a quartered onion, cumin seeds, coriander seeds, dried oregano, chipotle chiles in adobo, a bay leaf, and chicken broth to cover. Bring to a boil, then reduce to low and simmer until very tender, about 3 hours. Toss the meat with melted pork lard and roast in a 450°F oven for 30 minutes.

Black Beans with Chiles

THIS BLACK BEAN preparation could be served alone, but it's great with pork carnitas. You can add nearly anything to it, and with a little extra cheese and a hot tortilla it makes a nice snack.

Makes 4 servings

1 cup dried black beans

1 small onion, quartered

1 large garlic clove, finely chopped

5 cups water

2 tablespoons pork lard (preferably) or unsalted butter

2 large fresh green serrano chiles, seeded and finely chopped

5 sprigs fresh epazote (optional)

Salt to taste

1 cup crumbled queso fresco or shredded Mexican 4-cheese blend (about 3½ ounces)

3 tablespoons finely chopped fresh cilantro (coriander leaf), for garnish

1. Place the beans in a saucepan with the onion and garlic, cover with the 5 cups of water, and bring to a boil. Reduce the heat to medium-low and cook until the beans are very tender, about 1½ hours. If the water has evaporated, add about ½ cup of boiling water to keep it moist.

2. Meanwhile, in a medium skillet, melt the lard over high heat with the chiles. Once the chiles are sizzling and soft and the beans are tender, add 2 ladlefuls of the beans to the skillet and cook, stirring, until softer, about 5 minutes. Mash the beans in the skillet with a potato masher and return the contents of the skillet to the saucepan with the remaining beans, along with the epazote, if using, and salt. Cook the beans over low heat for 30 minutes, stirring occasionally. Transfer the beans to a serving plate or platter and sprinkle the cheese on top. Serve with a sprinkling of cilantro.

Black Beans with Habanero Chile

One 15-ounce can black beans, drained

2 fresh habanero chiles, seeds and membranes removed, chopped or cut into thin slivers

1 cup shredded Mexican 4-cheese blend (about 3½ ounces)

Salt to taste

THIS QUICK LITTLE DISH is one I will make for breakfast and serve with scrambled eggs and bacon. It's simple and delicious beyond what you would imagine for its humble ingredients.

Makes 4 small servings

1. Preheat the oven to 350°F.

2. Pour the beans into an ungreased 9-inch baking casserole. Stir in the habanero chiles, cheese, and salt and bake until the cheese is completely melted, 12 to 15 minutes. Serve hot.

Black Beans and Nopalitos with Cheese

THIS VEGETABLE STEW is satisfying both as a vegetable main course and as a dish that packs a lot of heat, thanks to the habanero chiles. *Nopalitos* is the Mexican Spanish word for the pads of cactus that are edible. They are usually sold already cleaned and cut up in bags in the supermarket. Rinse them well in cold water to remove some of the viscosity. You could also serve this dish as a first course with some corn tortillas.

Makes 4 servings

In a stockpot, heat the olive oil over medium-high heat. Add the tomato, scallions, garlic, and habanero chiles and cook, stirring, until softened, about 4 minutes. Add the black beans, cactus, cumin, and chili powder and cook until most of the liquid has evaporated, about 25 minutes. Season with salt, add the cheese, and cook only until it starts to melt, about 5 minutes. Serve hot.

2 tablespoons extra-virgin olive oil

1 plum tomato, chopped

3 scallions, chopped

2 large garlic cloves, finely chopped

2 fresh habanero chiles, seeded and finely chopped

One 15-ounce can black beans, drained and rinsed

1 pound chopped prepared cactus (nopalitos), rinsed and drained

1 teaspoon ground cumin

1 teaspoon chili powder

Salt to taste

4 ounces queso Oaxaca or mozzarella cheese, diced

Broccoli Cheese Dish

Salt, as needed

1 pound broccoli florets

2 cups heavy cream

2 large eggs, beaten

1 small onion,
finely chopped

1½ cups grated white
cheddar cheese
(about 5 ounces)

⅛ teaspoon ground nutmeg

6 tablespoons
unsalted butter

1 sleeve Ritz crackers
(4 ounces), crumbled

THERE'S NO DENYING that this rich casserole is a favorite. It's an old-fashioned Midwestern dish typical at a church supper. You can use bread crumbs instead of Ritz crackers for the au gratin finish. If you want to accompany it with something, think light, such as chicken breasts. You do not use the broccoli stems in this preparation; save them for Broccoli Stems Pistachio au Gratin on page 279. *Makes 6 servings*

1. Preheat the oven to 325°F.

2. Bring a saucepan of water to a boil, salt lightly, then cook the broccoli until tender but still bright green, about 6 minutes, but not more. Drain and immediately cool under cold running water. Let drain some more in a colander.

3. In a bowl, stir together the cream, eggs, onion, cheese, and nutmeg. Pour this mixture into a 12 × 9 × 2-inch baking casserole. Add the broccoli.

4. Meanwhile, in a large skillet, melt the butter over medium-high heat, then cook the crumbled Ritz crackers, stirring, until crispy and fragrant, about 3 minutes. Sprinkle the crackers over the broccoli, place in the oven, and bake until bubbly, about 30 minutes. Serve hot.

Broccoli Stems Pistachio au Gratin

I MAKE THIS DISH usually when I need the florets for an-other purpose, such as Baked Rigatoni with Broccoli (page 226) or Broccoli Cheese Dish (page 278). It makes for a nice little tapas or appetizer. *Makes 2 to 4 servings*

3 thick broccoli stems peeled and quartered lengthwise

3 tablespoons ground pistachios

3 tablespoons freshly and finely grated Parmesan cheese

Extra-virgin olive oil, for oiling the casserole and for drizzling

Salt to taste

1. Preheat the oven to 400°F.

2. Bring a pot of water to a rolling boil over high heat, then cook the broccoli stems until cooked but slightly firm, 5 min-utes. Drain. In a bowl, toss the pistachios and Parmesan cheese together.

3. Lightly oil a 7-inch baking casserole. Toss the stems in all but 1 tablespoon of the pistachio-Parmesan mixture and arrange in the casserole. Sprinkle the remaining ground mixture on top and season with salt. Drizzle with a little olive oil and bake until golden on top, 20 minutes. Serve hot.

Brussels Sprouts with Caraway Cheese Sauce

Salt, as needed

1 pound fresh Brussels sprouts, trimmed

¾ cup evaporated milk

1 cup cubed sharp cheddar cheese (4 ounces)

¾ teaspoon caraway seeds

½ teaspoon Worcestershire sauce

¼ teaspoon dry mustard

¼ teaspoon Tabasco sauce

THIS CAJUN RECIPE is adapted from Merlin Bodin's *A Cajun Family's Recipe Collection*, a compilation of south Louisiana family recipes collected over twenty years. It's delicious, and the secret, if it can be called that, is to make sure that the Brussels sprouts are not cooked more than 8 minutes.

Makes 6 servings

1. In a saucepan, bring an inch of salted water to a boil over high heat, then add the Brussels sprouts and cook until tender, 7 to 8 minutes. Drain well and keep warm if they finish cooking before the cheese sauce, but make sure they don't continue cooking.

2. Meanwhile, in a small saucepan, heat the evaporated milk, cheddar cheese, caraway seeds, Worcestershire sauce, dry mustard, and Tabasco sauce over medium heat, stirring constantly in a figure-8 motion, until the cheese melts. Transfer the Brussels sprouts to a serving bowl or platter and spoon the cheese sauce over them. Serve hot.

Stuffed Cabbage with Mozzarella in Tomato Sauce

STUFFED VEGETABLES ARE POPULAR in southern Italy. In this recipe, you'll stuff cabbage leaves with scamorza and mozzarella cheese and bake them with tomato sauce. Scamorza is a soft mozzarella-type cheese originally made in the Abruzzo and Molise provinces of Italy with water buffalo's milk. Scamorza is hard to find, but good Italian markets will have it and you can order it at www.realmozzarella.com, www.mozzco.com, or www.igourmet.com. If you can't find it, replace it with provolone cheese. *Makes 4 to 6 servings*

1 savoy cabbage (about 2 pounds), any damaged outer leaves removed

4 ounces scamorza, smoked scamorza, or provolone cheese, cut into 18 tiny wedges

4 ounces fresh mozzarella cheese, cut into 18 tiny wedges

2½ cups Tomato Sauce (page 235)

Salt and freshly ground black pepper to taste

3 tablespoons freshly grated Parmesan cheese

1. Place the cabbage in the top portion of a steamer pot, filling the bottom with several inches of water. Cover, bring to a boil, and steam until a skewer glides into the center of the core with a little resistance and the cabbage is still firm, about 35 minutes. Cool and remove the leaves carefully so they don't rip. Arrange the cabbage leaves in front of you with the stem end closest to you and lay pieces of scamorza and mozzarella in the center. Roll once away from you, tuck the sides over, and continue rolling. You should have about 18 rolls.

2. Meanwhile, preheat the oven to 350°F.

3. Pour half of the tomato sauce on the bottom of a 13 × 10 × 2-inch baking casserole and lay all the rolled-up cabbage leaves on top in 2 rows. Season with salt and pepper. Cover the cabbage with the remaining tomato sauce and sprinkle the Parmesan on top. Bake until the top is dappled black and the sauce is bubbling, 12 to 15 minutes. Serve immediately.

Cauliflower Casserole

1 cauliflower (about
1½ pounds), trimmed

1 cup sour cream

1 cup shredded mild cheddar
cheese (about 3 ounces)

½ cup crushed corn
flakes cereal

¼ cup chopped green
bell pepper

¼ cup chopped red
bell pepper

1 teaspoon salt

Unsalted butter, for
greasing the casserole

¼ cup freshly grated
Parmesan cheese

1 teaspoon hot paprika

ANOTHER CLASSIC CHEESY American casserole is the cauliflower casserole, made all the better with its crisp au gratin topping prepared, in this case, with corn flakes cereal for a real old-timey comfort food taste like grandma used to make.

Makes 4 servings

1. Preheat the oven to 325°F.

2. Place the cauliflower in a steamer basket and steam over boiling water until tender but slightly firm, about 15 minutes. Remove the cauliflower and cool slightly. Break the cauliflower into florets and slice the thicker stems.

3. In a large bowl, stir together the sour cream, cheddar cheese, corn flakes, green and red bell peppers, and salt. Add the cauliflower and mix well, but gently.

4. Butter a 13 × 10 × 2-inch casserole. Transfer the cauliflower to the casserole. Sprinkle the Parmesan cheese and paprika on top. Bake until crispy golden on top, 30 to 35 minutes. Serve hot.

Jalapeño Chiles and Tomatoes with Boiled Cheese

NOT ANY CHEESE will work in this recipe, which requires you to boil the cheese. You'll need a firm white cheese such as a Mexican queso blanco, paneer cheese, or Syrian white cheese. It's a spicy hot dish, so if you like fire you'll love this. You can eat raw chiles to accompany it or serve it with steamed rice on the side. *Makes 4 servings*

Put the jalapeños, onion, and vegetable oil in a medium saucepan and pour in the water. Bring to a boil, then reduce the heat to medium and cook for 8 minutes. Add the tomatoes and garlic and boil for another 2 minutes. Stir in the cheese and cook for 3 minutes. Stir in the cilantro, then turn off the heat, stir, cover, and let sit for 2 minutes. Serve hot.

8 ounces fresh green jalapeño chiles, seeded and quartered lengthwise

1 medium onion, chopped

1 tablespoon vegetable oil

1¾ cups water

1 pound tomatoes, peeled, seeded, and chopped

5 large garlic cloves, smashed

8 ounces firm queso blanco or Syrian white cheese, cut into small cubes

1 tablespoon finely chopped fresh cilantro (coriander leaf)

Mild Chiles Stuffed with Feta Cheese

8 fresh mild green long chiles (New Mexico, Anaheim, Italian frying peppers, or peperoncini)

¼ cup extra-virgin olive oil, plus more for oiling the casserole and for drizzling

3 scallions, white part only, finely chopped

2 tablespoons tomato paste

½ teaspoon freshly ground black pepper

½ teaspoon dried oregano

⅛ teaspoon cayenne pepper

8 ounces Bulgarian or Greek feta cheese (preferably), crumbled

1 tablespoon finely chopped fresh flat-leaf parsley

ALL "PEPPERS" ARE A FORM OF CHILE, ranging from those with no piquancy at all, such as bell peppers, to those with a little to a lot of heat, which tend to be called chiles. The chiles called for in this recipe are quite mild. They are stuffed with feta cheese, baked, and eaten as a meze with some ouzo. You'll want to be just a bit careful when removing the seeds from the chiles so that you don't split them. There are other ways of making this. One of my favorites is using red bell peppers and stuffing them with manouri cheese.

Makes 4 to 8 servings

1. Cut the stem end off the chiles and, with a paring knife, carefully cut out and remove the seeds without splitting the chiles.

2. Bring a large pot of water to a boil over high heat and blanch the peppers for 5 minutes. Drain and cool.

3. In a pot, heat the oil over medium heat. Add the scallions and cook, stirring, until softened, about 6 minutes. Add the tomato paste, black pepper, oregano, and cayenne, stir, and cook for 2 minutes, stirring constantly, then remove from the heat. Transfer to a bowl and let cool.

4. Preheat the broiler.

5. In the bowl, mix the feta cheese and parsley together with the tomato paste mixture. Stuff the peppers with the cheese mixture and arrange in a lightly oiled 13 × 10 × 2-inch baking casserole that will hold the chiles snugly but without their touching each other. Drizzle a little more oil over the chiles and broil, turning several times, until the chiles are blistering black on all sides, 6 to 8 minutes. Serve hot or cold.

Poblano Chile Strips in Cheese

4 fresh poblano chiles
or green bell peppers

3 tablespoons pork lard
(preferably) or vegetable oil

2 medium onions, sliced

4 medium tomatoes
(about 1 pound), peeled,
seeded, and chopped

¼ cup water

1 teaspoon salt

4 ounces cream cheese

4 ounces queso blanco
or Mexican shredded
4-cheese blend

Corn tortillas, for serving

RAJAS CON QUESO is a classic Mexican preparation for chiles. *Rajas* means "strips" or "rags" in Spanish, and that's how you'll cut them for this preparation, which can be eaten as an appetizer, a side dish, or a vegetarian main course wrapped in corn tortillas. No matter how you serve it, you'll find people asking for more. Poblano chiles are dark green and mildly hot chiles that are heart shaped and labeled, incorrectly, pasilla chiles in California supermarkets (I have no idea why). If you use sweet bell peppers, the taste will be quite mild.

Makes 4 servings

1. Place the chiles on a wire rack over a burner on high heat and roast until their skins blister black on all sides, turning occasionally with tongs. Remove the chiles and place in a paper or heavy plastic bag to steam for 20 minutes, which will make peeling them easier. When cool enough to handle, rub off as much blackened peel as you can and remove the seeds by rubbing with a paper towel (to avoid washing away flavorful juices) or by rinsing under running water (to remove more easily). Cut into strips.

2. In a skillet, melt the lard over medium heat. Add the onions and cook, stirring frequently, until yellow and slightly caramelized, about 10 minutes. Add the chiles, tomatoes, water, and salt, reduce the heat to low, and simmer until it reaches a boil, about 5 minutes. Add the cheeses and simmer, stirring constantly, until melted and bubbling a bit, about 10 minutes. Serve with corn tortillas.

Chile con Queso

IF YOU LOVE CHILES and you love cheese, this is your dish, called, appropriately enough, *chile con queso* (chiles with cheese). What makes it so appealing is that the bland cheeses moderate the blistering hot chiles. The cheeses used are the Mexican cheeses queso Chihuahua and queso asadero, both of which may be available in supermarkets. You can substitute both with mild white cheddar and Monterey Jack cheese. To start, place a wire rack over the burner and blister the chiles black. If you have a grill going, do that step over the open fire. Serve as an appetizer. *Makes 6 servings*

30 fresh green jalapeño chiles

¼ cup vegetable oil

1 medium onion, thinly sliced

1 medium ripe tomato, peeled, seeded, and coarsely chopped

¾ cup half-and-half

8 ounces mixed queso Chihuahua and queso asadero or mixed mild white cheddar and Monterey Jack cheese, diced

Salt to taste

1. Place the chiles on a wire rack over a burner on high heat and roast, turning occasionally with tongs, until their skins blister black on all sides. Remove the chiles and place in a paper or heavy plastic bag to steam for 20 minutes, which will make peeling them easier. When cool enough to handle, rub off as much blackened peel as you can and remove the seeds by rubbing with a paper towel (to avoid washing away flavorful juices) or by rinsing under running water (to remove more easily). Slice into thin strips.

2. In a medium skillet, heat the vegetable oil over medium heat, then add the onion and cook, stirring, until translucent, about 7 minutes. Add the chile strips and tomato to the skillet, cover, and cook, stirring occasionally, until softened, about 8 minutes, stirring occasionally. Add the half-and-half and cook for another 2 minutes. Stir in the cheese until it melts. Season with salt and serve.

Queso Fundido with Chiles
and Chorizo Sausage

3 large fresh jalapeño chiles

2 tablespoons vegetable oil

½ small onion, thinly sliced

4 ounces Mexican chorizo sausage, removed from the casing and crumbled

8 ounces Monterey Jack cheese, cut into ½-inch cubes

Tortillas, for serving

WHEN I SEE THIS PREPARATION of roasted chiles with chorizo sausage in melted cheese on a restaurant menu, I order it without hesitation. The dish resembles a fondue, but in this case you spread a little in a tortilla and eat it as a snack or appetizer. I'm crazy about this preparation and always eat too much. This recipe is adapted from the one in *Authentic Mexican* by Rick and Deann Bayless, whose method of heating the pan first in the oven assures that the cheese melts quickly and evenly.

Makes 4 to 6 servings

1. Preheat the oven to 375°F.

2. Place the chiles on a wire rack over a burner on high heat and roast, turning occasionally with tongs, until their skins blister black on all sides. Remove the chiles and place in a paper or heavy plastic bag to steam for 20 minutes, which will make peeling them easier. When cool enough to handle, rub off as much blackened peel as you can and remove the seeds by rubbing with a paper towel (to avoid washing away flavorful juices) or by rinsing under running water (to remove more easily). Slice into thin strips and set aside.

3. Place an 8-inch square or round baking dish or pie pan in the oven and let it heat until needed in step 6.

4. In a medium skillet, heat 1 tablespoon of the vegetable oil over medium heat, then add the onion and cook, stirring occasionally, until translucent, about 8 minutes. Add the chile strips and cook,

stirring occasionally, until they are a little soft, about 4 minutes. Remove the vegetables from the skillet and set aside.

5. Add the remaining 1 tablespoon vegetable oil to the skillet, reduce the heat to medium-low, and cook the chorizo sausage until cooked through, about 10 minutes, breaking up clumps with a wooden spoon as it cooks. Drain the fat out, but leave a little for coloring and flavor.

6. Remove the baking dish from the oven. Scatter the cheese cubes on the bottom of the baking dish and return to the oven until the cheese has melted but is not bubbling, about 10 minutes. Sprinkle the chile-onion mixture and the crumbled chorizo on top, return to the oven, and bake until bubbling, about 5 minutes. Serve with tortillas.

Queso Fundido with Chiles and Mushrooms

2 large fresh poblano chiles

1 tablespoon vegetable oil

4 ounces fresh oyster mushrooms, chopped

2 large garlic cloves, finely chopped

2½ cups shredded Monterey Jack cheese (8 ounces)

2 green onions or scallions, thinly sliced

2 fresh jalapeño chiles, preferably 1 red and 1 green, seeded and chopped

Salt to taste

Corn tortillas, for serving

THERE ARE TWO FAMOUS queso fundidos, one made with chorizo and chiles (page 288) and this one. Many recipes for queso fundido suggest using manchego cheese but fail to mention that they mean Mexican-style queso manchego, a young, soft, and meltable cheese better replaced with Monterey Jack than the aged Spanish-style manchego cheese from La Mancha that is usually grated. I've adapted this recipe from one by food writer Karen Hursh Graber. *Makes 4 servings*

1. Place the poblano chiles on a wire rack over a burner on high heat and roast, turning occasionally with tongs, until their skins blister black on all sides. Remove the chiles and place in a paper or heavy plastic bag to steam for 20 minutes, which will make peeling them easier. When cool enough to handle, rub off as much blackened peel as you can and remove the seeds by rubbing with a paper towel (to avoid washing away flavorful juices) or by rinsing under running water (to remove more easily). Slice into thin strips and set aside.

2. Preheat the oven to 325°F.

3. In a large cast-iron skillet or clay cazuela, heat the vegetable oil over medium heat. Add the chile strips, mushrooms, and garlic and cook, stirring, until softened, about 5 minutes. Add the cheese, scallions, jalapeño chiles, and salt. Stir to blend well and simmer, stirring frequently, until the cheese melts.

4. Place the skillet in the oven, or transfer to small, individual ramekins, and bake until bubbling, 2 to 3 minutes. Serve immediately with corn tortillas.

Chiles Rellenos

1 pound ripe tomatoes, peeled and seeded

½ small onion, quartered

2 large garlic cloves, chopped

1½ tablespoons pork lard or unsalted butter

2 cups chicken broth

3 cloves

4 black peppercorns

1 bay leaf

1 cinnamon stick

⅛ teaspoon dried thyme

4 large fresh poblano chiles or New Mexico (also called Anaheim or Hatch) chiles

1½ cups shredded combined Monterey Jack and white cheddar cheese (5 ounces)

2 cups vegetable oil, for frying

3 large eggs, separated

Salt to taste

All-purpose flour, for dredging

CHILES RELLENOS is one of my favorite dishes. I almost always order it in Mexican restaurants. The chiles can be stuffed with cheese or ground pork. I love them both, but I lean toward cheese. I usually use poblano chiles with cheese, although you can also use New Mexico (Anaheim) chiles. As far as the cheese to use, I prefer the Mexican cheeses such as queso blanco, a firm white cheese, or queso Chihuahua, a cheese like mild cheddar, but Monterey Jack and mild white cheddar are also good melting cheeses and are readily available.

Makes 4 servings

1. Put the tomatoes, onion, and garlic in a blender and blend until very smooth. In a large skillet, melt the lard over high heat, then add the tomato purée and cook until bubbling vigorously, about 3 minutes. Add the chicken broth, cloves, peppercorns, bay leaf, cinnamon stick, and thyme, bring to a boil, and cook at a boil for 3 minutes. Reduce the heat to medium and cook until it is a slightly dense, smooth sauce, about 25 minutes. Keep hot over low heat while you continue the preparation.

2. Meanwhile, place the chiles on a wire rack over a burner on high heat and roast until their skins blister black on all sides, turning occasionally with tongs. Remove the chiles and place in a paper or heavy plastic bag to steam for 20 minutes, which will make peeling them easier. When cool enough to handle, rub off as much blackened peel as you can and remove the seeds by rubbing with a paper towel (to avoid washing away flavorful juices) or by rinsing under running water (to remove more easily).

3. Make a T-shaped slit running three-quarters down one side of each chile, starting the "T" at the stem, and carefully remove the seeds and any thick white veins with a sharp paring knife, making sure that you don't cut all the way through the flesh of the chile when you are removing the sturdily attached seeds and making sure that the stem remains intact. Pat the chiles dry with paper towels and stuff the slit with the cheese, evenly divided and molded with your hands into an oval shape to fit into the opening. Set aside on a paper towel–lined plate and cover with paper towels to absorb more water. If the chiles are wet, the batter will not adhere to them properly for frying.

4. Preheat the frying oil in a large skillet for 10 minutes over medium-high heat or to 360°F.

5. Prepare the batter by beating the egg whites in a bowl until they form stiff peaks. Add the salt and the yolks, one at a time, beating each one in before adding the next one. Pat the chiles dry again, making sure the outside is completely dry, then dredge in the flour, tapping off any excess, and dip into the batter completely. Cook the chiles, in batches if necessary so that skillet isn't crowded, turning once with tongs, until golden, about 4 minutes. Remove to an ovenproof dish to keep warm in a low oven as you continue cooking the chiles.

6. Transfer a few ladlefuls of sauce to a wide, shallow platter and place the fried chiles in the center so the sauce comes up about halfway. Serve immediately.

Firecrackers

12 large fresh green
jalapeño chiles

4 ounces Monterey Jack
cheese, cut into 1-inch-
long, ¼-inch-thick sticks

6 cups vegetable
oil, for frying

All-purpose flour or fine
blue corn flour, for dredging

2 large eggs, beaten

Salt to taste

FIRECRACKERS, also called poppers, are nothing but stuffed jalapeños. This is the fried version, and there is a baked version, too (page 296). Firecrackers are always party favorites because you can prepare them ahead of time and then fry them at the last minute. Although they are very spicy hot, they'll disappear quickly.

Makes 6 servings

1. Place the chiles on a wire rack over a burner on high heat and roast until their skins blister black on all sides, turning occasionally with tongs. Remove the chiles and place in a paper or heavy plastic bag to steam for 20 minutes, which will make peeling them easier. When cool enough to handle, rub off as much blackened peel as you can and remove the seeds by rubbing with a paper towel (to avoid washing away flavorful juices) or by rinsing under running water (to remove more easily).

2. Make a T-shaped slit running three-quarters down one side of each chile, starting the "T" at the stem and carefully remove the seeds and any thick white veins with a sharp paring knife, making sure that you don't cut all the way through the flesh of the chile when you are removing the sturdily attached seeds and making sure that the stem remains intact. Set aside on a paper towel–lined plate and cover with paper towels to absorb more water. If the chiles are wet, the batter will not adhere to them properly for frying. Stuff the chiles with the cheese, securing the opening with a toothpick if necessary.

3. Preheat the frying oil to 360°F in a deep fryer or an 8-inch saucepan fitted with a basket insert.

4. Dredge the chiles in the flour, then dip them in the egg and back in the flour again. Cook the stuffed chiles in batches without crowding the fryer until golden, 3 to 4 minutes. Drain, season with salt, and serve.

Stuffed Jalapeños with Chorizo Sausage

12 fresh green
jalapeño chiles

6 ounces cream cheese

6 ounces fresh Mexican-
style chorizo sausage

THIS IS MY GIRLFRIEND Michelle van Vliet's recipe for poppers (and her variation) and the recipe we make more often for ourselves than for guests, although they're terrific party snacks, too. When buying Mexican chorizo sausage (Spanish chorizo is entirely different), and for a better-quality preparation, make sure you get the ones made with natural pork skins and fresh pork and not the ones wrapped in plastic and stapled and made with pig parts. These stuffed jalapeños are dangerously good: I once made this recipe and ate half before any guests arrived.

Makes 6 servings

1. Cut the chiles in entirely half lengthwise with a small paring knife and remove the seeds. Stuff the chiles with the cream cheese and push a piece of chorizo into the cheese on top.

2. Preheat the oven to 425°F.

3. Place the chiles on a baking tray and bake until semisoft, about 15 minutes. Serve hot or warm.

VARIATION: Replace the chorizo sausage with half a slice of bacon wrapped around the chile.

Spring Onions
with Garrotxa Cheese

GARROTXA CHEESE (pronounced gah-ROTCH-ah) is a goat's milk cheese produced in Catalonia. The flavor is milky and delicate, with a hint of nuttiness. Sprinkled on top of caramelized spring onions until melted, it is just about perfect. Spring onions are not scallions, but the onions that push through the ground in the spring with immature bulbs and long green shoots. When supermarkets sell them they're labeled as "spring onions," "green onions," and sometimes "Mexican spring onions" and "Cambray onions." This dish can be made with the white part of young leeks, too. You need to cook the onions over very low heat, so use a heat diffuser if your burner doesn't go low enough. *Makes 4 side-dish servings*

3 tablespoons extra-virgin olive oil

2 pounds spring onions, white and very light green parts only, split lengthwise

Salt and freshly ground black pepper to taste

3 ounces garrotxa cheese, grated

In a large skillet, heat the olive oil over very low heat. Add the onions and cook, turning them now and then, until softened and caramelized, about 3 hours. Season with salt and pepper. Sprinkle the garrotxa cheese on top, cover, and cook until melted, about 3 minutes. Serve hot or warm.

Dal with Cheese

2 tablespoons (1 ounce) dried yellow split peas, picked over

2 tablespoons (1 ounce) dried black lentils, picked over

2 tablespoons (1 ounce) dried green gram or dried mung beans

2 tablespoons (1 ounce) dried red gram or pigeon peas

2 tablespoons (1 ounce) dried split black gram or brown lentils

3 cups water

1 tablespoon clarified butter (ghee; page 171)

½ small onion, thinly sliced

One ½-inch cube fresh ginger, peeled and thinly sliced

3 large garlic cloves, finely chopped

3 fresh green serrano chiles, finely chopped

1 bay leaf

1 tablespoon ground coriander seeds

1 teaspoon salt

(continued)

THE WORD *DAL* REFERS TO a variety of different legumes, of which lentils are one. This dal is made with five different legumes. These five dried legumes are sold in Indian and specialty markets almost exclusively but are available from Internet sources, too; see www.indianfoodsco.com, or www.indianblend.com for the different legumes and the spices. If you want to make this dish but are simply unable to get these particular legumes, then replace them with supermarket choices, such as green split peas, red lentils, brown lentils, black lentils, and dried chickpeas (and try looking for yellow split peas in the Spanish foods aisle). The garam masala called for can be purchased online at www.penzeys.com. Don't use anything labeled "curry powder," which is a turmeric-heavy spice mix.

Makes 4 servings

1. Place the first five ingredients in a bowl, cover with water, and soak for 1 hour. Drain, place in a large saucepan, and pour in the 3 cups water. Bring to a boil over high heat, then reduce the heat to medium-high and boil until the liquid is almost half evaporated and the dals are nearly tender, 25 to 30 minutes. Reduce the heat to low until needed.

2. Meanwhile, melt the clarified butter in a small skillet over medium-high heat. Add the onion and ginger and cook, stirring frequently, until golden, 3 to 4 minutes. Add the garlic, serrano chiles, and bay leaf and cook, stirring, for 1 minute. Add to the dal. Add the coriander, salt, turmeric, and red chile, stir, reduce the heat to low, and cook, stirring occasionally, for 15 minutes. Stir in the cheese and chopped tomatoes and cook for 10 minutes. Stir in the garam masala and cook for 2 minutes. Serve hot.

¼ teaspoon ground turmeric

1 dried red chile, crumbled

2½ ounces fresh white cheese (such as queso blanco, paneer, tuma, Syrian white cheese, frying cheese, farmer's cheese), cut into ¼-inch cubes

2 large ripe plum tomatoes (about 6 ounces), peeled, seeded, and chopped

½ teaspoon garam masala

A HISTORY OF EGGPLANT PARMESAN

The first mention of something resembling eggplant Parmesan is found in *Il saporetto* by Simone Prudenzani (1387–1440), where the recipe refers to Parmesan cheese. The eighteenth-century Neapolitan chef Vincenzo Corrado mentions in his book *Il cuoco galante*, published in 1786, that eggplant can be cooked "alla Parmegiana," meaning the eggplant was seasoned with butter, herbs, cinnamon, and other spices and grated Parmesan cheese and covered with a cream sauce made with egg yolks before being oven-baked.

There are several theories—or, better, apocrypha—about the origin of eggplant Parmesan. The most obvious is that it derives from Parmesan cheese, the predominant cheese used in the dish and a cheese that gets its name from the city of Parma, in Emilia-Romagna, where it has been produced for perhaps a thousand years; and therefore the dish is from Parma. Many food writers believe this explanation because, although the dish is thought to originate in Campania or Sicily, Parmesan cheese is not native to the south of Italy. I've never been persuaded by that line of thinking because from at least the fourteenth century onward, Parmesan was a widely traded cheese and found throughout Italy in quantity.

Other ideas abound. The Sicilian food authority Pino Correnti suggests that the word actually comes from *damigiana*, a sleeve made of wicker where you put a wine bottle, or in this case, the hot casserole. Another explanation is reported by cookbook authors Mary Taylor Simeti and the late Vincent Schiavelli, among several others. They suggest that the name has nothing to do with Parmesan cheese nor Parma the city, but derives instead from the Sicilian word *palmigiana*, meaning "shutters," the louvered panes of shutters or palm-thatched roofs that the layered eggplant slices are meant to resemble. Simeti suggests that since the Sicilian have a "probrem" pronouncing the "l," it became "parmigiana." Another Sicilian food writer, Franca Colonna Romano Apostolo, suggests that the name is *parmiciana*, the equivalent in Sicilian dialect to "Persian," and not parmigiano, a cheese that is not important to the original dish.

Eggplant Parmesan

THE CLASSIC eggplant Parmesan, *parmigiana di melanzane*, is not only a famous southern Italian dish but equally well known here because of Italian Americans. This recipe was published first in my book *Mediterranean Vegetables* (Harvard Common Press, 2001), but I include it again here because the recipe is perfected and one cannot not include it in a book called *Hot & Cheesy*.

Eggplant Parmesan is made a bit differently by Italian Americans, many of whom bread the eggplant before frying it. The traditional eggplant Parmesan is a heavy dish because the eggplant absorbs an enormous amount of oil even after you have blotted and drained it. For this reason one normally does not serve huge portions but, rather, smaller portions that are very filling and usually eaten as a first course. Alternatively, some cooks don't bother to fry the eggplants at all, and that will make for a much lighter preparation. *Makes 8 servings*

4 large eggplants (about 4 pounds), sliced ¼ inch thick

Salt, as needed

4 pounds ripe tomatoes, peeled, seeded, and chopped

3 cups olive oil, for frying

All-purpose flour, for dredging

¼ cup extra-virgin olive oil

1 medium onion, peeled and chopped

1 bunch fresh basil leaves, chopped

Freshly ground black pepper to taste

1 pound fresh mozzarella cheese, very thinly sliced or chopped

4 ounces Parmesan cheese (preferably Parmigiano-Reggiano cheese), freshly grated

4 large hard-boiled eggs, shelled and sliced, or 4 large eggs, beaten one at a time as needed

1. Lay the eggplant pieces on some paper towels and sprinkle with salt. Leave them to drain of their bitter juices for 30 minutes, then pat dry with paper towels. (This step is not needed with modern eggplants as they are selected and grown for lack of bitterness, but is done out of habit by Italian-American cooks.) Place the chopped tomatoes in a colander or strainer and drain for 1 hour.

2. Preheat the oil for frying in a 12-inch skillet to 375°F over medium-high heat, about 10 minutes of preheating. Dredge the eggplant slices in the flour, patting off any excess, and fry the egg-
(continued)

plants until golden brown, about 4 minutes per side. Drain on paper towels. Change the paper towels at least once; this way you will remove a good deal of residual olive oil.

3. In a large skillet or casserole, heat the olive oil over medium-high heat. Add the onion and cook, stirring frequently, until translucent, about 5 minutes. Add the tomatoes and 2 table-spoons chopped basil, reduce the heat to low, and simmer, stirring occasionally, until quite dense, about 30 minutes. Pass the tomato sauce through a food mill and then add to a medium saucepan. Season with salt and pepper and heat over medium heat until the remaining water is nearly gone, 8 to 10 minutes. Meanwhile, pre-heat the oven to 400°F.

4. Cover the bottom of a large baking casserole with a few table-spoons of the tomato sauce and cover it with eggplant slices. Sprinkle on some mozzarella, Parmesan cheese, basil, a few egg slices or some of the beaten egg, salt, pepper, and tomato sauce. Continue in this order until the eggplant slices are used up, fin-ishing the last layer with a sprinkling of Parmesan cheese. Bake until bubbling and the Parmesan top is beginning to brown slightly, about 2 minutes. Serve hot or at room temperature.

"Coupled" Eggplants

THIS WONDERFUL INVENTION of an unknown Sicilian cook is called *'ccucchiati* in Sicilian, which means "coupled." Two eggplant slices are coupled by melted mozzarella to form a sort of *melanzane in carozza*, meant to resemble the more famous Mozzarella in Carozza, a standard offering in so many Italian restaurants.

Makes 6 servings

2 cups olive oil

2 large eggplants (about 2½ pounds), peeled and cut into twenty ¼-inch-thick slices of about the same diameter

Salt, as needed

10 slices mortadella (about 5 ounces)

10 slices fresh mozzarella cheese (about 1 pound)

All-purpose flour, for dredging

2 large eggs, beaten

Dried bread crumbs, for dredging

1. In a skillet, heat 1 cup of the olive oil over medium-high heat. Once it starts to smoke, fry the eggplant slices on one side only until golden, about 3 minutes. Remove and set aside on a paper towel–lined platter to drain. Season with salt. Place a slice of mortadella on the fried side of one eggplant slice and then a slice of fresh mozzarella on top of the mortadella. Place another fried eggplant slice on top of the mozzarella with the fried side facing inward. Trim any overhanging pieces of mortadella. Repeat with the remaining ingredients.

2. Press the coupled eggplant slices together gently by pressing down slightly. Pick them up carefully and dredge in the flour, tapping off any excess, then dip them into the beaten egg on both sides, including their sides. Finally, dredge them in the bread crumbs. Refrigerate for 30 minutes.

3. Add the remaining 1 cup of olive oil to the skillet you fried the eggplants in the first time and heat over medium heat. When the oil is about to smoke, fry the eggplants, turning once with tongs, until golden brown on both sides, 3 to 4 minutes in all. Drain on paper towels and serve hot.

Eggplant with Cheese

2½ pounds eggplant, peeled and chopped

Salt, as needed

1 tablespoon extra-virgin olive oil

1 medium onion, finely chopped

1 large egg, hard-boiled, shelled, and chopped

½ cup dried bread crumbs

4 ounces manchego, Idiazábal, or Ibores cheese freshly grated

1 teaspoon dried mint

⅛ teaspoon ground cloves

⅛ teaspoon ground cinnamon

1 teaspoon sugar

Pinch of ground nutmeg

Salt and freshly ground black pepper to taste

6 to 8 cups olive oil, for frying

1 cup all-purpose flour

2 large eggs, beaten

Freshly ground cumin, for sprinkling

THIS PREPARATION FROM SPAIN'S southernmost region, Andalusia, called *berenjenas con queso*, has roots in the thirteenth century. At that time, the Arab-introduced eggplant was a never-before-seen vegetable in the Mediterranean. The sixteenth-century chef Ruperto de Nola called a nearly identical dish "Moorish eggplant." Eggplant became popular in Spain and Italy, but only after a time, as in the beginning it was thought to be poisonous. These fritters make a quite nice tapas offering or hors d'oeuvre at a party. They freeze well, too. The Spanish cheeses called for can be ordered online at either www.donajuana.com or www.tienda.com.

Makes 6 tapas servings

1. Boil the eggplant in salted water to cover for 10 minutes. Drain very well, pressing out all liquid; otherwise you will be unable to form the eggplant into patties in the next step. Process the eggplant in a food processor until smooth. Transfer to a fine-mesh strainer and leave to drain for another 45 minutes or more if it still looks liquidy. Transfer to a large bowl.

2. In a small skillet, heat the 1 tablespoon extra-virgin olive oil over medium-high heat. Add the onion and cook, stirring, until yellow, 3 to 4 minutes. Add the onion to the eggplant and mix well. Add the hard-boiled egg, bread crumbs, cheese, and mint and mix again. Season with the cloves, cinnamon, sugar, nutmeg, and salt and pepper, and mix well. Form the mixture into patties about 2½ inches in diameter.

3. Preheat the frying oil in a deep fryer or an 8-inch saucepan fitted with a basket insert to 360°F.

4. Dredge the eggplant patties in the flour, tapping off any excess, then dip into the beaten eggs and dredge again in the flour. Deep-fry the eggplant patties in batches until golden, 7 to 8 minutes. Drain of excess oil on paper towels and serve hot or lukewarm with a sprinkle of cumin.

Eggplant with Mozzarella and Béchamel Sauce

2 cups olive oil, plus more for oiling the casserole

3 pounds eggplant, sliced ¼ inch thick

3 large eggs, beaten

1 cup dried bread crumbs, or more as needed

2 tablespoons unsalted butter

Salt, as needed

2 tablespoons all-purpose flour

2 cups milk

Pinch of ground nutmeg

Freshly ground black pepper to taste

9 ounces fresh mozzarella cheese, sliced

1½ cups freshly grated Parmesan cheese (about 5 ounces)

THIS PREPARATION for eggplant is typical of the village of Pago Veiano in the Campania region of Italy, where my grandfather was born. It is served as a first course and known as *melanzane alla besciamella* or *timballo di melanzane.* I learned how to make it from my second cousin Carlo De Ieso. At his house we ate it as a first course followed by fried chicken. The sliced eggplant was dipped in egg, dredged in bread crumbs, and fried in olive oil. It is layered with béchamel sauce, sliced mozzarella, and Parmesan cheese and baked until golden brown.

Makes 6 servings

1. In a large skillet, heat the olive oil over medium-high heat. Dip the eggplant slices in the egg and then dredge in the bread crumbs. Cook the eggplant slices, in batches, until crispy golden brown on both sides, turning only once, 3 to 4 minutes in all for each batch. Remove and drain on paper towels. Season with salt.

2. To prepare the béchamel sauce. in a small saucepan, melt the butter over medium-high heat, then add the flour to form a roux and stir until golden, about 2 minutes. Season with salt, remove the saucepan from the heat, and pour in the milk, stirring constantly. Return to medium-low heat and cook, stirring, until thick, about 10 minutes. Season with nutmeg and black pepper.

3. Preheat the oven to 350°F.

4. Lightly oil a 13 × 10 × 2-inch baking casserole and cover the bottom with a layer of cooked eggplant. Lay some slices of mozzarella on top and a film of béchamel sauce. Sprinkle with Parmesan cheese. Continue in this order until all ingredients are layered. Bake until golden brown on top, about 45 minutes. Serve hot.

Green Bean Casserole

Salt, as needed

2 pounds fresh green beans, trimmed

6 slices bacon (about 4 ounces)

1 medium onion, chopped

Freshly ground black pepper to taste

2 cups sour cream or crème fraîche

8 ounces Swiss (Emmenthaler) cheese, shredded

2 tablespoons unsalted butter, melted

½ cup fresh bread crumbs (see Note)

IN THE AMERICAN MIDWEST, the green bean casserole is a favorite at Thanksgiving. In New England, where I lived for many years, it is not a classic Thanksgiving dish. In any case, "classic" is a bit pretentious, since the green bean casserole was invented in the test kitchen of the Campbell Soup Company in Camden, New Jersey, in 1955. There are literally hundreds of recipes posted online, most calling for frozen green beans, canned soup, and Durkee French Fried Onions. Although I eschew those ingredients—and my recipe is fresher—the casserole is still quite rich, which I guess explains why it's popular.

Makes 6 servings

1. Preheat the oven to 350°F.

2. Bring a large saucepan of water to a boil, salt lightly, then blanch the green beans by plunging them into the boiling water for 3 minutes. Remove with a skimmer and let the water continue boiling while you rinse the beans under cold water in a colander. Return the green beans to the boiling water and cook until tender but with a slight crunch, about 6 minutes. Drain and immediately run under cold water in a colander to stop their cooking. Place the green beans in a large bowl.

3. In a skillet, cook the bacon over medium heat until crispy, about 15 minutes, then crumble once the bacon is cool enough to handle and place in the bowl with the green beans. Discard all but 3 tablespoons of bacon fat from the skillet, then add the onion and cook over medium-high heat, stirring, until softened, about 4 minutes. Transfer the onion to the bowl with the beans and toss well with salt and pepper.

4. In a bowl, stir together the sour cream with the Swiss cheese. Transfer to the bowl with the beans and fold together. Butter a 12 × 9 × 2-inch casserole with 1 tablespoon of the melted butter and transfer the green bean mixture into it, spreading it flat. Toss the bread crumbs with the remaining 1 tablespoon of melted butter and sprinkle the top with them. Bake until golden brown on top, about 25 minutes. Serve hot.

NOTE: This amount of bread crumbs can be made from one ½-inch-thick slice of 5¼ × 3-inch French or Italian bread crumbled in a food processor.

Mushrooms Stuffed with Goat Cheese

5 large (2½ to 3 inches in diameter) portobello mushrooms, stems removed and reserved

1 shallot, finely chopped

1 tablespoon extra-virgin olive oil

Salt and freshly ground black pepper to taste

2 ounces smoked pork, cut into thin strips

1 Crottin de Chavignol cheese (about 3 ounces), or 1 Chèvre de Rocamadour, or 4 thick slices goat cheese log

THIS DELIGHTFUL FRENCH hors d'oeuvre is made with either the small round of goat cheese called Crottin de Chavignol, made near the town of Sancerre in the Loire Valley, or Chèvre de Rocamadour, from the Lot and surrounding region. Both cheeses are made in the form of small rounds that would fit nicely into a large mushroom. They have the nutty flavors that marry well with mushrooms. These cheeses can be ordered via the Internet at www.murrayscheese.com and sometimes will be found at better supermarkets. The smoked pork is sold in your supermarket near the bacon and frankfurters; it is often labeled "smoked pork chops," sold on or off the bone.

Makes 4 first-course servings

1. Preheat the oven to 350°F.

2. Finely chop the mushroom stems and 1 whole mushroom. In a bowl, mix together the chopped mushrooms and the shallot.

3. In a skillet, heat the olive oil over medium-high heat, then add the mushrooms-shallot mixture and cook, stirring, until softened, about 3 minutes. Season with salt and pepper. Stuff the 4 mushroom caps with this mixture.

4. Divide three-quarters of the smoked pork strips and lay them in the mushrooms. Cut the cheese into 4 slices and lay on top of the pork strips. Sprinkle the remaining one-quarter of the pork strips on top and bake until the cheese is very soft and the mushrooms cooked, 25 to 30 minutes. Serve hot.

Mushrooms Stuffed with Gruyère Cheese

12 button (white) mushrooms, stems removed carefully and reserved

Salt and freshly ground black pepper to taste

3 ounces prosciutto, finely chopped

2 tablespoons crème fraîche or sour cream

2 small tomatoes, cut into 12 slices (easier with a serrated knife)

3 ounces Gruyère cheese, cut into 12 squares

THESE STUFFED MUSHROOMS are the perfect little party appetizer, as they are finger food par excellence. Use bulbous button mushrooms whose caps, when removed, leave a nice-size well for stuffing. If they don't sit straight, slice a tiny section off the top to let them sit steady. *Makes 6 appetizer servings*

1. Preheat the oven to 425°F.

2. Season the inside of the mushrooms with salt and pepper. Finely chop the mushroom stems and mix them with the prosciutto and crème fraîche. Stuff this mixture tightly into the mushroom caps. Lay a slice of tomato on top and a piece of Gruyère cheese on top of the tomato. Bake until the mushrooms are soft and brown and the cheese completely melts, 12 to 15 minutes.

Potato, Bacon, and Gruyère Casserole

MANY PEOPLE FEEL that the finest combinations of food involve potatoes, bacon, and cheese. Make this and you'll agree. This combination is appealing on a cold day and needs only the simplest of accompaniments, such as roast game hens or pan-seared chicken breasts. Make sure you use slab bacon.

Makes 4 servings

3 tablespoons unsalted butter

2 large baking potatoes (about 1¾ pounds), peeled and cut into ¼-inch-thick slices

¼ cup finely chopped onion

Salt and freshly ground black pepper to taste

4 ounces Gruyère cheese, shredded

4 ounces slab bacon, cut into 6 slices

1 cup half-and-half

½ cup crème fraîche or sour cream

1. Preheat the oven to 325°F.

2. Coat a 10-inch diameter round casserole with 1 tablespoon of the butter. Arrange half of the potato slices in the buttered casserole, slightly overlapping each other. Sprinkle with half of the onion, season with salt and pepper, and top with half of the cheese. Dot with the remaining butter.

3. Arrange the remaining potato slices over the first layer, sprinkle the remaining onion over the potatoes, season lightly with salt and pepper, and cover with the remaining cheese. Arrange the bacon over the cheese.

4. In a small bowl, whisk together the half-and-half and crème fraîche, then pour over the casserole. Bake until the top is dappled golden brown and bubbling, about 1½ hours. Serve hot.

Baked Potato Skins

2 baking potatoes
(about 1¼ pounds)

2 teaspoons extra-
virgin olive oil

6 slices bacon

Salt to taste

1 fresh jalapeño chile, sliced

4 ounces cheddar cheese,
grated, or shredded
Mexican 4-cheese blend

Freshly ground black
pepper to taste

½ cup sour cream

2 scallions, thinly sliced

I SEEM TO REMEMBER that the first time I had baked potato skins with melted cheese, bacon, and sour cream was in the late 1970s and it was most definitely served as pub food. In fact, the preparation is so much associated with pub grub that normally one drinks a beer with it. There's no reason we can't make these at home, although when I do I tend to serve them as an accompaniment rather than as an appetizer because they are substantial and work well with other foods Some cooks deep-fry the potatoes, but I think the baked version is just fine and easier.

Makes 4 servings

1. Preheat the oven to 400°F.

2. Rub the potatoes with 1 teaspoon of the olive oil, place in a baking pan, and bake until tender, about 1 hour.

3. Meanwhile, in a skillet, cook the bacon over medium-low heat until crisp, about 10 minutes. Remove and drain on paper towels. Let cool, then crumble into large pieces.

4. Remove the potatoes from the oven and let cool enough to handle. Cut in half lengthwise. Carefully scoop out the insides, reserving the scooped potatoes for another use, leaving about ¼ inch of potato on the skin so it looks like a canoe.

5. Increase the heat of the oven to 450°F.

6. Brush the potato skins with the remaining teaspoon of oil and season the inside with salt. Place the potatoes in a baking pan, skin side up, and return to the oven to bake until a little crispier, about 10 minutes. Turn the potatoes and sprinkle the jalapeño

inside. Return to the oven and bake for another 10 minutes. Remove from the oven and let cool enough to handle.

7. Sprinkle the cheese inside the potatoes and top with freshly ground black pepper and the crumbled bacon. Return to the oven. Bake until the cheese is bubbly, about 10 minutes. Remove from the oven and transfer to a serving platter or individual plates. Spoon a dollop of sour cream onto each skin and sprinkle with scallions. Serve hot.

Cheese-Stuffed
Mashed Potato Terrine

2 pounds baking potatoes

12 ounces ricotta cheese

3 large eggs, beaten

Salt and freshly ground
black pepper to taste

Pinch of ground nutmeg

2 tablespoons extra-
virgin olive oil, plus
more for drizzling

Unsalted butter,
for the mold

Dried bread crumbs,
for sprinkling

8 ounces fresh mozzarella
cheese, sliced

½ cup cooked peas

6 ounces salami, thinly
sliced and cut into strips

2 large hard-boiled eggs,
shelled and thinly sliced

ALTHOUGH THIS PREPARATION is made in a terrine, it's a kind of salami, mozzarella, egg, and pea-stuffed potato cake. One could also make this terrine in small tartlet molds, but that's up to you. It is best served as a first course.

Makes 8 servings

1. Place the potatoes in a large saucepan with water to cover and bring to a boil, about 20 minutes, then boil until a skewer glides easily to the center, about 20 minutes more. Drain and when cool enough to handle, peel and mash the potatoes.

2. Preheat the oven to 350°F.

3. In a large bowl, mix the mashed potatoes, ricotta, beaten eggs, salt, pepper, and nutmeg until relatively smooth. Stir in the 2 tablespoons of olive oil.

4. Grease a 2-quart mold or terrine with butter and sprinkle with enough bread crumbs so that when you shake and tilt the terrine they coat the bottom and sides with a thin film of bread crumbs. Put in two-thirds of the potato mixture, making a well in the center and having the sides of the walls about ½ inch thick. In the cavity that remains, arrange the mozzarella, peas, salami,

and sliced eggs, and then cover with the remaining potato mixture. Seal the edges carefully so the stuffing remains closed off.

5. Drizzle some olive oil over the top of the terrine, then sprinkle with some bread crumbs. Bake until golden on top, about 45 minutes. Remove from the oven and let cool for 15 minutes. Unmold if desired, slice into small serving portions, and serve hot or warm.

Gratin Savoyard

2 tablespoons
unsalted butter

2 pounds baking potatoes,
peeled and cut into
$\frac{1}{16}$-inch-thick slices

Salt to taste

4 ounces Gruyère
cheese, shredded

1¼ cup raw unpasteurized
milk, or ¾ cup pasteurized
milk mixed with
½ cup heavy cream

IN THE SAVOY REGION OF FRANCE, this preparation is well known. Traditionally, Savoyard cooks make this gratin with raw unpasteurized milk. You will be able to find such cheese and milk at Whole Foods supermarkets and similar stores, cheese stores, farmers markets, and Web sites such as www.igourmet.com or www.markys.com. If raw milk is not available, then use half pasteurized milk and half heavy cream.

Makes 4 to 6 servings

1. Preheat the oven to 350°F.

2. Butter a medium baking casserole with the butter. Lay some of the sliced potatoes in the casserole, season with salt, and sprinkle with about one-quarter of the cheese and a little milk. Make at least 4 layers, covering each layer with a quarter of the cheese, salt, and a little milk. Make sure to top the last layer with cheese. Pour the remaining milk over the potatoes. Bake until brown on top, 55 to 60 minutes. Serve hot.

Spicy Potatoes with Creamy Cheese Sauce

THIS PERUVIAN DISH requires a dried ground native South American chile called ají limo or ají amarillo. The easiest place to find this chile is under Groceries & Gourmet Foods at www.Amazon.com. Cayenne pepper makes a more than acceptable substitute here. Serve the spicy potatoes as a first course rather than as a side dish. *Makes 8 appetizer servings*

1. Place the whole potatoes in a large saucepan and cover with cold water. Bring to a boil over medium heat, then continue boiling until a skewer glides easily to the center of the potato, 40 to 45 minutes in all. Drain, peel, and slice the potatoes about ½ inch thick.

2. Meanwhile, in a saucepan, melt the cheese with the evaporated milk, vegetable oil, onion, garlic, and chile over medium heat, stirring in a figure-8 pattern until the sauce is creamy and smooth, about 8 minutes. Arrange the lettuce leaves on a serving plate, then lay the sliced potatoes on top of the lettuce and spoon the cheese sauce over the potatoes to cover. Garnish with the egg and black olives. Serve at room temperature.

2 pounds medium Yukon Gold potatoes

12 ounces white cheese (such as farmer's cheese or queso blanco)

One 12-ounce can evaporated milk

3 tablespoons vegetable oil

1 small slice onion

1 large garlic clove, crushed

3 tablespoons ground yellow chile (ají amarillo) or cayenne pepper

For the garnish

1 head Boston or butter lettuce, leaves separated, for garnish

3 large eggs, hard-boiled, shelled, and quartered or sliced

10 black olives, pitted and cut in half

Potato Fondue

1 pound large red potatoes, cut into 1-inch pieces

2 tablespoons extra-virgin olive oil

1 tablespoon chopped fresh flat-leaf parsley

1 teaspoon salt

Freshly ground black pepper to taste

½ cup chopped onion

One 8-ounce package cream cheese, at room temperature

1 cup freshly grated Parmesan cheese (about 3 ounces)

½ cup grated Gruyère cheese (about 1½ ounces)

1¼ cups heavy cream

¼ teaspoon ground nutmeg

THE PARTICULAR COMBINATION of cheese in this recipe is a very appealing taste for perfectly cooked potatoes that remain firm enough not to break apart when you dip them. The preparation can be served either as a party dip or as a dinner accompaniment. If serving as a party dip, you will need a tabletop burner to keep the cheese bubbling gently while you swirl the skewered potato pieces. As an accompaniment, it would be best to pour the cheese sauce over the potatoes, and you would not need a burner.

Makes 10 hors d'oeuvres servings or
6 side-dish servings

1. Place the potatoes in a large saucepan and cover with cold water. Bring to a boil over high heat, about 15 minutes, then reduce the heat to medium and cook until potatoes are just tender with some firmness when pierced with skewer, about another 10 minutes. Drain and transfer the potatoes to a bowl. Toss with 1 tablespoon of the olive oil, the parsley, salt, and pepper.

2. Meanwhile, in a medium saucepan or fondue pot, heat the remaining 1 tablespoon of oil over medium heat. Add the onion and cook, stirring, until softened, about 4 minutes. Reduce the heat to low and add the cream cheese, Parmesan cheese, Gruyère cheese, and cream, whisking until smooth, about 3 minutes. Season with salt, pepper, and the nutmeg. Keep warm and melted until the potatoes are ready.

3. If serving at a party, place the fondue pot on a burner and skewer each potato piece with a short skewer or thick toothpick. If serving as an accompaniment, arrange the potatoes on a serving platter, spoon the fondue over them, and serve immediately.

Aligot

1¼ pounds baking potatoes, peeled and quartered

Salt to taste

3 tablespoons unsalted butter

½ cup heavy cream

3 cups grated Cantal cheese (about 12 ounces)

Freshly ground black pepper to taste

ALIGOT IS ONE OF the famous dishes from the Auvergne region of France. I first had it when my dad, who had retired to France, took me to one of his favorite restaurants in Paris, the Ambassade d'Auvergne. It is the potato-and-cheese lover's dream come true. It's luscious and rib-sticking, and you'll find you can't stop eating it. Mash the potatoes until creamy and then blend in a copious amount of Cantal cheese until the concoction is elastic and very cheesy and smooth. Cantal cheese can be replaced with Gruyère cheese. *Makes 4 servings*

1. Put the potatoes in a saucepan with cold water to cover, salt lightly, and bring to a boil over medium heat. Once they reach a boil, cook until they fall apart when pierced with a fork, about 20 minutes. Drain and push through a food mill back into the empty saucepan you used to boil them.

2. Beat in the butter and cream a little at a time over low heat until the potatoes are soft. Beat in the cheese and continue stirring slowly until the cheese melts, about 8 minutes. Season with pepper, then check the seasoning and correct if desired.

Potato and Cheese Cakes

THESE DELICIOUS little patties are so simple to make that you might just start popping them into your mouth as an appetizer. If you can hold off a little, serve them as a side dish to roast pork or pan-seared pork chops. They freeze well.

Makes 4 servings

1 pound all-purpose potatoes, peeled and quartered

Salt, as needed

3 ounces Edam cheese, grated

2 large egg yolks

Freshly ground black pepper to taste

All-purpose flour, for dredging

6 tablespoons pork lard or unsalted butter

1. Place the potatoes in a saucepan and cover with cold water. Bring to a boil over medium heat, salt lightly, then cook until tender, about 40 minutes in all. Drain and pass the potatoes while still hot through a sieve or ricer into a bowl. Blend in the cheese, egg yolks, salt, and pepper. Knead thoroughly with a fork to mix well. Form the potato dough into patties on a flour-strewn counter. Dredge the patties in flour, tapping off any excess.

2. In a large skillet, melt the lard over medium heat, then cook the patties on both sides until golden brown, about 5 minutes in all. Serve hot.

Cheese- and Bacon-Stuffed Hash Browns

6 ounces thick-cut bacon, cut into 1-inch pieces

Pork lard or unsalted butter, if needed

2 Yukon Gold or russet potatoes (about 1¼ pounds), peeled

Salt to taste

6 ounces cheddar cheese, shredded

FOR A HEARTY BREAKFAST, this dish needs only some eggs on the side or on top. Plan to shovel snow afterward.

Makes 4 servings

1. In a large nonstick skillet, cook the bacon over medium-low heat until crispy and a few tablespoons of fat are in the skillet. If there isn't enough fat, add a couple of tablespoons of lard or butter to the skillet. Remove the bacon.

2. Increase the heat to medium. Using the large hole of a standing box grater, grate 1 of the potatoes directly into the skillet. Flatten and spread out until 9 inches in diameter with a spatula and season with salt. Sprinkle the bacon over the potato. Cover with the cheese. Grate the remaining potato onto a plate and then sprinkle it over the cheese in the skillet, covering all the cheese. Tamp down the edges with a spatula and cook until golden brown and crispy on the bottom, about 15 minutes. Turn with a wide spatula. Don't worry if it breaks. Cook the other side until golden, about 10 minutes. Serve hot.

Pumpkin and Cheese Stew

THIS VEGETABLE STEW is luscious but also very hot from the chiles. It makes for a nice presentation too, as it is colorfully orange and white. Many supermarkets sell peeled and cut-up fresh pumpkin flesh as a convenience so you don't have to buy a whole huge pumpkin. You will not want to use canned pumpkin in this recipe. Pumpkin stew can easily be served as a main course with a green salad on the side.　*Makes 6 servings*

1 tablespoon vegetable or safflower oil

1 medium onion, finely chopped

2 large garlic cloves, finely chopped

6 fresh green serrano chiles, finely chopped

1¾ pounds pumpkin flesh, cubed

2 medium white potatoes, peeled and cubed

1 cup water

2 teaspoons salt, plus more to taste

½ teaspoon freshly ground black pepper, plus more to taste

¼ cup half-and-half

1¼ cups diced queso blanco, queso fresco, or farmer's cheese (about 6 ounces)

1. In a casserole, heat the vegetable oil over medium-high heat, then add the onion, garlic, and chiles and cook, stirring, until softened, about 5 minutes. Add the pumpkin, potatoes, water, salt, and pepper. Stir, cover, reduce the heat to low, and simmer until the pumpkin and potatoes are tender, 40 to 45 minutes.

2. Add the half-and-half and 1 cup of the cheese and cook, stirring gently, until the cheese has melted, about 5 minutes. Season with more salt and pepper, if desired, and garnish with the remaining cheese. Serve immediately.

Pumpkin with Ricotta Salata

6 tablespoons extra-
virgin olive oil

1 medium onion, peeled
and thinly sliced

1 celery stalk, chopped

1 large garlic clove,
lightly crushed

4 salted anchovy
fillets, rinsed

2 tablespoons capers,
chopped if large

2 pounds pumpkin
flesh, cut into pieces

1½ cups pitted imported
black olives (about 8 ounces)

1 tablespoon freshly
grated ricotta salata,
plus more as needed

Salt and freshly ground
black pepper to taste

Toasted bread, for
serving (optional)

IN THE SOUTHERN ITALIAN REGION of Apulia, pumpkin is prepared using a strongly flavored dried ricotta cheese called ricotta salata or cacioricotta. This fragrant dish, seasoned with anchovy, capers, garlic, onion, and olives, is usually served at room temperature, which allows the flavors to mellow nicely.

Makes 4 to 6 servings

1. In a large casserole, heat the olive oil over medium-high heat, then add the onion, celery, garlic, anchovies, and capers and cook, stirring so the garlic doesn't burn, until the onions are translucent, about 5 minutes. Remove and discard the garlic.

2. Add the pumpkin, cover, reduce the heat to medium-low, and cook until tender, about 25 minutes. Add the olives and cook until heated through, about 8 minutes. Turn off the heat, sprinkle with the ricotta salata, season with salt and pepper, and serve at room temperature on toasted bread if desired. Serve extra ricotta salata on the side.

Saag Paneer

MOST AMERICANS who love this dish first ate it in an Indian restaurant. However, they think of it as a creamy spinach curry with cheese, which it is, except that saag paneer is actually made with mustard greens. The version made with spinach is called palak paneer. In any case, the two dishes are almost identical, and no one will notice what you use.   *Makes 3 servings*

1½ pounds mustard greens, heaviest part of stems removed

8 ounces spinach, heavy stems removed

3 tablespoons vegetable oil

1 teaspoon cumin seeds

8 large garlic cloves, lightly crushed

1 small onion, finely chopped

3 tablespoons chickpea flour

1 teaspoon salt

1 teaspoon red chile flakes

8 ounces paneer cheese, queso blanco, or queso fresco, cubed

2 tablespoons heavy cream

One 1-inch cube fresh ginger, peeled and finely julienned

1. Place the mustard and spinach in a large saucepan with only the water adhering to it from its last rinsing, cover, and wilt over high heat, turning once or twice, about 5 minutes. Remove and finely chop.

2. In a skillet, heat the vegetable oil over medium-high heat, then add the cumin seeds and when they start to crackle, add the garlic and cook until it turns light brown in a minute; reduce the heat if it is turning brown too quickly. Add the onion and cook, stirring, until golden, 3 to 4 minutes. Add the chickpea flour and cook, stirring constantly, until it is blended without any lumps, about 3 minutes. Add the chopped greens and cook, adding up to ¼ cup water if it is too dry, until all the liquid is evaporated but the spinach is still wet, about 10 minutes. Add the salt, red chile flakes, and cheese, and cook until the cheese is soft, about 3 minutes. Stir in the cream and add the ginger, stir well, cook for 1 minute, and serve.

Rutabagas au Gratin

1½ pounds rutabagas, peeled and diced

½ teaspoon salt

½ teaspoon sugar

1 tablespoon unsalted butter

1 tablespoon all-purpose flour

¾ cup milk

½ cup shredded cheddar cheese (about 1½ ounces)

1 teaspoon seasoning salt, such as Dash or Accent

Pinch of freshly ground black pepper

2 tablespoons dried bread crumbs

RUTABAGAS GET THEIR NAME from the Swedish for "root bag." These root vegetables are similar to turnips but larger, yellower, and sweeter. They're a big favorite in the Scandinavian countries. Nutritionally, they are good source of beta carotene and have more vitamin C than turnips.

Makes 4 side-dish servings

1. Preheat the oven to 350°F.

2. In a large saucepan, combine the rutabagas, salt, and sugar and cover with water. Bring to a boil over high heat, reduce the heat to low, cover, and cook until tender, about 12 minutes. Drain well.

3. In the same saucepan, melt the butter over low heat. Add the flour to form a roux and cook, stirring constantly, for 1 minute. Gradually add the milk while stirring, then cook, stirring constantly, over medium heat until thickened and bubbly. Add the cheese, seasoning salt, and pepper, stirring until the cheese melts. Remove from the heat and stir in the rutabagas. Transfer the rutabaga mixture to a lightly buttered 1-quart baking casserole, sprinkle with the bread crumbs, and bake until the top is golden, 20 to 25 minutes. Serve hot.

Spinach Raclette

THIS RIDICULOUSLY SIMPLE recipe pleases everyone both in taste and in the disbelief about its simplicity. It's simply a matter of laying the spinach in a casserole, topping it with the raclette cheese, and placing it under the broiler. That's all. However, there's a trick and that is that the spinach must be completely dry, so either buy a bag of prewashed spinach leaves or spin-dry the washed bunch of spinach and then pat dry with paper towels. The Swiss cheese known as raclette is perfect for this preparation, but you could also use Gruyère, Appenzeller, Comté, Cantal, or Emmenthaler (Swiss cheese).

Makes 4 servings

1 tablespoon unsalted butter

1½ pounds spinach, heavy stems removed and dried very well

Salt to taste

8 ounces raclette cheese, shredded

1. Preheat the broiler.

2. Butter the bottom and sides of a 12 × 9 × 2-inch baking casserole. Add the spinach, covering the casserole evenly. Season with salt. Sprinkle the cheese on top, then broil until the cheese is melted and lightly dappled golden, 4 to 6 minutes. Serve hot.

Swiss Chard with Swiss Cheese

Salt, as needed

2 bunches Swiss chard (about 2½ pounds), stems cut into 1-inch pieces, leaves sliced into 1-inch strips

4 slices bacon, cut into ½-inch pieces

Freshly ground black pepper to taste

6 ounces Swiss (Emmenthaler) cheese, shredded

THIS IS A SIMPLE PREPARATION with a great taste that's perfect for those who want more dark leafy greens in their diet. Red-stemmed Swiss chard, in particular, makes this preparation also look very pretty. *Makes 4 or 5 servings*

1. Preheat the oven to 350°F.

2. Bring a large pot of salted water to a boil over high heat, and cook the Swiss chard until softened but still bright green, about 8 minutes. Drain well in a colander, pressing out excess water with the back of a wooden spoon.

3. In a skillet, cook the bacon over medium heat until nearly crispy, stirring occasionally, about 6 minutes.

4. Pour some of the bacon fat into a 10-inch baking casserole. Lay the Swiss chard in the casserole with the bacon, mixing slightly. Sprinkle with salt and pepper. Sprinkle the Swiss cheese on top and bake until the cheese melts and the chard is hot, 10 minutes. Serve hot.

Swiss Chard Stems on Fondue of Ham and Cheese

ONE OF THE CHALLENGES for the cook when it comes to Swiss chard is what to do with the stems, which are rarely called for in recipes. This Provençal preparation is called *côtes de blettes sur fondue de fromage et jambon cru* and is an ingenious way to use the stems not used in, for instance, the Swiss Chard Tart (page 86). *Makes 4 servings*

Salt, as needed

1 pound Swiss chard stems, cut into 1-inch pieces

2 tablespoons extra-virgin olive oil, plus more to taste

1 medium onion, chopped

3 medium tomatoes, peeled, seeded, and diced

2 teaspoons herbes de Provence

Freshly ground black pepper to taste

1 cup pitted black olives

3 slices cooked ham, sliced into thin strips

2 ounces Swiss (Emmenthaler) cheese, shredded

4 tablespoons heavy cream

1. Bring a pot of water to a boil over high heat, salt lightly, and cook the Swiss chard stems until softened, about 10 minutes. Drain.

2. In a large skillet, heat the olive oil over medium heat. Add the onion and cook, stirring, until softened, about 7 minutes. Add the Swiss chard stems and the tomatoes and continue cooking for 1 minute. Season with the herbes de Provence, salt, and pepper and then add the olives. Reduce the heat to low, cover, and simmer, stirring occasionally, until softened, about 10 minutes.

3. Meanwhile, in a small skillet over medium high-heat, cook the ham on both sides until crispy golden brown in parts, 2 to 3 minutes.

4. In a small saucepan, melt the cheese with the cream over low heat, stirring constantly. Add the ham and cook for 1 minute. Pour a puddle of cheese sauce on 4 individual serving plates and spoon the Swiss chard mixture on top. Serve immediately.

White Cheese in Tomatoes and Cream Sauce

2½ pounds ripe tomatoes, cut in half, seeds squeezed out, and grated against the largest holes of a box grater

¼ cup vegetable oil

One 1-inch cube fresh ginger, peeled and finely chopped

1 bay leaf

Seeds from 2 cardamom pods, crushed

2 teaspoons ground fenugreek

1 teaspoon ground red chile or cayenne pepper

¼ cup heavy cream

½ teaspoon garam masala

Salt to taste

8 ounces paneer cheese, queso blanco, queso asadero, farmer's cheese, well-soaked feta cheese, or cottage cheese drained by squeezing out liquid and formed into lumps by squeezing in your hand, cubed

1 tablespoon finely chopped fresh cilantro (coriander leaf)

THE CHEESE USED IN THIS Mogul dish from northern India is called *paneer*, a word that means "cheese," an unsalted firm white cheese that can be found in some supermarkets with Whole Foods–type variety. You could replace it with Mexican queso blanco, Syrian white cheese, well-soaked feta cheese (to remove all brining salts), or cottage cheese drained and pressed together to form lumps. The cubes of soft cheese are embedded in tomato sauce, which should be made from fresh tomatoes in the summer for an extraordinary dish. The garam masala called for can be purchased online at www.penzeys.com.

Makes 4 servings

1. Place the tomatoes in a food processor and blend until a smooth purée. In a large skillet, heat the vegetable oil over medium-high heat, then add the tomato purée, ginger, bay leaf, cardamom seeds, fenugreek, and ground chile. Cover and cook until bubbling furiously for a few minutes, about 6 minutes in all. Reduce the heat to low, add the cream, garam masala, and salt, stir, and simmer until dense, about 45 minutes, stirring occasionally.

2. Add the cheese and cook until it is soft and hot, about 5 minutes. Transfer to a serving platter or bowl and garnish with the cilantro leaves. Serve immediately.

Baked Zucchini with Tomato and Fontina Cheese

THIS PREPARATION can be served as an antipasto or as a side dish. Although I prefer it piping hot right out of the oven, it can be served in a more relaxed way as a room temperature appetizer. The finished dish will be topped by an attractive golden crust and redolent with oregano. *Makes 6 servings*

1. Preheat the oven to 375°F.

2. In a medium skillet, melt 2 tablespoons of the butter over medium heat, then add the bread strips and cook until golden, about 5 minutes.

3. Spread a little olive oil over the bottom of 12 × 9-inch a baking casserole, then arrange the pieces of tomato, zucchini, and bread in alternating strips. Top everything with the fontina cheese, pushing it down into the other ingredients. Season with the oregano, salt, and pepper. Drizzle some olive oil on top, then sprinkle with the bread crumbs and dot the top with thin slivers of the remaining 1 tablespoon butter. Cover with aluminum foil and bake for 25 minutes. Remove the foil and continue to bake until the top is golden and crusty, about 15 minutes more. Serve hot, warm, or at room temperature.

3 tablespoons unsalted butter

Two ½-inch-thick slices Italian bread, cut into 3 × ¼-inch strips

Extra-virgin olive oil, for oiling the baking dish and drizzling

1 large, ripe but firm tomato (about 12 ounces), peeled, seeded, and cut into strips

3 medium zucchini, cut in half, then each half cut into ¼-inch-wide strips

2 ounces Fontina Val d'Aosta cheese, cut into 3 × ¼-inch strips

1 to 2 teaspoons dried oregano, to your taste

Salt and freshly ground black pepper to taste

3 tablespoons dried bread crumbs

Baked Stuffed Zucchini with Cheese

½ teaspoon salt, plus more as needed

6 zucchini (about 2 pounds)

Six ½-inch-thick slices French or Italian country bread (8 ounces), crust removed

1 cup milk

1 cup ricotta cheese (page 65)

¼ cup freshly grated Parmesan cheese

2 large eggs, beaten

1 teaspoon extra-virgin olive oil, for oiling the casserole

3 ounces dried bread crumbs

3 tablespoons unsalted butter, cut into thin slivers

THIS RICOTTA- AND BREAD-STUFFED zucchini is a luscious dish that is a very nice accompaniment to Veal Parmesan (page 348). It's quite easy to assemble and prepare.

Makes 8 to 10 servings

1. Preheat the oven to 350°F.

2. Bring a large saucepan of water to a boil and salt lightly. Add the zucchini and boil for 5 minutes. Remove the zucchini and let cool, then cut lengthwise. Scoop out some of the pulp with a spoon, being careful not to cut into the shell, and chop the pulp.

3. In a bowl, soak the bread in the milk for a minute or two. Remove the bread and squeeze out the milk. Transfer the bread to a large bowl and mix with the ricotta cheese, Parmesan cheese, half of the zucchini pulp, the eggs, and with the ½ teaspoon salt. Stuff the zucchini shells with this mixture and place in a lightly oiled 13 × 10-inch baking casserole. Sprinkle the tops of the zucchini with the bread crumbs and thin slivers of butter. Bake until golden brown on top, about 30 minutes. Serve hot.

NOTE: The half of the zucchini pulp you don't use can be mixed with some grated pecorino cheese, an egg, and some bread crumbs and fried in oil in the form of patties.

Meat and Seafood
with Cheese

The very first recipe in this chapter, Filet Mignon with Roquefort Butter (page 336), is my go-to dish when I don't want to make too much of an effort. It's simple and delicious. A delightful and surprising preparation is Stuffed Meatballs with Mozzarella and Pistachios (page 340) because hidden inside is this green cheese—that is, mozzarella that has been turned green by the pistachios. Further along is an Italian-American classic, Veal Parmesan (page 348), whose leftovers can be turned into a Veal Parmesan Hero (page 134). Seafood and cheese is not that common a combination, but the New England–style Haddock and Cheddar Casserole (page 369) will surely delight in its flavor and simplicity.

Filet Mignon with Roquefort Butter

For the Roquefort butter

½ cup crumbled Roquefort cheese (about 2 ounces)

4 tablespoons unsalted butter, at room temperature

2 tablespoons sour cream

1 tablespoon chopped fresh chives

For the steak

4 filet mignon steaks (about 1½ pounds in all)

1 tablespoons extra-virgin olive oil

Freshly ground black pepper to taste

THIS IS A POPULAR BISTRO DISH in France's southwest, especially in Languedoc. Roquefort cheese, which is produced in Languedoc, is a much-loved ingredient in many local recipes, such as this sauce. It's ideal with filet mignon because the meat is so tender and lean. You can also use rib eye for this dish.

Makes 4 servings

1. For the butter, combine the Roquefort cheese, butter, sour cream, and chives and beat well until smooth. Keep at room temperature and stir before using.

2. Prepare a hot charcoal fire to one side of the grill box, preheat a gas grill on high for 20 minutes, or preheat a cast-iron or carbon-steel skillet on high.

3. Brush the steaks with the olive oil and season with pepper. Grill the steaks, turning once, until rare, about 4 minutes per side directly over the fire, a little longer if cooking indirectly, and about the same time if cooking in a skillet. Place the steaks on individual serving plates and serve with a dollop of Roquefort butter in the center. Pass the remaining butter at the table.

Fajitas al Sombrero

THIS DISH COMES FROM a restaurant in the small town of San Fernando, in the region of northern Mexico along the Tamaulipas coast close to the Texas border. A specialty there is a dish called *fajitas al sombrero*, the "sombrero" being the tortilla that tops the dish. I've adapted the recipe from Mexican food authority Karen Hursh Graber, whose knowledgeable writings on the regional foods of Mexico are always enlightening.

Makes 4 servings

1 pound skirt steak

Salt and freshly ground black pepper to taste

4 slices bacon

1 large onion, cut in half widthwise, halves thinly sliced

2 fresh poblano chiles, seeded and cut into strips

6 ounces Mexican-style manchego, queso Chihuahua, or Monterey Jack cheese, shredded

4 small flour tortillas, plus more for serving

Salsa, for garnish

Sour cream, for garnish

1. Preheat a cast-iron skillet over high heat for 10 minutes. Add the steak to the hot skillet and cook, turning once, until very rare, about 4 minutes in all. Remove the steak, season with salt and pepper, and let rest while you continue the preparation.

2. Add the bacon to the skillet and remove once it is almost crispy, about 3 minutes, leaving the fat in the pan. Add the onion and poblano chiles and cook, stirring frequently, until the onion is softened, about 7 minutes.

3. Thinly slice the skirt steak and add the slices to the skillet. Toss well with the vegetables and cook for 1 to 2 minutes. Flatten the vegetable mixture to cover the bottom of the skillet to its sides and then top with the shredded cheese. Once the cheese has melted, divide the meat mixture onto 4 plates and top each serving with a strip of bacon and a tortilla. Serve with additional tortillas, salsa, and sour cream on the side.

Gravy Meatballs on Spinach Mashed Potatoes

One 2-inch-thick slice
Italian or French country
bread, crust removed

1 cup milk

1 pound ground beef

1 large egg

Salt and freshly ground
black pepper to taste

5 tablespoons
unsalted butter

1 cup sour cream

½ cup mascarpone
cheese (4 ounces)

¼ cup freshly grated
Parmesan cheese

8 ounces spinach leaves

2 russet potatoes
(about 1¼ pounds)

4 large garlic cloves,
mashed in a mortar
with ½ teaspoon salt

10 tablespoons heavy
cream or milk

1 cup shredded Gruyère
cheese (about 2¼ ounces)

THIS RECIPE IS an entire meal, so as you go through the method, remember that you are presenting one big dinner. This is rib-sticking food too, luscious and inviting.

Makes 4 servings

1. Soak the bread in the milk for a few minutes, then squeeze the bread out and discard the milk. Place the bread in a bowl with the ground beef, egg, salt, and pepper. Knead the mixture with your hands and form into 32 small meatballs.

2. In a large skillet, melt 1 tablespoon of the butter over medium-low heat. Add the meatballs to the skillet and cook, shaking the skillet occasionally, until the meatballs are golden brown, about 25 minutes. Add the sour cream, mascarpone cheese, and Parmesan cheese and continue cooking until smooth and hot, about 8 minutes. Keep warm.

3. In a large pot, add the spinach with only the water adhering to it from its last rinsing, cover, turn the heat to medium-high, and cook until it wilts, turning a few times, about 5 minutes. Drain well. Finely chop.

4. In a large pot, place the whole potatoes and cover by several inches with water. Bring to a boil over high heat, then reduce the heat to medium and cook until pierced easily with a skewer, about

45 minutes. Drain, cool, peel, and mash into a saucepan with the remaining 4 tablespoons butter, the spinach, and garlic. Cook over low heat, stirring in the cream and Gruyère cheese until both are smooth, about 5 minutes. Season with salt and pepper.

5. Spread some mashed potatoes on a plate. Place the meatballs over the potatoes and spoon some gravy on top. Serve hot.

Stuffed Meatballs with Mozzarella and Pistachios

1 large egg

1 pound ground beef or bison

1 thick slice French or Italian country bread, soaked in milk for 5 minutes and squeezed dry

2 tablespoons finely chopped fresh flat-leaf parsley

1 teaspoon salt

¼ cup ground pistachios

One 4-ounce ball fresh mozzarella cheese, quartered

1½ cups Tomato Sauce (page 235; optional)

THIS IS A DELIGHTFUL PREPARATION because hidden inside is this green cheese. No, it's not really green cheese but fresh mozzarella encased in ground pistachios encased in ground meat, the pistachios turning the cheese green. If you like, you can serve this with tomato sauce or any leftover sauce you have in the refrigerator. I also like to cook the meatballs at a low temperature, but you can cook them at a higher temperature if you are pressed for time. *Makes 4 servings*

1. Preheat the oven to 325°F.

2. Place the egg in a food processor and run for 15 seconds. Add the meat, bread, parsley, and salt and run until almost pasty. If you don't have a food processor, you can mix everything in a bowl with your hands. Divide the mixture into 4 equal pieces. Flatten each like a hamburger with wet hands so they don't stick. Sprinkle 1 tablespoon of the pistachios over each hamburger. Place a piece of mozzarella in the middle and, using your hands, cup and form the meat around the cheese, enclosing it entirely. Mold the ball with your hands, like making a snowball, until there are no cracks or seams.

3. Put the meatballs in a baking dish and bake until golden brown, about 1 hour. Serve with the tomato sauce if desired.

Baked Lamb with Potatoes and Cheese

THIS WEEKEND TREAT is an oven-baked delight begging to be made in the early spring. It's an easy dish because everything goes into the casserole and you bake away until the two different cuts of lamb, the potatoes, and the cheese melt together. A side dish of a spinach and arugula salad with light vinaigrette would complete the meal. *Makes 8 servings*

4 cups freshly and very finely grated pecorino cheese (about 12 ounces)

⅓ cup finely chopped fresh flat-leaf parsley

3 tablespoons extra-virgin olive oil

1 large white onion, sliced about ¼ inch thick

2 pounds blade lamb chops

1½ pounds rib lamb chops

3 fresh rosemary sprigs

3 baking potatoes (about 2¾ pounds), peeled and cut into wedges

1. In a bowl, mix together the cheese and parsley.

2. Preheat the oven to 325°F.

3. In a 12- to-14-inch round (preferably) baking casserole, drizzle 1 tablespoon of the olive oil to coat the bottom, then arrange the onion slices to cover the bottom. Dredge the lamb pieces on all sides in the cheese mixture and lay it on top of the onion. Place the rosemary sprigs in the casserole. Dredge the potato wedges in the cheese mixture too and use them to cover the lamb completely. Sprinkle any remaining cheese over the potatoes. Drizzle the remaining olive oil over the top and bake until tender and golden, 2½ to 3 hours.

Kofta Curry

For the meatballs

1 pound ground lamb

1 large egg, beaten

2 tablespoons finely chopped fresh cilantro

1 teaspoon all-purpose flour

1½ teaspoons grated fresh ginger

¾ teaspoon salt

⅛ teaspoon ground cloves

⅛ teaspoon ground cinnamon

3 tablespoons vegetable oil

(continued)

THIS IS ONE OF THOSE Indian dishes that I like so much and find myself ordering when I go to Indian restaurants. Once you get the hang of it—and "it" is mostly the use of spices—Indian food is quite easy to make. You just can't beat the flavor and subtlety of dishes like this, made with ground lamb in a richly spiced curry with coconut, tomato, and cheese.

Makes 4 servings

1. For the meatballs, in a bowl, combine the lamb, egg, cilantro, flour, ginger, salt, cloves, and cinnamon. Mix well with your hands until blended, then shape into meatballs about the size of a golf ball using wet hands so they don't stick.

2. In a skillet, heat the vegetable oil over medium heat, then add the meatballs and cook, shaking the skillet and turning the meatballs with a spatula so they don't stick, until browned all over, about 8 minutes. Turn off the heat and leave in the pan.

3. For the curry, in another skillet, heat the vegetable oil over medium heat. Add the onion and cook, stirring, until softened, about 7 minutes. Add the coconut, garlic, coriander, paprika, green chile, chile flakes, and turmeric. Cook, stirring, for 3 minutes. Add the tomatoes, boiling water, and salt. Reduce the heat to low and simmer, stirring gently occasionally, until softened and thickened, about 15 minutes. Add the cooked meatballs and cheese and simmer until the cheese is very soft, about 10 minutes. Stir in the lemon juice and serve.

For the curry

3 tablespoons vegetable oil

1 medium onion,
thinly sliced

2 tablespoons grated
unsweetened coconut

2 large garlic cloves, crushed

1 tablespoon ground
coriander seeds

1 teaspoon hot paprika

2 teaspoons finely chopped
fresh green chile

¼ teaspoon red chile flakes

¼ teaspoon ground turmeric

3 large tomatoes,
peeled and chopped

½ cup boiling water

½ teaspoon salt

5 ounces fresh white cheese
(such as paneer cheese,
queso blanco, Syrian white
cheese, or frying cheese),
cut into ¾-inch cubes

Juice of ½ lemon

Lamb and Feta Cheese Burgers

Unsalted butter, for greasing the skillet

4 kaiser rolls or sesame seed hamburger buns

2 large garlic cloves

Salt to taste

½ cucumber, peeled and grated

6 tablespoons thick yogurt or strained yogurt (*labna*)

3 tablespoons finely chopped fresh mint

1 teaspoon extra-virgin olive oil, plus more for greasing the skillet

1 pound ground lamb

¼ cup finely chopped red onion

1 teaspoon dried oregano

½ teaspoon freshly ground black pepper

4 ounces feta cheese in one piece, cut into 4 equal slices

4 slices red onion

1 small tomato, sliced

THIS POPULAR DISH gets its inspiration from Greek food; it's not a traditional dish in Greece but is an American favorite. There are any number of ways of making it. For example, some cooks mix the feta cheese into the ground lamb, while others use black olives and fresh mint in abundance. I like this recipe because it keeps the concept closer to what it is: a burger! Serve with french fries, potato chips, or a cucumber salad.

Makes 4 servings

1. Preheat a large cast-iron skillet over medium heat for 10 minutes.

2. Lightly butter the skillet and place the hamburger buns down to make crispy on the inside. Remove and set aside.

3. In a mortar, pound the garlic with ½ teaspoon salt until mushy, then transfer to a bowl and stir together with the grated cucumber, yogurt, and mint. Stir in the olive oil and season with salt if necessary. Refrigerate until needed.

4. In a bowl, mix the lamb with the chopped red onion, oregano, some salt, and the pepper. Form the lamb into 4 quarter-pound patties, without handling the meat excessively. Make an indentation in the middle of the patty with your thumb, which will help it maintain its shape while cooking. Put a little olive oil in the

skillet, then cook the lamb until golden brown on the bottom, about 8 minutes. Turn, then lay the feta cheese on top, cover the skillet, and cook until the feta cheese is soft, about 5 minutes.

5. Lay the red onion and tomato slices on the bottom buns. Spoon some cucumber sauce over, place the patties on top, and cover with the other bun halves. Serve immediately.

Veal Chops with Cantal Cheese and Mushroom Sauce

2 veal chops (about 1½ pounds), bone removed

All-purpose flour, for dredging

4 tablespoons unsalted butter

14 ounces cremini mushrooms, thinly sliced

8 ounces small zucchini, thinly sliced into rounds

4 ounces tomatoes, peeled and chopped

½ cup white wine

Salt and freshly ground black pepper to taste

3 ounces Cantal cheese, raclette cheese, or Saint-Nectaire cheese, diced

½ cup chopped fresh chives

THIS LUSCIOUS PREPARATION, which I also make with pork chops or turkey breast, is a mainstay winter dish in our house. Each different cheese gives a slightly different taste to this dish, so experiment. It's rich, so you may want to accompany it with something much lighter, such as a simple garden salad or sautéed spinach. *Makes 4 servings*

1. Dredge the veal chops in the flour, tapping off any excess. In a skillet, melt the butter over high heat, then add the veal chops and cook, turning once, until browned on both sides, about 2 minutes. Add the mushrooms, zucchini, and tomatoes and cook, stirring, until mixed well, about 2 minutes.

2. Pour in the wine, reduce the heat to low, and cook until the wine is nearly evaporated and the mushrooms and zucchini are softened, about 20 minutes. Season with salt and pepper, add the cheese, and cook until the cheese is almost all melted, about 3 minutes. Sprinkle with the chives, stirring, then serve.

Stuffed Veal Chops Valdostana

THIS DELICIOUS VEAL CHOP cooked in butter comes from the Val d'Aosta region of northern Italy, where the famous Fontina Val d'Aosta cheese is made, which is featured in this preparation. Curiously, in the 1960s, this preparation was popular on menus of restaurants in New York serving "continental cuisine." *Makes 4 servings*

4 veal chops (about 1 inch thick, about 2 pounds in all)

4 ounces Fontina Val d'Aosta cheese, cut into thin strips

8 slices prosciutto (about 2 ounces)

Salt and freshly ground black pepper to taste

All-purpose flour, for dredging

1 large egg, beaten

Dried bread crumbs, for dredging

4 tablespoons unsalted butter

1. With a sharp paring knife, make an incision along the side of the chop through its surrounding fat and then widen it with the knife to form a pocket. Divide the cheese into quarters, wrap each quarter in 2 slices of prosciutto, then flatten slightly and stuff inside the pockets of the veal chops. Pound the edge of the pocket opening with your hand so the opening will stay closed, or seal with a toothpick. Season the chops with salt and pepper. Place the flour, egg, and bread crumbs in separate shallow dishes. Dredge the chops in the flour, patting off any excess; dip in the egg; and then dredge in the bread crumbs on all sides.

2. In a large skillet, melt the butter over low heat, then cook the chops, turning only once, until golden brown, about 35 minutes in all. Serve immediately.

Veal Parmesan

For the marinara sauce

One 28-ounce can peeled
whole plum tomatoes

3 tablespoons extra-
virgin olive oil

½ small onion,
finely chopped

1 large garlic clove,
finely chopped

1 bay leaf

½ teaspoon dried oregano

¼ teaspoon dried thyme

1 tablespoon finely chopped
fresh flat-leaf parsley

½ teaspoon salt

¼ teaspoon freshly
ground black pepper,
or more to taste

½ teaspoon sugar (optional)

(continued)

I FONDLY REMEMBER ordering veal Parmesan when I was a teenager on Long Island, and we would go to those wonderful Italian-American restaurants with their red-checked tablecloths and wicker-basket chianti bottle candle holders. In those days we called them Italian restaurants because we did not yet know they had little to do with the food of Italy. But they were great. In the supermarkets, we would buy veal scaloppine that was pounded to about a ⅛-inch thickness. They were usually cut from the top round, although fancy restaurants would cut them from the filet. Typically, an Italian-American family would use leftovers to make Veal Parmesan Heros (page 134).

Makes 6 to 8 servings

1. For the marinara sauce, put the tomatoes and their liquid into a food processor and pulse until coarsely chopped, or chop by hand.

2. In a 4-quart saucepan, heat the olive oil over medium heat. Add the onion, garlic, and bay leaf and cook, stirring occasionally, until the onion is translucent, about 10 minutes. Add the tomatoes, oregano, and thyme and cook, stirring occasionally, until the sauce thickens slightly, about 20 minutes. Stir in the parsley and season with salt and pepper. Taste and if the sauce is bitter, add the sugar.

3. For the veal, season the veal with salt and pepper. Place the flour, eggs, and bread crumbs in separate shallow dishes. Working with one piece at a time, dredge the veal in the flour, then eggs, and then the bread crumbs and transfer to a parchment paper–lined baking sheet.

4. In a 12-inch skillet, heat the olive oil over medium-high heat. Add 2 pieces of breaded veal at a time and cook, turning once with tongs, until golden brown, about 3 minutes. Transfer the veal to a baking sheet. Cook the remaining veal.

5. Set an oven rack 10 inches from the heating element. Preheat the broiler.

6. Top each piece of veal with ⅓ cup of the marinara sauce, cover with provolone cheese, and sprinkle with 1½ tablespoons of the Parmesan. Broil until the cheese is golden and bubbly, about 5 minutes. Sprinkle with the parsley. Serve the veal whole or cut in half depending on the desired portion size.

For the veal

6 veal scaloppine
(about 2 pounds), cut
in half if desired

Salt and freshly ground
black pepper to taste

½ cup all-purpose flour

2 large eggs, beaten

2 cups dried bread crumbs

½ cup extra-virgin olive oil

8 ounces provolone
cheese, sliced

¾ cup freshly grated
Parmesan cheese
(about 2½ ounces)

2 tablespoons chopped
fresh flat-leaf parsley

Vols-au-Vent with Ham, Mushroom, and Cheese

4 vols-au-vent frozen
pastry shells

3 tablespoons
unsalted butter

1 cup (about 3 ounces) sliced
button (white) mushrooms

½ medium zucchini,
cut into small dice

1 large shallot,
finely chopped

1 cup (about 6 ounces)
diced cooked ham

3 tablespoons all-
purpose flour

1 tablespoon chopped
fresh rosemary

1 cup milk

½ cup chicken broth

1 cup diced vacherin cheese
or Brillat-Savarin cheese or
Brie cheese (about 5 ounces)

Salt and freshly ground
black pepper to taste

A VOL-AU-VENT is a hollow, light puff pastry shell stuffed with usually savory ingredients. It means "windblown" in French, to capture the idea of its lightness. They are sold in packages of six in the frozen dessert section of supermarkets. This is a Canadian recipe found in the blog "Dans la cuisine de Julie" written by a home cook in Quebec. Vacherin is a washed-rind soft cow's milk cheese made in the Jura and Fribourg regions of France and Switzerland, respectively. You could replace it with two other Canadian cheeses: fou du roy cheese, an organic semisoft raw-milk washed-rind artisanal farmhouse cheese with a rust-colored rind; or freddo, a semifirm, washed-rind cheese made with cow's milk that has a delightful aroma of milk and wildflowers. Both Canadian cheeses can be purchased online at www.fromagesduquebec.qc.ca. The vacherin can be purchased at www.artisanalcheese.com. This preparation is very nice served with sautéed zucchini and/or grilled sweet bell peppers. *Makes 4 first-course servings*

1. Preheat the oven and prepare the vols-au-vent pastry shells according to the package instructions.

2. In a saucepan, melt the butter over medium heat. Add the mushrooms, zucchini, and shallot and cook, stirring, until golden, about 5 minutes. Add the ham and cook, stirring, for 2 more minutes. Add the flour and rosemary and stir to mix well. Add the milk and broth and cook until it thickens, about 5 minutes. Stir in half the cheese and season with salt and pepper.

3. Increase the oven temperature to 425°F.

4. Place the vols-au-vent on a baking sheet and fill them with the ham mixture. Put the remaining cheese on top and place the pastry cap on top of the cheese. Bake just until the cheese is melted, about 4 minutes. Serve hot.

Pork Strips with Carrot and Leeks in Chèvre Sauce

Salt, as needed

12 ounces small carrots, peeled and split lengthwise

1 tablespoon unsalted butter

1 tablespoon walnut oil (optional)

14 ounces pork loin, cut into strips

2 small leeks, white and light greens part only, split lengthwise, washed well, cut in half lengthwise, and thinly sliced

¼ cup dry white wine

4 ounces chèvre cheese

¼ cup crème fraîche or sour cream

¼ cup finely chopped fresh flat-leaf parsley

Freshly ground black pepper to taste

THIS SIMPLE EVERYDAY DINNER preparation is full of flavor and very appealing on a cold day. It sounds sophisticated and complex, but I assure you only the flavor is, not its preparation.

Makes 3 servings

1. Bring a small saucepan of water to a boil over high heat, add salt, add the carrots, and cook until tender but firm, about 4 minutes. Drain.

2. In a skillet, melt the butter with the walnut oil, if using, over high heat. Add the pork and cook, stirring, until it loses its color, about 2 minutes. Add the leeks, stir, reduce the heat to low, and continue cooking until softened, about 8 minutes. Add the carrots and wine and cook for 5 minutes. Add the chèvre, crème fraîche, and parsley; season with salt and pepper, and cook, stirring to blend well, until tender and syrupy, about 10 minutes. Serve hot.

Pork Chops with Gorgonzola and Pears

YOUR FAMILY WILL GO WILD over this preparation, as the flavors are extraordinarily complementary. The two elements for success are firm, not-quite-ripe pears and remembering to let the skillet cool down just a bit before moving to the next step. I like to serve this next to Baked Rice with Three Cheeses (page 257). *Makes 4 servings*

4 pork chops (about 1¾ pounds), cut ¾ to 1 inch thick

Salt to taste

2 tablespoons extra-virgin olive oil

2 tablespoons unsalted butter

2 pears, peeled, cored, and each cut into 8 wedges

¼ cup dry white wine

¼ cup heavy cream

8 ounces Gorgonzola or blue cheese, at room temperature, cut up

Freshly ground black pepper to taste

1. Preheat the oven to 200°F.

2. Season the pork chops with salt. In a large skillet, heat the olive oil over medium heat. Add the pork chops and cook, turning once, until golden brown and the juices run clear, about 10 minutes in all. Transfer the chops to an ovenproof serving platter and place in the oven to keep warm. Drain the fat from the skillet. Remove the skillet from the heat and let cool for 3 to 4 minutes.

3. In the same skillet, melt the butter over medium-high heat. Add the pear wedges and cook, turning once, until browned, about 5 minutes. Transfer the pears on top of the pork chops and return to the oven to keep warm.

4. Remove the skillet from the heat and let cool for 3 to 4 minutes. Return to the heat, add the wine and cream, bring to a boil over high heat, then immediately reduce the heat to low and let bubble, uncovered, for 1 to 2 minutes while stirring. Add the Gorgonzola cheese and stir until cheese is almost melted. Remove the skillet from heat and spoon the sauce over the pork and pears. Season with black pepper and serve hot.

Pork Chops Stuffed with Pecans and Blue Cheese

4 pork loin rib chops (about 2 pounds in all)

¾ cup crumbled blue cheese (about 6 ounces)

¼ cup chopped pecans

1 scallion, finely chopped

1 teaspoon Worcestershire sauce

1 tablespoon unsalted butter

1 tablespoon all-purpose flour

½ cup sour cream

⅛ teaspoon cayenne pepper

Salt and freshly ground black pepper to taste

CUTTING A POCKET into a pork chop is not as difficult as it sounds. You want to start an incision with a sharp paring or utility knife and then enlarge the pocket with quick slashing strokes to widen the pocket right to the bone, making sure you don't cut through the meat and make a hole for the cheese to escape. Blue cheese is ideal in this recipe, and you can use any kind of blue cheese you desire. This recipe is adapted from Derrick Riches, who writes about barbecue for About.com.

Makes 4 servings

1. Lay each pork chop on a surface in front of you with the bone side away from you. With a sharp paring knife or small utility knife, cut a pocket from the fat side almost to the bone, widening the pocket carefully with slashes from the knife.

2. In a bowl, stir together ½ cup of the blue cheese, the pecans, scallion, and Worcestershire sauce. Divide the blue cheese stuffing among the 4 chops, spoon into the pockets, and close up using toothpicks.

3. In a small saucepan, melt the butter over medium-high heat, then stir in the flour to form a roux and cook, stirring, for 2 minutes. Remove the saucepan from the heat and stir in the sour cream and the remaining ¼ cup blue cheese. Return to the heat and cook, stirring, until saucy, 2 to 3 minutes. Season with the cayenne and salt and pepper. Keep warm.

4. Preheat a large cast-iron skillet over high heat. Add the pork chops and cook for 2 minutes on each side. Reduce the heat to medium-low and continue cooking, partially covered and turning only once more, until springy to the touch, about 15 minutes. Transfer the pork chops to a platter or individual plates, spoon the sauce over them, and serve hot.

Greek Chicken Stew

6 tablespoons
unsalted butter

1 tablespoon extra-
virgin olive oil

One 4-pound chicken,
cut into serving pieces

3 medium onions, grated on
the largest holes of a grater

1 tablespoon tomato paste
dissolved in ½ cup water

Bouquet garni, tied in
cheesecloth, consisting
of 1 teaspoon cumin
seeds, 1 cinnamon stick,
3 allspice berries, 1 clove,
and 2 bay leaves

12 to 14 small red and
white onions (1 to
1¼ pounds), peeled

6 ounces kefalotyri or
kashkaval cheese, cut
in ½-inch cubes

IN THIS GREEK CHICKEN STEW called *kota stifado*, the gravy is a delicately perfumed one achieved through a spice bouquet consisting of cumin, cinnamon, cloves, and allspice. When stewing the chicken, be careful that the sauce never comes to boil, or the chicken will toughen. It's best to let it simmer gently and, if it doesn't appear to be done in the time recommended, continue simmering until it is. I like to serve the chicken with rice pilaf, but you could also serve it with pasta such as orzo. For this stew you will fry the cubes of cheese in a skillet until they are brown and crunchy, and then they are turned into the stew. The best cheese to use is either a kefalotyri, which is a hard, salty, light yellow cheese made of sheep's or goat's milk (you could use a young pecorino cheese in its place), or a kashkaval, which is a mild, creamy, provolone-like cheese in texture, but saltier, made of sheep's milk. Both cheeses are found in Greek or Middle Eastern markets and at www.christosmarket.com. *Makes 4 to 6 servings*

1. In a large casserole, melt 4 tablespoons of the butter over medium-high heat with the olive oil. Once the butter stops sizzling and is beginning to turn light brown, brown the chicken pieces on all sides, 8 to 10 minutes. Add the grated onions, cook for 1 to 2 minutes, then add the tomato paste and water. Add the bouquet garni, reduce the heat to low, cover, and simmer for 45 minutes. Add the whole onions and cook, covered, until the chicken and onions are fork-tender, 45 to 60 minutes more.

2. Meanwhile, in a skillet, heat the remaining 2 tablespoons butter over medium-high heat, then cook the cheese cubes until crispy golden on one side, about 1 minute. Scrape them up with a spatula (make sure the crust doesn't come off) and cook the other side until crispy, too. Remove and add to the chicken stew. Cook until they are beginning to melt, about 5 minutes, then serve.

Cheese-Coated Fried Chicken Breasts

4 boneless, skinless chicken breast halves (about 2 pounds)

All-purpose flour, for dredging

2 large eggs, beaten

2 cups finely grated manchego cheese

6 to 8 cups olive oil, for frying

THIS SIMPLE SPANISH RECIPE for chicken breast scaloppine coated in manchego cheese, called *pechugas de gallina panadas*, uses the cheese as one would use bread crumbs. The recipe is associated with the cooking of the Andalusian city of Cordoba. It appears on the menu of a luncheon given by the Marquis de la Vega de Armijo for King Alfonso XII in 1877. The cheese should be finely grated, and the chicken should cook at a low temperature so the cheese doesn't burn. Serve with a side of finely cut french fries. *Makes 4 servings*

1. Gently pound the chicken breasts thinner between sheets of wax paper with a mallet. Place the flour in one shallow plate and the eggs in another. Dredge a breast in the flour, tapping off any excess. Dip in the egg. Spread a few tablespoons of the cheese over the surface of a dinner plate and dredge a breast in the cheese. Lift up and sprinkle some more cheese evenly over the surface of the plate and dredge the other side, pressing down. The breast cannot really be "dredged" since the cheese is too moist, so it must be pressed into the flesh. Repeat with the remaining breasts and refrigerate for 30 minutes before cooking.

2. Preheat the frying oil in a deep-fryer or an 8-inch saucepan fitted with a basket insert to 320°F. Cook the breasts until golden, 4 to 5 minutes, turning once. Serve hot.

Turkey Sausages with Hatch Chiles and Queso Blanco

HATCH CHILES, also called New Mexico chiles and Anaheim chiles, are a cultivar of New Mexico chiles that are grown around Hatch, New Mexico. You'll find them in the farmers markets and supermarkets in August and September. You could also use Italian long frying peppers or fresh peperoncino chiles. Serve with warm tortillas. *Makes 4 servings*

1¾ pounds Hatch chiles (also called New Mexico or Anaheim chiles)

3 tablespoons extra-virgin olive oil

1½ pounds turkey sausage, links cut in half

1 fresh habanero chile or uvilla grande chile, finely chopped

1 fresh jalapeño chile, seeded and slivered

1 large garlic clove, finely chopped

8 ounces queso blanco or queso fresco, cut into 9 cubes

1. Place the Hatch chiles on a wire rack over a burner on high heat and roast until their skins blister black on all sides, turning occasionally with tongs. Remove the chiles and place in a paper or heavy plastic bag to steam for 20 minutes, which will make peeling them easier. When cool enough to handle, rub off as much blackened skin as you can and remove the seeds by rubbing with a paper towel (to avoid washing away flavorful juices) or by rinsing under running water (to remove more easily). Cut into strips.

2. In a large skillet, heat the olive oil over medium heat. Add the turkey sausage, roasted chiles, habanero chile, jalapeño chile, and garlic and cook, stirring occasionally, until the sausages are firm and cooked through, about 20 minutes. Add the cubed cheese, cover, and cook until the cheese is soft. Serve hot.

Chicken in Jalapeño Cream Sauce

8 large fresh jalapeño chiles, seeded and chopped

½ cup whole milk

4 tablespoons unsalted butter, plus more for greasing the casserole

1 tablespoon all-purpose flour

1 cup Mexican crema or heavy cream

1 teaspoon salt

4 boneless, skinless chicken breast halves (about 2 pounds)

1½ cups grated Monterey Jack cheese (about 5 ounces)

THIS DISH IS A BEAUTY TO BEHOLD. It comes out of the oven resembling a painting, with its lime green and white color. It's also a very piquant dish, so I prefer to serve it with either plain rice or cauliflower with Chef Thijs's Cheese Sauce (page 20). You could also serve the chicken with corn tortillas.

Makes 4 to 6 servings

1. Preheat the oven to 350°F.

2. Put the jalapeño chiles and milk in a blender and run until smooth. In a medium saucepan, melt 2 tablespoons of the butter over medium-high heat, then add the flour and brown lightly while stirring for 1 minute to form a roux. Add the chile purée, stirring constantly, until smooth. Reduce the heat to medium-low, add the crema, and stir constantly until the sauce begins to bubble, about 4 minutes. Remove from the heat and add the salt. The sauce can be refrigerated at this point and used later or the next day.

3. In a large skillet, melt the remaining 2 tablespoons of butter over medium-high heat. Add the chicken breast halves and cook, turning once, until golden brown, about 4 minutes on each side.

4. Transfer the chicken to a buttered 12 × 9-inch baking casserole, pour the jalapeño cream sauce over the chicken, and top with the grated cheese. Bake, uncovered, until the cheese is golden and bubbling, about 20 minutes. Serve hot.

Grilled Chicken Breast Rolls with Ham and Cheese

A GRILLED CHICKEN ROLL-UP is a nice alternative to a hot dog or a hamburger for a summer barbecue. They're called *involtini di pollo* in Italian and can also be cooked in a skillet with sauce. Once you've got them stuffed, rolled, and closed up, they can rest in the refrigerator for several hours until you're ready to grill. *Makes 6 servings*

3 boneless, skinless chicken breast halves (about 1½ pounds), each cut in half sideways to form 6 scaloppine in all

Salt and freshly ground black pepper to taste

6 thin slices cooked ham

2 teaspoons finely chopped fresh rosemary

4 ounces soft cheese, such as mozzarella, young provolone, truffle cheese, etc., cut into sticks

Extra-virgin olive oil, for drizzling

¼ cup ground pistachios

1. Lay a piece of chicken in front of you on a surface between pieces of plastic wrap or wax paper. Gently pound a little thinner with a mallet or the side of a cleaver. Repeat with the remaining chicken.

2. Prepare a hot charcoal fire to one side of the grill box or pre-heat a gas grill on high for 20 minutes.

3. Season the chicken with salt and pepper, lay a slice of ham on top, sprinkle with the rosemary, and then add a piece of the cheese. Roll up tightly and secure with toothpicks. Drizzle with olive oil. Sprinkle the roll-ups with the ground pistachios.

4. Place the chicken breast roll-ups directly over the hottest part of the fire and once they develop black grid marks, after about 1 minute, move to the indirect fire area of the grill and continue cooking, partially covered, until cooked through, about 20 minutes. Serve hot.

Chicken Coconut Curry
with Paneer Cheese

¼ cup whole unsalted cashews

2¼ cups vegetable oil

8 ounces paneer cheese or queso blanco, cut into small cubes

All-purpose flour, for dredging

Salt to taste

1 pound boneless, skinless chicken breast halves, cut into 1-inch pieces

¼ teaspoon black mustard seeds

1 tablespoon garam masala

¼ teaspoon black cumin seeds

¼ teaspoon ground coriander seeds

1 medium onion, thinly sliced

1 teaspoon finely grated fresh ginger

1 large garlic clove, finely chopped

One 14-ounce can unsweetened coconut milk

¼ cup frozen peas

2 tablespoons finely chopped fresh cilantro

PANEER CHEESE IS A DENSE, unsalted cow's milk cheese that does not melt and maintains its shape when cooked. It is not aged or salted. Although Whole Foods markets carry it, the Mexican queso blanco is very similar and is what I recommend as a substitute. The coconut milk used in this recipe comes from a can, but to make your own is easy; just soak grated unsweetened coconut in hot water until its water is very cloudy. The various spices called for can be bought at www.penzeys.com. The success of the preparation depends on not overcooking the chicken, so take the times listed seriously. It is best accompanied with Chenna Pulao (page 256). *Makes 4 servings*

1. Preheat the oven to 350°F.

2. Spread the cashews on a baking sheet or pie plate and bake until fragrant and lightly toasted, about 7 minutes. (You could also use a toaster oven for this step.) Transfer to a plate to cool.

3. In a small saucepan, heat 2 cups of the vegetable oil over medium-high heat until nearly smoking. Dredge the paneer cheese in flour, tapping off any excess, and fry the cheese cubes until golden brown, 1 to 2 minutes. Set aside.

4. Lightly salt the chicken. In a large, deep skillet, heat 3 tablespoons of the vegetable oil over medium-high heat until nearly smoking. Add the chicken and cook until golden brown, about 3 minutes. Remove the chicken and set aside.

5. Reduce the heat to medium. Add the remaining 1 tablespoon oil to the skillet, and heat until nearly smoking. Add the mustard seeds and cook until they start to pop, about 1 minute. Add the garam masala, cumin seeds, and coriander seeds and cook, stirring, for 30 seconds. Add the onion, ginger, and garlic and cook, stirring, until the onion is softened, about 7 minutes. Stir in the coconut milk and bring to a boil. Reduce the heat to low.

6. Return the chicken to the skillet with the peas and fried paneer cheese and simmer until cooked through, about 10 minutes. Transfer the coconut chicken curry to a bowl, sprinkle with the cilantro and cashews, and serve.

Pan-Fried Spring Rolls with Duck and White Cheese

3 tablespoons vegetable oil

6 ounces fresh white cheese, such as queso fresco, queso blanco, or Syrian white cheese, sliced ½ inch thick

6 ounces cooked duck meat, chopped

8 ounces bean sprouts, blanched in boiling water for 3 minutes and drained

4 scallions, finely chopped

1 tablespoon soy sauce

½ teaspoon salt

15 rice spring roll wrappers (8½ inches in diameter)

THERE IS NO CHEESE IN SOUTHEAST ASIAN cooking, so this preparation may look a little strange. However, if you love spring rolls of any kind, then this is oh-so-good. I usually make this when I have leftover roast duck. If you don't have leftover duck, then you need to cook up some or use some turkey or chicken thigh. I serve these spring rolls as an appetizer, and they are very popular. Spring roll wrappers are sold in supermarkets' Asian or international aisle. Serve with soy sauce, prepared mustard, and chile oil.

Makes 12 large egg rolls to serve 4 as a main course or 12 as an appetizer

1. In a large nonstick skillet, heat 1 tablespoon of the oil over medium-high heat. Add the slices of cheese and cook on both sides until golden brown, about 2 minutes. Remove and cut into small dice.

2. In a wok, heat 1 tablespoon of the oil over high heat. Add the duck, bean sprouts, and scallions and stir-fry for 2 minutes. Add the soy sauce and salt and stir-fry until blended. Transfer the mixture to a strainer and let drain and cool. Add the fried cheese and toss.

3. Rice spring roll wrappers are sold dry, like sheets of very thin lasagne. Soak the wrapper in a plate of water until malleable, about 10 seconds. Place a spring roll wrapper on a wet kitchen towel on the surface in front of you. Place about 2 tablespoons filling below the center of the skin. Fold the bottom over the filling tightly to cover it, then fold the left and right sides over and roll the spring roll up, making sure that you wrap as tightly as possible. Continue with the remaining wrappers and filling.

4. Wipe out the large nonstick skillet you used to cook the cheese with a paper towel, then heat the remaining 1 tablespoon oil over medium heat. Cook the spring rolls, making sure they don't touch each other, until crispy golden on both sides, about 5 minutes. (Cook in batches if necessary. Keep in a warm oven as you prepare the rest.) Serve hot.

Oysters au Gratin Roquefort

24 raw oysters, very well cleaned

1 tablespoon baking soda

¾ cup dry sherry

7 ounces Roquefort cheese

6 egg yolks

3 tablespoons heavy cream

Juice from 1 lemon

Salt and freshly ground black pepper to taste

WHEN I WAS RESEARCHING my book *A Mediterranean Feast*, a number of French chefs in Languedoc helped with explanations of the local cuisine and some provided recipes. In the end, the book I wrote was not about restaurant cooking, but I held onto the recipes because they were intriguing. Many years ago, this recipe was provided to me by Chef Patrick Lenfant, then of the Grand Hotel in Roquefort-sur-Soulzon, the home of Roquefort cheese; it is called *huitres gratinées au Roquefort "Société."* I've adapted the recipe slightly to make it more appropriate to an appetizer you might serve at home. In the restaurant, they served the oysters in the shells on a bed of rock salt and endive leaves.   *Makes 4 servings*

1. Soak the oysters in cold water to cover with the baking soda for 2 hours.

2. Place an oven rack 5 inches from the broiler heat source. Preheat the broiler.

3. In a large casserole, place all the oysters, cover, and cook over medium heat until all the oysters are just open enough to pry them open further, 3 to 5 minutes. Remove the oysters and strain the oyster juice remaining in the casserole. Remove the oysters from the shell, saving the less uneven half of the shell and reserving the oysters. Transfer the oyster juice to a smaller saucepan. Add the sherry to the strained oyster juice and cook over medium-high heat until reduced by about three-quarters.

4. In a bowl, stir together the Roquefort, egg yolks, cream, lemon juice, salt, and pepper and blend well until it is nearly smooth. Pour into a saucepan and simmer, shaking constantly, until smooth, about 2 minutes. Combine the cheese sauce with the oyster sauce.

5. Place the reserved shells on 4 broiler-proof plates, 6 to each. Place an oyster on each shell and spoon a generous amount of sauce over each oyster. Place under the broiler until slightly brown on top, 1 to 2 minutes, but watch carefully. Serve hot.

Crab au Gratin

4 tablespoons unsalted butter, plus more for greasing the casserole

2 large egg yolks

1½ cups heavy cream

1 large yellow onion, chopped

1 celery stalk, chopped

1 teaspoon garlic powder

1 teaspoon Creole seasoning (such as Tony Chachere's or Paul Prudhomme's Creole seasoning)

1 teaspoon salt, or to taste

½ teaspoon cayenne pepper

¼ cup all-purpose flour

1½ cups shredded cheddar cheese, at room temperature (about 3½ ounces)

½ cup shredded Monterey Jack or Edam cheese (about 1½ ounces)

1 pound cooked lump crabmeat

1 bunch scallions, trimmed and chopped

CRAB AND CRAWFISH are popular shellfish in Louisiana, and crab au gratin is one of the most famous dishes to combine shellfish and cheese in the Creole tradition. The secret in this preparation is to allow the onion and celery to become very soft before you make the roux with the flour. This recipe, adapted from Louisiana-born Dennis Morazan, is as rich as they get, so a nice green salad is the perfect accompaniment.

Makes 4 to 6 servings

1. Preheat oven to 400°F. Lightly butter a 9-inch square baking casserole.

2. In a bowl, whisk together the egg yolks and heavy cream.

3. In a large saucepan, melt the butter over medium heat, then add the onion and celery and cook, stirring, until softened, about 5 minutes. Season with the garlic powder, Creole seasoning, salt, and cayenne. Reduce the heat to low, cover, and simmer, stirring occasionally, until very tender, about 20 minutes.

4. Stir the flour into the saucepan and cook, stirring continuously, for 5 minutes. Stir in the egg yolk mixture. Stir in ½ cup of the cheddar cheese and the Monterey Jack cheese until melted. Remove from heat and fold in the crabmeat. Transfer the mixture to the prepared baking casserole. Bake until bubbly and lightly browned, about 25 minutes. Remove from heat and top with the remaining cheddar cheese and the scallions. Allow the cheese to melt before serving. Serve hot.

Haddock and Cheddar Casserole

I ALWAYS ASSOCIATE fish and cheese with old dishes from New England. A cursory examination of nineteenth-century New England cookbooks confirms that cooks combined fish and cheese and that haddock and cheddar were favorites. It's a delicious and satisfying dish on a cold night and it doesn't need much in the way of an accompaniment—perhaps some chewy biscuits or boiled rice and fresh green beans. *Makes 4 servings*

2 tablespoons unsalted butter, plus more for greasing the casserole

2 tablespoons all-purpose flour

1½ cups whole milk

Salt and freshly ground black pepper to taste

¾ cup shredded mild white cheddar cheese (about 2½ ounces)

1 pound fish fillets, such as haddock, sole, red snapper, flounder, or fluke

A few gratings of whole nutmeg or a pinch of ground nutmeg

1. Preheat the oven to 450°F. Lightly butter a 13 × 9 × 2-inch casserole.

2. In a saucepan, melt the butter over medium heat, then add the flour and stir to form a roux. Reduce the heat to medium-low and continue to cook, stirring, for 2 minutes. Remove the saucepan from the heat, then slowly whisk in the milk. Return the saucepan to medium heat and continue to cook, stirring, until it is smooth and a little denser, about 7 minutes. Season with salt and pepper. Stir in the cheese until it melts, 4 to 5 minutes.

3. Arrange the fish fillets in the casserole. Spread the white sauce over the fillets and sprinkle with nutmeg. Bake until bubbling and dappled golden brown, 20 to 25 minutes. Serve hot.

Puff Pastry with Salmon and Roquefort

10 ounces puff pastry, defrosted according to package instructions

1 cup crème fraîche

7 ounces Roquefort cheese

1 tablespoon cognac

Salt and freshly ground black pepper to taste

1 pound fresh spinach, stems removed

3 tablespoons extra-virgin olive oil

1 garlic clove, finely chopped

One 1¾-pound skinless salmon fillet, cut into 6 equal pieces

THIS ELEGANT DISH, called *pavé croustillant de saumon au Roquefort effeuillé d'épinards* by its creator, Chef Patrick Lenfant, then of the Michelin-starred Grand Hotel in Roquefort-sur-Soulzon, combines some traditional ingredients of this region of Aveyron in the Languedoc of France—namely, the spinach, the Roquefort, and the puff pastry. Roquefort-sur-Soulzon is the town from which the world-famous Roquefort cheese comes. *Makes 6 servings*

1. Preheat the oven to 350°F.

2. Roll the sheet of pastry out a bit, following the instructions on the package, and cut into 12 equal triangles. Place on an ungreased baking sheet and bake until golden brown, about 20 minutes. Transfer to a wire rack to cool and set aside. Leave the oven on.

3. In a medium, heavy saucepan, warm the crème fraîche, then crumble the Roquefort into it with the cognac. Lightly salt and pepper the sauce. Keep warm, not letting it get too hot, and never letting it boil.

4. Meanwhile, bring a large saucepan of lightly salted water to a boil, add the spinach, and cook for 1 to 2 minutes. Drain the spinach and plunge into ice water to stop the cooking. Drain very well, pressing out as much liquid as you can with the back of a wooden spoon, and then blot with paper towels.

5. In a small, heavy saucepan, heat the spinach over medium-low heat with 1 tablespoon of the olive oil, the garlic, and 2 tablespoons of the Roquefort sauce. Keep warm.

6. In a large skillet, heat the remaining 2 tablespoons olive oil over medium heat. Lightly season the salmon with salt and pepper, add to the skillet, and cook until the fish can be flaked, about 10 minutes, turning only once and lifting with a spatula occasionally to avoid sticking. Remove from the skillet and keep warm covered with a sheet of aluminum foil.

7. Re-warm the pastry triangles in the oven for a few minutes. On 6 individual plates or a serving platter, arrange 6 triangles of baked pastry. Layer them with the spinach and place a salmon piece on top. Place the 6 remaining pastry triangles on top of each piece of salmon and pour the Roquefort sauce over. Serve immediately.

Halibut and Blue Cheese Bake

6 ounces blue cheese,
crumbled

2 cups buttermilk

1½ cups mayonnaise

1 large garlic clove,
mashed in a mortar with
½ teaspoon salt until mushy

½ teaspoon freshly
ground black pepper

½ teaspoon freshly
ground white pepper

2 pounds halibut,
cut into 6 pieces

1 small red onion,
thinly sliced

DON'T BE TEMPTED to cut corners and pour some bottled salad dressing on top of the halibut in this recipe. There's a difference, and remember to use good-quality blue cheese, preferably Roquefort, and very fresh fish, and you can't go wrong.

Makes 6 servings

1. In a bowl, mix 4 ounces (that is, two-thirds) of the blue cheese with the buttermilk, mayonnaise, mashed garlic, black pepper, and white pepper. Chill for 2 hours.

2. Preheat the oven to 350°F.

3. In a 13 × 10 × 2-inch casserole, spoon some of the blue cheese dressing to form a thin layer on the bottom of the casserole. Arrange the fish on top, cover with the remaining blue cheese dressing, and layer the red onion on top. Crumble the remaining 2 ounces blue cheese on top and bake until the fish flakes, about 20 minutes. Serve hot.

Sweets with Cheese

In this chapter, you will find the greatest desserts invented using cheese. I had to pick and choose carefully, but in a way the recipes were self-selecting. After all, how could one not have cheesecake in a book called *Hot & Cheesy*? Not all these desserts are served hot, of course, but they are all made with cheese in one form or another. Besides the famous Lindy's New York–Style Cheesecake (page 375), the recipe here being as authentic as one can get, you'll also find some delightful surprises such as Beet Cake (page 379) and the Neapolitan Easter treat Pastiera alla Napoletana (page 380). One of my favorite kinds of cheese desserts are the cheese crêpes so popular in Eastern Europe, and you'll find them all here. If you want to put no effort into dessert at all, then Mascarpone Cream with Rum (page 387) is for you.

Cheesecake Torte

For the torte

1½ tablespoons
unsalted butter

¾ cup graham
cracker crumbs

1½ pounds cream cheese,
at room temperature

4 large egg whites

1 cup sugar

1 teaspoon pure
vanilla extract

For the frosting

2 cups sour cream

2 tablespoons sugar

½ teaspoon pure
vanilla extract

THIS DELIGHTFUL CHEESECAKE is much lighter than a traditional cheesecake (see page 375). After baking, it goes to the refrigerator and then is served either cold or cool. You will need a springform pan to make it. *Makes 10 servings*

1. Preheat the oven to 350°F.

2. For the torte, butter a 9-inch springform pan, using all the butter. Sprinkle the cracker crumbs on the bottom and sides of the pan, shaking the pan so all sides are covered.

3. In a bowl, cream the softened cream cheese with a fork. In another bowl, beat the egg whites until frothy. Gradually add the sugar and continue beating until the egg whites form stiff peaks. Gradually add the egg white mixture to the cheese and blend. Add the vanilla and blend. Pour the cheese mixture into the pan. Bake until solid, about 25 minutes.

4. Meanwhile, for the frosting, mix the sour cream, sugar, and vanilla. When the cheesecake is done, remove from the oven and increase the heat to 475°F. Spread the sour cream mixture over the cake while it's still hot and bake for 5 minutes more. Remove and let cool. Place in the refrigerator until cold, then remove the springform and serve cold or cool.

Lindy's New York–Style Cheesecake

MY MOTHER WAS BORN in the Hell's Kitchen section of New York City in 1919, not too far from Lindy's, which was at 1626 Broadway. I asked her one day if she had ever eaten Lindy's cheesecake. And she related the following: "Are you kidding? One day in 1936 we played hooky from school and went to a movie at the Paramount and afterwards went to Lindy's for cheesecake. Many famous people went to Lindy's for their cheesecake and that day we shook hands with Franchot Tone [the George Clooney of the 1930s]."

In his book *Jewish Home Cooking*, Arthur Schwartz tells some interesting stories about this most famous cheesecake in the world. Leo "Lindy" Lindermann opened Lindy's deli on August 20, 1921, on Broadway at Times Square, and it soon become known as offering a "world famous cheesecake."

It was over Lindy's cheesecake, transformed to "Mindy's," that Nathan Detroit made a bet with Sky Masterson in the Broadway musical *Guys and Dolls*. In the New York of the 1930s, though, it was not Lindy's that was the most famous cheesecake but Arnold Reuben's, served at his Turf Restaurant at 49th and Broadway. However, Lindy Lindermann understood publicity, so he gave the cheesecake recipe to one of his important customers in the 1950s, the very popular restaurant critic Duncan Hines. The rest is history, as they say.

(continued)

For the pastry

½ cup sugar

Finely grated zest of 1 lemon

4 tablespoons cold unsalted butter, cut into 4 pieces

1 large egg yolk

1 tablespoon water

1 teaspoon pure vanilla extract

1 cup all-purpose flour

For the cheese filling

Five 8-ounce packages Neufchâtel cream cheese or low-fat Philadelphia cream cheese, at room temperature

1¾ cups sugar

3 tablespoons all-purpose flour

¼ teaspoon salt

Finely grated zest of 1 orange, spread on a plate to dry a bit

Finely grated zest of 1 lemon, spread on a plate to dry a bit

1 tablespoon pure vanilla extract

5 large eggs

2 large egg yolks

¼ cup heavy cream

(continued)

For the strawberry sauce

1 pound ripe strawberries, stems removed

¾ cup sugar

⅓ cup water

Pinch of salt

1½ tablespoons cornstarch

2 teaspoons unsalted butter

1 teaspoon fresh lemon juice

It is the most famous cheesecake and the most imitated, and that has presented a problem. There are a million recipes out there, and it's frightfully difficult to tell which one is original and authentic. I concluded that the one offered by Greg Patent in his *Baking in America*, published by Houghton Mifflin in 2002, was the best one, and his is the one I've adapted for this book. He wrote that the late Helen McCully, food editor of *House Beautiful* magazine for many years, claimed to have gotten the recipe from Lindy himself, and Patent adapted his recipe from her 1978 version in *Cooking* magazine. It is a dense and creamy cake that has become known as New York–style cheesecake. The original Lindy's restaurant closed in 1967, luckily after I had had a slice with my father when I was a teenager. Greg Patent advises: "The recipe calls for a pastry crust and an unusual method of baking. Both are essential to the success of the recipe. For baking, the cake is started at a temperature of 525°F, then the oven temperature is reduced to a cool 200°F. The high temperature gives the top of the cheesecake a rich brown color, and the low temperature assures a creamy texture. Be sure to use an oven thermometer to make certain your oven can accommodate these swings in temperature. I've made this with regular and reduced-fat cream cheese and can honestly say I prefer the texture and feel of the latter. A fresh strawberry sauce brings out the flavors of the cheesecake."

Remember to take the cheesecake out of the refrigerator about an hour before serving. *Makes 16 servings*

1. For the pastry, place the sugar and lemon zest in a food processor and process for 5 seconds. (You may want to grate the second lemon and the orange for its zest used in the cheese filling at this time, too.) Add the butter, egg yolk, water, and vanilla and pulse until the mixture looks granular and lumpy; the butter should be in about ¼-inch pieces. Add the flour and pulse rapidly 20 to 30 times, stopping occasionally to scrape the sides and bottom of the bowl, until the mixture almost gathers into a ball. Turn the dough out onto a piece of plastic wrap and press the dough into a 1-inch-thick disk. Wrap and refrigerate for 1 hour.

2. Adjust an oven rack to the lower third position and preheat the oven to 400°F. Butter a 9-inch springform pan. Detach the sides; set aside.

3. Cut off slightly less than one-half of the dough. Break it into pieces, and scatter them over the springform bottom. Press firmly and evenly with your fingertips to make a thin layer. Set the bottom crust in the oven and bake until pale golden brown, about minutes. Remove from the oven with a wide metal spatula and set on a cooling rack to cool completely. Increase the oven temperature to 525°F.

4. Shape the remaining pastry into a square. Roll it out on a lightly floured surface to a rectangle slightly larger than 10 × 6 inches. With a large sharp knife, trim away the edges so that the pastry measures 10 × 6 inches. Cut the pastry crosswise into five 2-inch strips. Reassemble the springform pan. Line the sides of the pan with 4 of the pastry strips, pressing the pieces firmly together where their edges meet and pressing the pastry firmly against the pan so that it will stay in place. Cut what you need from the last strip to fill in the last gap. Refrigerate while you prepare the filling.

5. For the filling, beat the cream cheese in a large bowl with an electric mixer on medium speed until smooth. Add the sugar,

(continued)

flour, salt, orange and lemon zests, and vanilla and beat until smooth, 2 to 3 minutes. Beat in the eggs and yolks one at a time, beating only until thoroughly incorporated, about 15 seconds after each. Beat for another 30 seconds. Remove the bowl from the mixer and incorporate any cream cheese at the bottom missed by the beaters. Also incorporate any zest sticking to the beaters. Return the bowl to the mixer and on low speed, beat in the heavy cream. Scrape the mixture into the pan and smooth the top.

6. Bake for 10 minutes, then reduce the oven temperature to 200°F and bake for 1 hour longer; the top will be golden brown. Let cool to room temperature on a rack. Do not remove the springform sides. Cover loosely and refrigerate overnight.

7. For the strawberry sauce, place three-quarters of the strawberries in a food processor and run until completely mashed. If the remaining strawberries are small, leave them whole; if they are large, slice enough to make 1 cup. Place the mashed berries in a medium saucepan. Add the sugar, water, salt, and cornstarch. Turn the heat to medium and bring to a boil, stirring well and constantly with a heatproof rubber spatula. Reduce the heat to low and continue cooking, stirring constantly, until the sauce is slightly thickened, about 2 minutes. Remove from the heat and add the butter, lemon juice, and reserved berries. Cool to room temperature, then refrigerate until chilled. (The sauce can be made a day ahead.)

8. To serve, remove the cheesecake about an hour before serving. Run a small sharp knife around the edges of the cake to release the pastry and carefully remove the sides of the pan. Rinse a knife in hot water, wipe dry, and slice. Repeat between cutting each piece. Serve each portion with a spoonful of the strawberry sauce. Refrigerate leftovers.

Beet Cake

I HEARD ABOUT the beet cake served at the now-closed Gorky's restaurant in downtown Los Angeles; however, I was unable to find anyone who could tell me anything about it. I found the idea of using raw beetroots in a dessert cake intriguing—after all, I love carrot cake. After making this recipe for the first time, I was totally delighted with how well it worked. You will be, too; if you like carrot cake, you'll love this cake. And it has to be healthy, too. *Makes 10 servings*

1. Preheat the oven to 350°F.

2. For the cake, in a bowl, beat together the eggs, sugar, and oil with a whisk until fluffy. In a large bowl, sift together the flour, baking powder, baking soda, cinnamon, and salt. Add the egg mixture to the dry ingredients and stir well to blend. Add the beetroots, walnuts, and vanilla and beat together for 1 minute.

3. Lightly grease a 2-quart Bundt pan. Dust with flour and shake out any excess. Pour in the batter and bake until puffed up, cracks appear, and a skewer comes out nearly clean, 40 to 45 minutes. Let cool completely in the pan.

4. Meanwhile, for the frosting, in an electric mixer (preferably), blend the cream cheese, heavy cream, and almond extract until fluffy. Blend in the confectioners' sugar. Once the cake is cool, remove the cake from the pan and spoon the frosting over the cake, spreading it evenly all over. You may refrigerate it at this point, but remove from the refrigerator 1 hour before serving.

For the cake

4 large eggs

2 cups granulated sugar

1 cup canola oil, plus more for greasing the pan

2 cups all-purpose flour, plus more for dusting the pan

2 teaspoons baking powder

1½ teaspoons baking soda

1 teaspoon ground cinnamon

½ teaspoon salt

3 cups (about 1 pound) shredded fresh uncooked red beetroots

1 cup chopped walnuts

1 teaspoon vanilla extract

For the cream cheese frosting

8 ounces cream cheese, at room temperature

¾ cup heavy cream

1 teaspoon almond extract

½ cup confectioners' sugar

Pastiera alla Napoletana

For the grain

1 cup whole wheat berries,
soaked in cold water
overnight, drained well

3 cups whole milk

1 tablespoon pork lard

1 teaspoon sugar

1 teaspoon vanilla extract

Grated zest of ½ orange

For the dough

2 cups all-purpose flour

6 ounces pork lard
or unsalted butter, at
room temperature

¾ cup sugar

3 large egg yolks

3 tablespoons or
more ice water

(continued)

THIS IS THE CLASSIC Neapolitan Easter sweet. For many Neapolitans, *pastiera* is not just a sweet but also a veritable ritual, with well-defined modalities of preparation. It is made on Holy Thursday, and as every family has its own recipe, there is no "right" way of making it.

As with so many sweets of southern Italy, *pastiera* probably had its origin with the sisters of a now-forgotten monastery of Naples. Just as every traditional preparation seems to have a legend behind it, so too does *pastiera*. One story relates how Maria Teresa of Austria, the consort of King Ferdinand II of Bourbon, who was nicknamed by Ferdinand's soldiers as "the queen who never smiles," did indeed smile when she tasted *pastiera*. The king exclaimed that he wanted *pastiera* served to his wife every day; otherwise he must wait until the following Easter before he could see her smile again.

The pie is prepared over the course of 2 days. Wheat berries are sold hulled and whole. The whole wheat berries will take much longer to cook but have a deeper flavor. If using hulled wheat berries, soak them for 1 hour, then cook in half the amount of milk called for, for about 4 hours. This makes a great breakfast. ***Makes 8 servings***

1. For the grain, on the first day, cook the wheat berries in a saucepan over very low heat with the milk, lard, sugar, vanilla, and orange zest, using a heat diffuser if necessary, until the milk has been absorbed and the mixture is dense and creamy, 6 to 7 hours. Let rest overnight in the refrigerator.

2. On the second day, make the crust. In a large bowl or on a work surface, make a mound with the flour and create a well in the middle. Fill the well with the lard, sugar, and egg yolks. Use forks or a pastry blender (preferably) to combine the ingredients and form a dough, using the ice water if necessary to form a ball of dough. Handle the dough as little as possible (don't knead it). Once you have obtained a uniform dough, press it into a ball, wrap it in plastic wrap, and refrigerate for 1 hour.

3. Meanwhile, for the filling, pass the ricotta through a strainer into a large bowl. Stir in the sugar and continue stirring until well blended, about 3 minutes. Stir in the egg yolks one at a time. Stir in the reserved cooked wheat berries and then the orange flower water. Stir in the candied fruit and squash, if using, and the cinnamon. Beat the egg whites to stiff peaks and fold into the filling with a rubber spatula.

4. Preheat the oven to 375°F.

5. Roll out two-thirds of the pastry dough with a floured rolling pin on a floured sheet of parchment paper until thin. Place an inverted 9-inch pie pan on top of the pie dough. Flip the parchment paper and pan over and press the dough into the pan. Carefully remove the parchment paper. If the dough is breaking apart too much, then place it in the pan in patchwork fashion until it evenly covers the pan. Pour the ricotta-wheat filling in. Roll out the remaining dough on a pastry cloth or parchment paper and cut it into strips, then lay them across the filling in a diagonal pattern (lift them from the pastry cloth with a long narrow spatula to keep them from breaking).

6. Bake until firm and golden on top, with an almost completely dry filling and a lightly brown crust, about 1 hour. Serve the pie directly from its pan.

For the filling

10 ounces ricotta cheese (page 65)

¾ cup sugar

3 large eggs, separated

5 tablespoons orange flower water

¼ cup chopped candied citron or cherries

¼ cup chopped candied orange peel

¼ cup chopped candied squash (optional)

1 teaspoon ground cinnamon

Palachinke

For the filling

16 ounces cottage cheese

3 ounces cream cheese,
at room temperature

¼ cup sugar

2 large eggs, beaten lightly

2 tablespoons tapioca

For the batter

1 cup all-purpose flour

1 cup whole milk

2 large eggs, beaten

1 teaspoon sugar

½ teaspoon salt

1 tablespoon unsalted
butter and 1 tablespoon
oil, for cooking the crêpes

For the topping

8 ounces sour cream

1 large egg yolk, beaten

2 tablespoons sugar

MY FIRST ENCOUNTER with these crêpes, or blintzes, popular throughout Eastern Europe was in Budapest in the 1970s. I've loved them ever since. This Serbo-Croatian *palachinke* are thin crêpe-like pancakes filled with cottage cheese and baked with a sour cream sauce. They can be filled with jam, fruit, or sweet or savory cheeses and rolled. Hungarians make these, too, and call them *palacsinta*, Poles call them *nalesniki*, Lithuanians call them *naliesnikai*, Ukrainians call them *nalysnyky*, and Romanians call them *clatita*. They are all the same. This recipe is adapted from Barbara Rolek from www.about.com.

Makes about twelve 7½-inch diameter palachinke to serve 6

1. For the filling, in a bowl, combine the cottage cheese, cream cheese, sugar, eggs, and tapioca. Cover and let rest in the refrigerator for 1½ hours.

2. Meanwhile, for the batter, in a blender, combine the flour, milk, eggs, sugar, and salt. Process until smooth. Leave in the blender, covered, and let rest for 30 minutes.

3. In a 7-inch nonstick skillet, heat only enough of the butter and oil to create a film on the bottom of the skillet over medium heat. Pour in a scant ¼ cup of batter and rotate the pan while swirling the batter to cover the bottom of the pan. Cook until lightly brown on the underside, then turn and cook the second side until light brown, 1 to 2 minutes in all (less time as the pan continues to heat).

4. Set out 2 greased plates and place the finished crêpes on the first greased plate. Move the crêpe to the second greased plate as it cools and as you cook the next crêpe. This technique will keep the crêpes from sticking to each other. (The crêpes can be used immediately or wrapped and frozen up to 3 months.) Place 2 heaping tablespoons of the filling on one edge of each crêpe and roll away from yourself. Continue making and rolling the remaining crêpes, greasing the skillet lightly each time, and place them on a large baking sheet lined with parchment paper.

5. Preheat the oven to 350°F.

6. For the topping, in a bowl, combine the sour cream, egg yolk, and sugar and spread on top of the filled crêpes. Bake until the topping is firm and the cheese is melted completely, about 20 minutes. Serve hot.

Cheese Blintz

For the blintzes

1¼ cups all-purpose flour, sifted

3 large egg yolks

10 tablespoons milk

10 tablespoons cold water

4 tablespoons unsalted butter, 3 tablespoons melted

2½ tablespoons Cointreau or similar orange liqueur

2½ teaspoons sugar

½ teaspoon salt

1 tablespoon unsalted butter or 1 tablespoon oil, for cooking the crêpes

For the filling

1¼ pounds ricotta cheese (page 65) or small-curd cottage cheese

1 large egg

5 teaspoons sugar

1¼ teaspoons pure vanilla extract

Fruit preserves or sour cream, for serving

CHEESE BLINTZES are a classic Eastern European Jewish food, although they are known throughout Eastern Europe and are popular among Russians, Ukrainians, Poles, Lithuanians, and others. *Blintz, blintze, blin, blynai, bliny,* and *mylintsi* are all words in a variety of languages for a thin pancake similar to a crêpe but sometimes made with yeast (while crêpes are not). The word *blintz* derives from an Old Slavic word (as does the Russian *blini*). Once the blintzes (crêpes) are filled, they can be stored in an airtight container or bag and frozen. Serve with fruit jams or sour cream. These blintzes can be eaten cold, warm, or hot. *Makes about 12 blintzes to serve 6*

1. For the blintzes, place the flour, egg yolks, milk, water, 3 tablespoons melted butter, Cointreau, sugar, and salt in a blender and run until smooth. Leave the blender with its cover on in the refrigerator for 2 hours.

2. Lightly butter or oil a 7-inch nonstick skillet and heat over medium-high heat. Add 2 to 3 tablespoons batter while holding the skillet tilted, and quickly rotate the skillet to spread the batter. If you've poured too much batter into the skillet, pour the excess back into blender. Cook until the top is dry, then lift the edges with a spatula and flip, cooking the other side for less than 30 seconds.

3. Set out 2 greased plates and place the finished crêpes on the first greased plate. Move the crêpe to the second greased plate as it cools and as you cook the next crêpe. This technique will keep the crêpes from sticking to each other. (The crêpes can be used immediately or wrapped and frozen up to 3 months.) Continue making the remaining crêpes, greasing the skillet lightly each time. You should have about 12 crêpes.

3. For the filling, in a bowl, mix together the ricotta cheese, egg, sugar, and vanilla. Put equal portions in each crêpe and roll up. The blintzes can be frozen at this point (see Note).

4. In a large skillet, melt the remaining 1 tablespoon butter over medium-high heat. Cook the rolled blintzes, in batches, until crispy on both sides, about 4 minutes. Serve with the preserves or sour cream.

NOTE: The blintzes freeze well. Arrange them on a double layer of aluminum foil next to each other in a single layer, cover with another piece of foil, crimp the edges closed, and freeze.

Sebadas

2 cups fine semolina

3½ tablespoons melted pork lard or unsalted butter

1 large egg

3 tablespoons water

½ cup diced young pecorino cheese (such as Pecorino Sarde or Pecorino Crotonese) (about 1½ ounces)

6 ounces provolone cheese, thinly sliced

2 to 3 cups vegetable oil or olive oil, for frying

Sardinian bitter honey, eucalyptus honey, mixed flower honey, or orange blossom honey, for drizzling

IN SARDINIA, sebadas are deep-fried cheese pies popular with both tourists and locals all over the island. They are made with short dough of fine semolina and stuffed with a young pecorino cheese and a cow's milk cheese called peretta, similar to provolone. After frying, the pies are served with Sardinian *miele amara*, a bitter honey, or with any good-quality honey. The Sardinian cook takes the strips of leftover dough and deep-fries them, too. This recipe is adapted from the one I first published in *Saveur* magazine in August 2003.   *Makes 8 servings*

1. Pour the semolina on a clean surface and make a well in the center. Pour the melted lard, egg, and the water into the well and begin to form a ball of dough by incorporating all the flour into the liquid with your fingers. Once a smooth ball of dough is formed, knead it for a few minutes and then leave it to rest for 1 hour, covered by a clean kitchen towel or wrapped in wax paper.

2. Roll the dough out into 16 disks 5 inches in diameter and about ⅛ inch thick. Lay a tablespoon of the diced pecorino and 2 small slices of the provolone on top of one disk. Cover with another disk and crimp the edges shut with a crimping wheel or the tines of a fork. Repeat with the remaining disks and cheese.

3. Preheat the vegetable oil in a skillet to 325°F.

4. Slide the sebadas into the oil, one or two at a time, as long as the skillet is not crowded. Cook, spooning hot oil over the tops as they cook, until light golden and the tops are blistering. Transfer to a serving platter, immediately spoon the honey over them, and let the heat of the sebadas melt the honey. Serve hot or very warm.

Mascarpone Cream with Rum

THIS IS SUCH A SIMPLE SWEET that it is perfect for a do-ahead dessert when you don't want to be bothered with last-minute preparation. It's very nice if you prepare it in martini glasses and refrigerate until needed. In Italy, this kind of sweet is known as a "spoon dessert." *Makes 6 servings*

1 pound mascarpone cheese

½ cup sugar

4 large eggs, separated, whites beaten to stiff peaks

½ cup rum

1 cup fresh raspberries

6 ladyfingers or butter cookies

1. In a bowl, mix together the mascarpone and sugar, then add the egg yolks, one at a time until absorbed, beating constantly. Stir in the rum. Fold in the egg whites.

2. Scoop the mixture into individual glasses and refrigerate for several hours. Serve with the raspberries and ladyfingers.

Cheese Kolache

For the dough

1 pound (4 sticks) unsalted butter, at room temperature

3 ounces cream cheese

3 cups all-purpose flour

6 tablespoons whole milk

For the cheese filling

8 ounces cream cheese, at room temperature

¼ cup sugar

3 tablespoons all-purpose flour

1 large egg yolk

½ teaspoon freshly grated lemon zest

1 tablespoon fresh lemon juice

Unsalted butter, for greasing the baking sheet

THE CZECH WORD *koláč* simply means any of a variety of sweet cakes, always sweet. However, Czech Americans use the plural, *kolache* (pronounced ko-LAHCH-kee), to refer to a specific type of small pastry with filling in the center indentation. This recipe is from Dolores Benes Duy of Illinois, who tells us there are many ways to make *kolache*. Interestingly, theses sweet are popular and much associated with a number of communities in Texas, Nebraska, and Minnesota, where Czechs immigrated in the nineteenth century. I'm pretty sure this is a Czech-American version. The dough is flakier than usual, although some cooks use yeasted dough.

Makes 16 to 18 kolache to serve 8

1. For the dough, in a bowl, cream the butter and cream cheese together. Add the flour and milk and mix well to form a ball of dough. Wrap in plastic wrap and refrigerate overnight or for a few hours.

2. For the cheese filling, in a bowl, combine the softened cream cheese and sugar and beat with a fork until light and fluffy. Stir in the flour, egg yolk, lemon zest, and lemon juice. Set aside.

3. Preheat the oven to 375°F.

4. Roll out half the dough like a pie crust on a floured counter surface until ¼ to ⅜ inch thick. Reserve the remaining dough for another batch, wrap well, and freeze for up to 6 months. Cut disks

out with a round 3-inch diameter cookie cutter. Make a small indentation in the center with your fingers, and fill the centers with 1 tablespoon of the cheese stuffing.

5. Arrange the kolache on a greased baking sheet and bake until golden brown on the bottoms and the cheese looks like custard, 15 to 20 minutes. Serve warm or at room temperature.

Ricotta Cheese Pudding

1 tablespoon golden raisins

3 tablespoons rum

¼ cup fine semolina

4 large eggs

1¾ cups ricotta cheese (page 65)

6 tablespoons confectioners' sugar

½ cup mixed candied citrus peel

Freshly grated zest from ½ lemon

Pinch of ground cinnamon

Unsalted butter, for greasing the mold

All-purpose flour, for dusting

Vanilla sugar, for dusting (see Note)

IN ITALIAN, THIS SWEET is called *budino di ricotta*, and it's a simple, sweet pudding one might find in Naples—perfect with a cup of espresso.

Makes 6 servings

1. Preheat the oven to 350°F.

2. Soak the raisins in the rum until needed.

3. Bring 1 cup of water to a boil over high heat in a small saucepan. Drizzle in the semolina, mix well, cook for 2 minutes, stirring quickly and constantly, then remove from the heat. Transfer to a bowl and leave to cool until needed.

4. Separate 3 of the eggs. Place the whites in one bowl and place the yolks in another bowl with the remaining whole egg, the ricotta, confectioners' sugar, candied peel, raisins and rum, zest, and cinnamon.

5. In another clean bowl, whip the egg whites until stiff. Add the semolina mixture to the ricotta mixture and mix well. Fold in the stiff egg whites. Butter a 2½-pint nonstick Bundt pan and then flour lightly, shaking out excess flour. Pour the mixture into the mold and bake for 1 hour. Remove and let cool completely. Turn over and let the pudding drop out of the mold onto a serving plate. Dust with vanilla sugar and serve.

NOTE: To make vanilla sugar, place a quarter of a vanilla bean in a jar with ½ cup confectioners' sugar and leave for 2 to 24 hours before using. You can leave the vanilla bean in the jar and replenish the sugar several times.

Index